Praise for

THE SAAD TRUTH ABOUT HAPPINESS

"No one is better at helping us laugh at the madness of today's modern world than my dear friend, podcaster, and therapist to us all, Dr. Gad Saad. Whether using his acerbic wit to address a public absurdity or broadcasting from under his desk in mock terror as he takes on the latest fear gripping the internet, Gad leads by example in showing us how humor is key to managing stress, upset, anger, and frustration. His new book, *The Saad Truth about Happiness*, reveals the secrets behind his optimistic approach to life and shows us how we can be happier people too."
— **Megyn Kelly,** journalist

"There is a virtual epidemic of unnecessary misery in the Western world at the present time. Much of it is the result of ideologies that stress victimization, insist on an external locus of control, and offer a borderless and unconstrained impulsive hedonism as a pathway to the good life. Professor Saad—who is, in truth, an engaging and happy person—offers a wiser alternative. Happiness is to be found, in Dr. Saad's well-founded estimation, in the spirit of free play; in responsible, altruistic, reciprocal social interactions; in the sense of awe and admiration available to anyone with open eyes. The idea that structureless freedom is anything other than the desert of the soul is harming people, young and old alike. Dr. Saad offers an alternative vision, laying out a more classic road to the good life, as is generally the case with wise people."
— **Dr. Jordan Peterson,** bestselling author

"With his characteristic wit, Professor Saad has produced an invaluable guide to the pursuit of happiness. In the glut of mostly worthless self-help books, this valuable gem stands apart. Instead of fly-by-night fads and paper-thin pop psychology, this book's sage and sane advice draws equally from the springs of ancient wisdom and modern science, grounding us in the eternal truths of human nature. Saad distills these sources into a winsome guide to a more flourishing life."

> —**Aaron Kheriaty**, M.D., psychiatrist and director of the Bioethics and American Democracy Program at the Ethics and Public Policy Institute

"Gad Saad knows that there is no magic formula for achieving happiness. But in this book he distills deep learning and practical wisdom to offer valuable insights grounded in science and experience. Written with warmth and humanity, the *Saad Truth*, it turns out, is a happy one."

> —**Dr. Darrin M. McMahon**, professor of history at Dartmouth College and author of *Happiness: A History*

"*The Saad Truth about Happiness* brims with insight into the journey we all take in life. Its engaging style and personal stories make the abstract principles vibrant. Amidst a flurry of books on happiness, Saad's evolutionary lens brims with wisdom and novel light on life's most ancient mystery—how to live an authentic life."

> —**David M. Buss**, author of *The Evolution of Desire: Strategies of Human Mating*, professor of psychology at the University of Texas at Austin, and founding member of the field of evolutionary psychology

"Embedded in his own lived experiences, his work as an academic, and the occasional advice from the likes of Aristotle and Viktor Frankl, Dr. Saad delivers a tour de force that will increase the likelihood that any of us should find our way to happiness."

—**Dr. Drew Pinsky**, physician and podcaster

"Evolutionary psychologist and wise man Professor Gad Saad knows how to be happy even amid controversy, turmoil, and danger. He is the epitome of a happy warrior, living up to the meaning of his last name, Saad, which translates to happiness and prosperity in Arabic. His new book, delightfully written, searches both ancient wisdom and modern social sciences for the answer. It has practical advice about finding the right life partner, the right job, and how to deal with failure. Ultimately, the answer Professor Saad provides lies more in the variety and depth of a person's life experiences than in the heft of a person's wallet. Read it if you want to learn how to be happy. It is written by someone who knows!"

—**Jay Bhattacharya**, M.D., Ph.D., professor of health policy at Stanford University School of Medicine

THE SAAD TRUTH ABOUT HAPPINESS

The Saad Truth about Happiness
8 Secrets for Leading the Good Life

Gad Saad

Since 1947
REGNERY
An Imprint of Skyhorse Publishing, Inc.

Regnery books may be purchased in bulk at special discounts for sales promotion, corporate gifts, fund-raising, or educational purposes. Special editions can also be created to specifications. For details, contact the Special Sales Department, Regnery, 307 West 36th Street, 11th Floor, New York, NY 10018 or info@skyhorsepublishing.com.

Regnery® is an imprint of Skyhorse Publishing, Inc.®, a Delaware corporation

Visit our website at www.regnery.com.

Please follow our publisher Tony Lyons on Instagram @tonylyonsisuncertain.

10 9 8 7 6 5 4 3 2 1

Library of Congress Cataloging-in-Publication Data is available on file.

Cover design by John Caruso
Cover photograph by Yvens Banatte

Paperback ISBN: 978-1-68451-528-8
Hardcover ISN: 978-1-68451-260-7
eBook ISBN: 978-1-68451-434-2

Printed in the United States of America

To all those who have enriched my life and made me happy

CONTENTS

CHAPTER ONE

On Being the Happy Professor

We hold these truths to be self-evident, that all men are created equal, that they are endowed by their Creator with certain unalienable Rights, that among these are Life, Liberty and the pursuit of Happiness.[1]

—The United States Declaration of Independence (July 4, 1776)

We naturally look for the ultimate goal that enables us to judge other goals by how they contribute to it. Happiness is that ultimate goal because, unlike other goals, it is self-evidently good. If we are asked why happiness matters, we can give no further, external reason. It just obviously does matter. As the American Declaration of Independence says, it is a "self-evident" objective.[2]

—Richard Layard, *Happiness: Lessons from a New Science*

If you ask people what they want to get out of life, many are likely to respond with "I want to be happy." A broad survey asked people to assort sixteen life goals in decreasing order of importance (these goals included "Being rich," "Physical health," and "Spiritual growth"). On top of the list, statistically tied with "great/fulfilling relationships," was "Being happy."[3] Of course, the challenge is: Can one identify what it means to live the optimal good life? Is there a reliable recipe for happiness? What constitutes happiness, well-being, and contentment? Is there a balance to be struck between competing goals? How much should one strive to maximize pleasure (or knowledge or wealth or inner peace) and minimize pain (or regret or struggle or apathy)? As is true for most things in life, there are countless relevant variables, some of which are part of our innate dispositions (our genes and temperaments), others that are situational (a bad marriage, a great job), and yet others that constitute winning mindsets that we might adopt, all of which contribute to our likelihood of being happy and content.

As a social scientist I can confirm that there is no magical formula for achieving the lofty objective of happiness. But one can identify many necessary ingredients that when combined properly increase the likelihood of being a fulfilled, happy individual.

The great ancient philosophers had an astute understanding of our universal human nature and how to achieve maximal happiness. In the chapters that follow, we will explore some of these ancient wisdoms as well as contemporary empirical research regarding the good life (happiness, contentment, and well-being). We will look at key life decisions that are the purveyors of either great misery or immense happiness. The two most important of these are choosing the right life partner and the ideal job or profession. We spend much of our days either at work or with our families. If these two domains engender joy, then we are well on our way to living a fulfilled life. We will scrutinize arguably the most universal law in nature regarding the good life—namely, that all good things take place in moderation. Mathematically, this is known as the inverted-U curve, which captures the fact that too little or too much of something is worse than having just the right amount, a sweet spot in the middle between dearth and excess, which can be applied in a wide variety of fields.

As our investigation proceeds, I will argue that the path to happiness requires that we construe life as a playground. We need not lose our childlike playful effervescence as we segue from our youth to our adult years. Adults can and should foster playfulness in most, if not all, of the endeavors in which they partake. In conducting my scientific research, I certainly take this approach. I view science as an intellectual playground replete with exciting twists and turns, as if on a roller coaster. Boredom, be it on a daily level or in a grand existential sense, is a bane of our existence. A rich life requires that we sample from a broad range of experiences. Variety is indeed the spice of life (in most instances), and this constitutes another topic that we will explore. I believe that he who experiences the most varied experiences from the buffet of life ultimately wins. That does not, however, mean that we go through life merely flitting from one thing to another. Many of the most transformational experiences of our lives require that we be dogged, persistent, and resilient as we take on a new challenge, be it starting a new business, beginning a new university degree, or simply losing weight. Without some optimal level of grit and persistence, few new businesses would ever have seen the light of day, and few New Year's resolutions would ever be kept. To be successful in our quest for happiness, we need to tackle life with the grit, determination, and persistence necessary to achieve meaningful goals, whilst possessing a protective armor against possible, even likely, failures. Successful individuals are almost always "anti-fragile" when it comes to failure. They learn from their failures but are not broken by them.

The ancient Greeks thought that to seek *ataraxia* (tranquility of mind) was an important objective to living the good life. Regret is one emotion that can create turmoil within our inner thoughts. It can eat away at us like a flesh-eating fungus. So, we will examine regret stemming both from actions ("I regret having cheated on my spouse") and inactions ("I regret that I never enrolled in medical school"), and argue for a strategy to avoid regret and achieve tranquility of mind. Finally, I intend to show how we are truly the architects and orchestrators of our happiness. Irrespective of whether you were born with a sunny disposition or a stark outlook on life, you always have the power to affect your well-being in positive ways.

In my 2011 book *The Consuming Instinct: What Juicy Burgers, Ferraris, Pornography, and Gift Giving Reveal about Human Nature*, I argued that self-help books are very successful because they offer supposed solutions to many of our most fundamental Darwinian-rooted insecurities. Is there a path to retaining one's youthful vigor in the bedroom? What are the secrets to being a better parent? Is there a strategy for becoming popular amongst a group of prospective friends? What is the recipe for eating healthily and averting disease? How can one lead a life filled with purpose and meaning? In some instances, self-help books are based on time-tested ancestral wisdom, up-to-date evidence-based findings, or poignant personal anecdotes. Regrettably, in other cases, the promissory solutions are rooted in quackery, faulty reasoning, and incomplete or missing evidence. And yet, millions of people purchase these books because hope is indeed useful to combat the challenges of life. In the classic 1994 movie *The Shawshank Redemption*, in a letter to his friend Red (played by Morgan Freeman), Andy Dufresne (played by Tim Robbins) opines on hope: "Remember Red, hope is a good thing, maybe the best of things, and no good thing ever dies. I will be hoping that this letter finds you and finds you well. Your friend, Andy." This is to be contrasted with something Red had told Andy earlier: "Hope? Let me tell you something my friend. Hope is a dangerous thing. Hope can drive a man insane." While it is true that false hope (hope that is easily falsified by unmet expectations) can be detrimental, genuine hope (or optimism) is an all-purpose elixir of life. It is positively linked to well-being on many levels, including improved academic and athletic performance, better rehabilitative recovery, better mental health, and greater happiness.[4] Real hope is the necessary optimism that encourages action to tackle life's obstacles, such as changing poor lifestyle choices to improve one's health. False hope is an illusory promise sold as definitive "life hacks." For instance, no amount of "age rejuvenation cream" is going to reverse aging. When it comes to self-help books, the Latin dictum *caveat emptor* ("let the buyer beware") is operative. But there is a sort of science to self-help, and it is possible to distinguish between valuable, veridical advice and specious, empty promises.[5] I trust readers will recognize that this book dispenses the former and not the latter.

On Becoming a De Facto Global Therapist

I have always had an interest in criminal psychology, clinical psychology, and psychiatry, and I toyed with the possibility of pursuing my studies in those areas. I opted against that for two reasons. First, I did not want to immerse myself in the dark aspects of the human condition, as I did not think that my personality would allow me to compartmentalize my professional work away from my personal feelings. The thought of dealing with people who impart misery onto others or those who are victims of other people's destructive behaviors did not sit well with me. Second, many of the therapeutic approaches in the mental health professions have historically been rooted in anti-scientific quackery.[6] (I would argue—and have argued—that the early psychoanalytic pioneers Sigmund Freud and Carl Jung fall into this category of highly celebrated quacks.)

Even though I eventually forged a career at the intersection of evolutionary psychology and consumer psychology, my earlier interests in mental health have materialized in several ways. In two of my previous books, I discussed the evolutionary roots of the dark side of consumption, to be found, for instance, in pathological gambling, eating disorders, compulsive buying, and pornographic addictions.[7] I have also published scientific papers on obsessive-compulsive disorder, suicide, and Munchausen syndrome by proxy, examining these topics through an evolutionary lens.[8] I soon discovered that because my work—including my popular YouTube program—positioned me as a public intellectual and afforded me a large public platform, I was often asked for my advice on innumerable topics ranging from personal relationships to fighting woke ideology, from life objectives and educational paths to diet tips. Moreover, I found that when I gave advice, it was among the popular content I offered over the internet. Without ever having aspired to this position, I found that I was becoming a personal therapist with a global reach. This book is one result of that—and a natural complement to my last book, *The Parasitic Mind: How Infectious Ideas Are Killing Common Sense*, which was about how to avoid the innumerable negative consequences of bad thinking. As a professional behavioral scientist my usual mode of analysis and presentation is descriptive. *The Saad Truth about Happiness* is much more prescriptive in my newfound role as a global therapist. This book is about how to improve your life—and be happier—by making smarter decisions. I should add that my last name, Saad, means "felicity, happiness, and prosperity" in Arabic, so if one were a fatalist he might conclude that I was meant to write a book about happiness.

Existential Gratitude and a Happy Disposition

In my book *The Parasitic Mind*, I recounted how my family and I escaped the brutality of the Lebanese civil war in the mid-1970s. I faced many brushes with death during my Lebanese childhood, and that has given me a tremendous appreciation for life, and a feeling of existential gratitude. Sure, I might face some trials and tribulations, as we all do, but at least I enjoy life in a free society. Another source of existential gratitude comes from this: My parents got married when my father was twenty and my mother nearly sixteen. They quickly had three children.

I came along ten years after that. I was an "accidental" pregnancy, and my mother was dead set on getting an abortion. As the story goes, my parents had an argument about it. My dad was opposed to abortion on principle, but my mother was insistent that she was going to abort me. Finally, my father asked my mother's best friend, a Syrian woman named Ihsan, to intervene. On the fateful day of the scheduled abortion, Ihsan pleaded with my mother: "Are you sure you want to do this? You don't know what this child might amount to in life." My mother proceeded to the clinic unmoved by this last-minute appeal. As they arrived at the top of the stairs, my mother stopped in her tracks and announced to her friend that she had changed her mind, and here I am typing these words nearly six decades later. My mother first told me this story as a means of reminding me that I owed her my life (a common trait among some Lebanese Jewish mothers!) and proceeded to tell me euphemistically that I had come very close to being "fish food." How lovely!

Life is a wondrous thing. It is statistically improbable that any one of us should exist. We are the result of a unique combination of DNA. And we should be grateful for it. We should be happy. And I can assure you, I am happy.

In the fall of 2021, I hosted media personality Glenn Beck on my show.[9] Our chat opened like this (edited slightly for clarity):

> **Glenn:** You know, Gad, I was just thinking as I was walking in the studio: I so enjoy you. I watch you. I listen to you. . . . And you know what's weird is, I associate you with "happy, joyful.". . . That's how I was just thinking: I was so excited to talk to you and I was thinking, like, why? What's the last time we talked? What were we talking about? . . . I cannot remember but I just remember it's associated in my head with happiness.
>
> **Me:** You know that is such a sweet thing of you to say . . . and not to engage in shameless plugging right after such a lovely

compliment, but my next book [this one] is about how to live the good happy life and it is precisely based on the fact that people say the types of things that you tell me; and I said, "Well, why don't I put it in a recipe book and see what comes out."

Or, as one individual wrote to me on Twitter: "I envy the way you have mastered the art of enjoying life."[10] Could my happy disposition work against me in writing this book? On one of my many trips to the university library to pick up a book on philosophical approaches to happiness, my wife, who had joined me on that outing, looked at me and said: "You need to be less happy and less smiley if you want people to follow your advice. No one wants to follow the advice of someone who is too comfortable and content." She thought that to be regarded as authentic and genuine, I needed to exude an austere aura of wisdom gained through suffering. But I disagree with this assessment. While I am fortunate enough to have been endowed with a sunny disposition, that is only half the equation (the half that comes, roughly speaking, from genes); the other half comes from conscious choices, our unique life trajectories, or environmental factors that we can, in part, control.[11] In other words, all people, from the most sullen and gloomy to the most effusive and effervescent, can implement behavioral and cognitive strategies that might augment their well-being irrespective of their starting set points.[12]

My wife has, herself, an uncanny ability to see the positive in most situations. She is much like the realtor who quickly comes up with positive rebuttals to counter any negative assessments from prospective home buyers. If a husband and wife complain that the house does not have a swimming pool, the realtor will remind them that they have young children and hence it might be safer that no pool is available. If the client complains about the highway noise, the realtor will suggest that the highway's proximity will allow for a quicker commute. Negatives can often be turned into positives, and this "silver lining" mindset is truly a vaccine against life's vagaries. It is well in line with a key precept from Stoicism. As Epictetus famously opined: "It's not what happens to you, but how you react to it that matters." He also stated: "There is only one way to happiness and that is to cease worrying about things which are beyond the power of our will."[13] These brilliant ancient insights are at the heart of one of the most empirically validated approaches in psychotherapy, namely cognitive behavior therapy, or CBT.[14] Many forms of suboptimal behavior or mental frailty stem from disordered thinking. CBT is a process by which a therapist helps a client identify faulty reasoning and the corresponding behavior patterns that ultimately lead to negative downstream effects. That Epictetus offered a precursor to CBT is a perfect segue to the next chapter, which explores ancient wisdom as well as current empirical insights on happiness. Thank you for joining me on this journey. I hope that this book offers you a pathway to being happier.

CHAPTER TWO

Ancient and Modern Wisdom
Regarding the Good Life

*There is not any thing in this world, perhaps, that is
more talked of, and less understood, than the business of
a* happy life *[emphasis in original]. It is every man's wish
and design; and yet not one of a thousand that knows
wherein that happiness consists.*[1]

—Seneca

*But it is a misfortune that the concept of happiness
is such an indeterminate concept that, although every
human being wishes to attain this, he can still never say
determinately and consistently with himself what he
really wishes and wills.*[2]

—Immanuel Kant

For thousands of years, philosophers and theologians have offered prescriptions for what makes a good life and how to pursue the good life. The emphases can differ, of course. If you are an orthodox Jew, for example, there are 613 mitzvot (religious rules) and 10 commandments. These do not guarantee you earthly happiness, but they will make God very happy. Christianity warns against the seven deadly sins (pride, lust, gluttony, envy, greed, wrath, and sloth) that are antithetical to a good life and separate one from God. But few, if any, philosophical traditions are as concerned with the good life as that produced by the ancient Greeks.[3]

After completing my MBA in 1990, I set off on a backpacking tour of six European countries (France, Switzerland, Germany, Austria, Italy, and Greece). While in Greece, my travel buddy and I visited five Greek islands (Corfu, Santorini, Naxos, Crete, and Folegandros). While sitting at a sleepy café on one of the islands (I can't remember which one), I struck up a conversation with a Greek individual who had lived in the United States. I teased him, saying, "How come we never hear of Greece in the news?" He paused for a moment and said: "When you are responsible for Socrates, Plato, and Aristotle, you don't need to do anything else. We've contributed more than enough to the enrichment of the world." He was right. But the Greeks did a lot more than offer us the three giants of philosophy; they created the philosophical, artistic, cultural, and political grounding of the Western world.

My friend and fellow Lebanese bestselling author Nassim Taleb has stated that the field of psychology is useless because all one needs to do to understand human nature is to study the ancient Greeks. He is perhaps playfully, bombastically overstating the case, but he is certainly correct that when it comes to philosophical treatises on the pursuit of a happy and enriched life, few traditions are as rich as that of the ancient Greeks, though they do, of course, have many competitors. Tim Lomas, a psychologist who specializes in the study of well-being, has, along with three of his coauthors, compiled a history of the philosophy of happiness from the ancient Egyptians to the Enlightenment.[4] He has also examined how happiness has been depicted in art over the past one thousand years in the West.[5] Another history of happiness comes from Darrin McMahon.[6] McMahon explains that the ancient Greeks started as fatalists, believing that a person's happiness was determined by the gods. But subsequent Greek philosophers—like Plato, Aristotle, and the Stoics—recognized that happiness could be achieved by human action. While many of these later philosophical schools contested with one another, they agreed that happiness was a result of human agency. This was a major advance in the study of happiness. In the Christian tradition, following the lead of Saint Augustine, happiness is to be found in an ever closer relationship with God, in prayer, in service to others, and in living the virtues taught by Jesus. Within the non-Western traditions, the ancient Chinese philosophies of Confucianism, Taoism, and Buddhism have their own varied guidelines for living the good life, from the importance of filial piety, to living in accord with nature, to transcending material problems through meditation.[7]

More recently, happiness has become a subject not just for philosophers and theologians but for scientists, armed with empirical studies. Over the past twenty-five years or so, many influential psychologists have turned their attention to an examination of happiness.[8] This includes the father of positive psychology, Martin Seligman, along with other leading academic psychologists including Laurie Santos (who created The Science of Well-Being course at Yale University and *The Happiness Lab* podcast), David Lykken (author of *Happiness: The Nature and Nurture of Joy and Contentment*), Sonja Lyubomirsky (author of *The How of Happiness*), Daniel Gilbert (author of *Stumbling on Happiness*), and Jonathan Haidt (author of *The Happiness Hypothesis*), among others. Much of the empirical research focuses on the various factors that are linked to happiness.[9] But there is also the question of what happiness produces. Perhaps the most concrete reason to be happy is that it affects our health.

Happiness as an Elixir of Health

Often, when we study human behavior, we see that something can be both the antecedent to an outcome as well as the result of an outcome, and it is important to distinguish between the two. For example, we know that men with higher levels of circulating testosterone (an antecedent variable) are more likely to be aggressive.[10] But we also know that men's testosterone levels increase when they drive a Porsche (an outcome effect).[11]

When we study the relationship between happiness and health, we can see both antecedent variables and outcome effects. It is not surprising to find that poor health (as an antecedent variable) can have a negative effect on one's happiness. But it is interesting to note that being happy can lead to better health outcomes.[12] How does happiness improve health? First, it has been shown that happy people are more likely to exercise, eat a healthy diet, and engage in other health-promoting behaviors.[13] Second, people who are happier exhibit a broad range of good health markers, from lower cortisol levels and less inflammation to lower blood pressure.[14]

Mental health is another benefit of happiness. Happy people are less likely to say, "I need to make the best possible decision" (fretting over getting a maximum benefit) and more likely to say, "I'll look for a winning alternative that is good enough" (being satisfied with an acceptable outcome). Happy people are also less likely to fall prey to the influence of social comparisons; their well-being is less contingent on the successes and failures of others. In their own lives, happy people tend to find the silver lining in whatever happens.[15] This is a trait, or a mindset, that can be nurtured or trained, as in cognitive behavior therapy; it can stand independent of genetics.

Do Some Personality Types Promote Happiness?

Certain things, of course, are genetically fixed. People are born with two eyes, two kidneys, one heart, ten fingers, and ten toes. These traits are now fixed within the human genome, defining human anatomy.[16]

While humans are identical to one another when it comes to fixed traits, the key variable on which we most clearly differ is our personality. Psychologists refer to personality traits as individual differences precisely because humans are extraordinarily heterogeneous in how they score on a very broad spectrum of such traits. How many personality traits are there? There have been many worthy attempts to create an exhaustive taxonomy of them. In 1936, Gordon W. Allport and Henry S. Odbert utilized a lexical analysis of the *Webster's New International Dictionary* (1925 edition) to generate 17,953 personality-related traits (out of roughly 400,000 words).[17] Of course, many of these words might be collapsed under a singular heading because they are essentially synonymous with one another. This has led several other psychologists to utilize various statistical techniques such as factor analysis to reduce the larger set of variables down to a much more manageable number, including Raymond Cattell's 16 Personality Factors model (consisting of 16 traits), and the now widely known Big Five test or OCEAN, which measures openness to experience, conscientiousness, extraversion, agreeableness, and neuroticism.[18]

Why has evolution retained a heterogeneity of personality traits? In other words, why do we not all have some fixed optimal personality profile in the same way that we have evolved other fixed traits that do not vary across people? Evolutionary psychologists have offered compelling adaptive reasons to explain personality differences,[19] human universals, cross-cultural differences due to biological reasons, and cross-cultural differences stemming from non-biological reasons.[20] It is clear that evolution has not selected a singular optimal personality profile because no such profile exists across all possible varied landscapes. Personality A might be optimal in environment Y whereas personality B might be best suited for environment X. In evolutionary terms, there are no universal selection pressures to eradicate individual personality differences among people across the globe.

That is not to say, however, that certain personality traits don't make us happier than others. A recent meta-analysis exploring the correlations between the Big Five character traits and well-being, and the traits of honesty-humility, emotionality, extraversion, agreeableness, conscientiousness, and openness (known as the HEXACO typology) and well-being, provided a resounding yes to the question of whether our personalities affect our subjective sense of happiness and psychological well-being.[21] Neuroticism and emotionality were negatively correlated with well-being, whereas the other traits were positively correlated with well-being. A person who is extraverted, agreeable, conscientious, open, and honest-humble and who scores low on neuroticism and emotionality has the ideal personality architecture to be happy. That our personality affects our well-being and happiness has been confirmed in an earlier meta-analysis examining 137 personality traits.[22]

Another way to divide the data is to separate out different aspects of life and see how much these weigh on one's sense of well-being. For example, a study in Mexico identified seven key domains of life: health, economic, job, family, personal, friendship, and community environment, and found that the first five were the most highly correlated to life satisfaction.[23] But it is also true that people with essentially the same life circumstances—the same levels of good health, prosperity, occupation, family concord, and personal achievement—can have very different levels of happiness. The data show that those who have a "good enough" mindset (who think scoring 70 out of 100 in satisfaction in these domains is fine) are happier than those with a "maximizing" mindset (who think they need to score 90 out of 100 in these domains).[24] Happiness is in part a product of our own decision-making and what we demand of life; it is part of a mindset. It might come to us naturally, or we can train ourselves to think in a more optimistic, happier fashion, and enjoy the resultant health benefits, just as we might train ourselves to diet and exercise. It's a choice.

Does Wealth Lead to Happiness?

I recently watched the first season of the documentary television series *Narco Wars* about narcotraffickers in Colombia and Mexico. The cartel leaders profiled in the show had amassed immense personal wealth and wielded extraordinary power, but I was struck at how similar their circumstances were before they were ultimately captured or killed. Whether we are referring to Pablo Escobar (Medellín Cartel), the brothers Gilberto José Rodríguez Orejuela and Miguel Ángel Rodríguez Orejuela (Cali Cartel), or more recently Joaquín "El Chapo" Guzmán (Sinaloa Cartel), they are always apprehended in some nondescript apartment cowering or hiding in some dark space, often a secret compartment or tunnel. The same was true when American soldiers captured the Iraqi dictator Saddam Hussein, who was hiding in an earthen hole. All of the wealth and power in the world was insufficient to protect these villains from their ignoble common destiny.

From an evolutionary perspective, it is easy to understand why these men would be driven to amass power and money. We can even explain their psychopathic brutality. But it seems unlikely that their power and money, and their amoral willingness to use any means necessary to acquire it, brought them happiness or contentment or even a sense of purpose or meaning once justice caught up with them. In the end, all they had was fear and humiliation.

These might be extreme examples, but they raise the perennial question: Does wealth make people happier? For nearly fifty years, economists who study the economics of personal happiness have been accumulating data on this question and debating what they have found. In 1974, economist Richard Easterlin showed that greater income was associated with greater happiness for individuals, but not so at the aggregate national level.[25] Therein lies the so-called Easterlin paradox, where wealthier individuals are generally happier, but wealthier nations are not—at least not necessarily, as several more recent studies have indicated that richer countries *do* produce happier individuals.[26] The question then becomes: Is there an inflection point after which more money does not lead to greater happiness? The relationship between money and happiness is not a straightforward one. If you are so poor that you are unable to meet your most basic needs, you are unlikely to be happy. But beyond a certain income level, can wealth actually decrease happiness? Was the late rapper The Notorious B.I.G. correct with his "Mo Money Mo Problems" song? Several studies have found that beyond a plateau of $75,000 per year, an individual's sense of well-being does not increase. This apparently well-grounded data has, however, itself been challenged by a more recent study arguing that higher levels of wealth correlate to greater well-being across the full range of income levels.[27]

Take all the big-picture data, and you could say: it all depends. But we can also consider the anecdotal evidence—or rather, a smaller set of data, involving lotteries. My father, for instance, is an avid purchaser of lottery tickets. One of his favorite games is Lotto 6/49. (Choose six numbers out of forty-nine; you hit the jackpot when you get all six numbers right.) One day, when I was talking with students in my office, my dad called me and asked me to recommend six numbers for him to pick. I said, "Dad, I'm busy." But he insisted: "Come on, just give me six numbers quickly!" I replied, "Okay, fine, 1-2-3-4-5-6," to which he said, "Well, if you are not going to answer me seriously, there is no point asking you." This combination of seemingly ordered numbers has the exact same probability of being generated as any other combination, even though people wrongly presume otherwise. I share this story because lottery winners offer one of the more interesting areas of research on the links between money and happiness. Early research found that lottery winners were not happier than a control group of individuals. More recent work has documented an increase in *life satisfaction* but *not* in a corresponding increase in *happiness*.[28] A windfall will undoubtedly reduce one's worries about financial security. But it will not necessarily improve one's long-term existential happiness, because choosing six lucky numbers and reaping the windfall does not, by itself, give one a resilient, optimistic mindset, or improve one's decision-making, or provide a sense of purpose, meaning, or accomplishment in life. When you achieve great things, be it launching a successful business, graduating from medical school, or raising a happy family, you experience a lasting sense of pride. Not so with having a winning lottery ticket.

Several members of my nuclear family have been quite wealthy at various times. One of my relatives owned several Ferraris, each of which he would dismantle upon receipt to customize it to his liking. He also owned an Aston Martin Lagonda and an outrageously detailed Jeep (with gigantic wheels). This was part and parcel of his extraordinarily lavish lifestyle. His entire identity was rooted in pecuniary pursuits. I warned him long ago that life should not be solely measured by an accumulation of conspicuous luxury items, but he ignored my pleas for temperance and perspective. Fast-forward two decades, he has lost his fortune and now lives a quiet, modest life—more modest than he would like. Still, it is hard to feel sorry for him, because he was financially irresponsible. He thought the money train would always be around, ready to take him to the next station of conspicuous debauchery. But eventually the money train derailed. This lavish spending explains how athletes, actors, and other obscenely wealthy people can accumulate unimaginable wealth and yet eventually file for bankruptcy. I was never impressed by the wealth of some of my family members. If anything, I was viewed as the black sheep because I seemed far less interested in material things than in ideas. Even as a young kid, I would rather discuss philosophy than the next model of Jaguar or Porsche someone was planning on leasing. Material possessions can be here today and gone tomorrow, and if your happiness is tied up in them, it too can be here today and gone tomorrow. But happiness, as a product of a mindset that combines curiosity, the joy of perpetual intellectual discovery, and an appreciation of life's experiences, can be more lasting.

A Nobel Prize or Money?

In my academic career, I have had the honor of meeting and interacting with several Nobel Prize winners (or eventual winners). My first such experience was as a first-year doctoral student at Cornell University when I took Richard Thaler's behavioral decision theory course. Thaler went on to win the Nobel Memorial Prize in Economic Sciences in 2017. In 1992, as a young doctoral student, if memory serves me right, I met Professor Daniel Kahneman (and/or perhaps his long-time collaborator Amos Tversky), one of the great thinkers on the topic of decision-making. In 2002, as a visiting professor at the University of California at Irvine, I predicted to my MBA class that Kahneman would win the Nobel Memorial Prize in Economic Sciences. Less than twenty-four hours later, I learned that he had. I also had brief communications with the other 2002 Nobel laureate in economics, Vernon L. Smith, as well as with Paul Greengard, a 2000 Nobel Prize winner in physiology/medicine, and with Kip Thorne, winner of the Nobel Prize in Physics in 2017.

While each of these encounters was memorable, none was quite as awe-inspiring as when Herb Simon, winner of the Nobel Memorial Prize in Economic Sciences in 1978, visited Cornell University in 1993. My doctoral supervisor knew him well and hence had met him for lunch. I was miffed at the time that I had not been invited to join them, but my disappointment was attenuated when my supervisor sent me a memo (which I still have somewhere) telling me how Simon had praised some of my work. I share these brushes with Nobel Prize winners to contrast how I define wealth (the richness of one's life experiences) with how my more materialistically inclined family members define wealth. During a trip to Rio de Janeiro, I had shared my excitement at meeting the great Herb Simon, one of the truly great polymaths of the twentieth century. Rather than sharing in my excitement, my relative smugly stated: "Who the hell is this guy? I can probably buy him five hundred times over." To which I retorted, "Perhaps, but while five hundred people will wait in line to hear him speak, no one cares what you have to say." So there you have it: two ways to accumulate wealth—through amassing brilliant moments or amassing piles of dollars. Both have their points, but the former can enrich your soul; the latter, if it is all you value, can rot it.

Cultural Determinants of Happiness

Is the pursuit of wealth as a proxy for happiness found in all cultures? What is the relationship between culture and happiness? In science we have what we call the WEIRD bias, which refers to an overreliance on research conducted in Western, Educated, Industrialized, Rich, and Democratic societies, and the presumption that those findings are then globally generalizable.[29] In research into happiness it is clear that while some factors are universally valid, others are dependent on culture.[30] Happiness itself is a universal desire. In a survey of forty-two countries, only 1 percent of respondents said they never thought of happiness as an ultimate life objective, while 69 percent said that happiness was highly important to them.[31] It is also universally true that married people are happier than single people and that extroverts are happier than introverts.[32] Culture, however, is a major factor in determining the extent to which happiness is shaped by eudaimonia (the pursuit of meaning) versus hedonism (the pursuit of pleasure).[33] Individualist cultures place greater importance on hedonistic pursuits than do their collectivist counterparts.

The *World Happiness Report*[34] provides a yearly ranking of countries on the basis of reported happiness. The Scandinavian countries consistently lead the world when it comes to national happiness. The top ten countries in the 2012 inaugural rankings were Denmark, Finland, Norway, the Netherlands, Canada, Switzerland, Sweden, New Zealand, Australia, and Ireland.[35] The 2021 rankings were strikingly similar: Finland, Denmark, Switzerland, Iceland, the Netherlands, Norway, Sweden, Luxembourg, New Zealand, and Austria.[36] The United States came in at #11 in 2012 and #19 in 2021. Not surprisingly, freer societies have happier people than do more repressive societies. One explanation for Nordic happiness was summarized thus: "The Nordic countries are characterized by a virtuous cycle in which various key institutional and cultural indicators of [a] good society feed into each other including well-functioning democracy, generous and effective social welfare benefits, low levels of crime and corruption, and satisfied citizens who feel free and trust each other and governmental institutions." The study also notes that "early analyses quantifying welfare as an aggregate measure of government welfare spending, like the percentage of GDP devoted to public welfare programs, tended to find no link between welfare expenditure and happiness, or even a negatively-correlated link. Government spending as such thus seems not to be clearly linked to greater or worse life satisfaction. . . ."[37] It seems, then, that when it comes to a welfare state, what matters to Scandinavian citizens is, for the most part, a generalized sense of economic security and the sense that the welfare state supports well-functioning public institutions, including education and public transport. But high government spending and the taxes that support them do not themselves produce happiness, and in fact can produce the exact opposite. I can say definitively as a highly productive resident of a deeply socialist society—in Quebec, Canada—that I have no such sense of economic security or of well-functioning institutions when the state's deeply confiscatory tax system "allows" me to retain only roughly one-third of my income (once all taxes are accounted for). Indeed, this makes me extremely depressed and unhappy and resentful that the government appears to think that it "owns" me, or at least most of my earnings. Personally, I believe that the only path to true happiness is one of minimal governmental intrusion into our lives and our bank accounts. In Canada, the income tax was originally levied in 1917 as a "temporary" measure, but as the economist and Nobel laureate Milton Friedman memorably opined, "Nothing is so permanent as a temporary government program."[38] I find such taxation more soul-destroying than life-affirming; it certainly does not make me happy! And that leads me to another point.

Happiness as a Positional Emotion

Some view happiness as a non-comparative metric. That is, my happiness and my standards for feeling happy have nothing to do with you or yours. But while this might be true for some contributing factors to happiness, the evidence seems pretty clear that happiness is also, in part, shaped by a comparative calculus. We are a social species that cares deeply about our relative standing when compared to relevant others. This is the whole premise behind social comparison theory[39] and what lies behind the adage "keeping up with the Joneses." It is also at the root of the concepts of "positional goods" and the "positional economy" as explained by Cornell economist Robert Frank in two of his books.[40] Take, for example, winner-take-all markets wherein countless individuals compete for one large reward that will ultimately go to one individual, or at best a few people (as in auditions for the leading roles in a blockbuster movie). Inherent to such markets is the relative performance of the competitors to one another rather than some absolute metric of success. The end result, though, is that one person or a few people will achieve maximal happiness whilst the others will be dejected by yet another rejection. From a collectivist perspective, this is a suboptimal allocation of happiness. Ecstasy for one or the few, and misery for many.

Particularly in the era of social media, social comparisons can lead to nefarious downstream effects. Everyone posts his best self on social media, so there is a tendency to overestimate how happy, successful, and content he is, and there is a danger, for some, in concluding, "Everyone on Facebook is travelling to exotic places, getting married, having wonderful promotions; and my life sucks!" For young people this is an especial problem, and the power of social comparison within cliques is oftentimes the central theme in films capturing teenage angst, because it is such a common occurrence. The 2015 film *The DUFF* (Designated Ugly Fat Friend) addresses this issue in a comical manner. Within any group of popular kids, there is always a "lesser" member, which serves to augment the attractiveness of the other group members via the contrast effect.

The extent to which people care about relative versus absolute metrics is captured well when it comes to one's salary. Suppose I were to ask you to choose between two options: 1) you receive a $600 salary increase and your colleague receives $800; or 2) you receive a $500 salary increase as does your colleague.[41] Note that if you choose option 1, you are left with more money in your pocket than if you were to choose option 2. From a strict income maximization perspective (the so-called rational choice), option 1 should always be preferred. But of course, humans are a social species endowed with a calculus for fairness and equitable distribution, so many people will end up preferring option 2. This is surprising to no one other than economists who preach the glory of *Homo economicus* (a mythical creature of hyperrationality that exists solely in their stunted imaginations). What applies to money applies also to the most basic of all Darwinian pursuits, sex. At first glance, it might be reasonable to assume that all other things being equal, the more sex we have, the happier we'll be.[42] But while our happiness is positively determined by the frequency of sex that we have, it is also negatively correlated to the frequency of sex that those around us are engaging in.[43] Hence, for people to be maximally happy, they should marry a spouse with a high libidinal drive and surround themselves with friends who are Catholic priests and nuns: a guaranteed pathway to happiness!

Happiness is not only a positional emotion, it is a *social contagion*. That is, it spreads through networks of friends. A network analysis on data from the Framingham Heart Study found that happiness spreads to up to three degrees of separation in a network.[44] In other words, beware of how unhappy or happy your friends are; their misery or elation might infect you!

Happiness is a comparative emotion in at least one additional way. In a study of Olympic medalists, bronze medalists were found to be happier than silver medalists.[45] At first, this might seem counterintuitive in that finishing second should trigger greater satisfaction and happiness than finishing third. If happiness in this case, however, is shaped by counterfactual thinking (comparing one's situation against what might have been), the silver medalist will likely compare herself against the gold medalist, while the bronze medalist will likely compare herself to those who received no medal at all. Viewed from this perspective, the silver medalist becomes disappointed whereas the bronze medalist is ecstatic. Our happiness is in part shaped by such comparative analyses. This is precisely why firms are so careful to manage their customers' expectations—because they know a consumer's satisfaction level is determined in part not by some preestablished absolute level of service, but by their expectations. So, if Amazon tells you this book is sold out, but Amazon has reordered it and it will be on your doorstep in four weeks, and then Amazon delivers it in one week—what do you think of Amazon?

The Peak-End Rule

The way we assess our happiness—as a measure of pleasurable or painful experiences—is hardly objective. Suppose that you went away on a one-week vacation, and at the end of each day, you ranked how great that day was. Now let's envision three scenarios. In scenario one, your first six days were horrible, marked by rainy weather and the flu. On the seventh day, however, the weather cleared, and you felt great. You gave the first six days 10 points each and the last day 100 (on a scale from 0–100 capturing "worst day ever" to "best day ever"). In scenario two, every day was wonderful with a consistent daily score of 80 points. In scenario three, your first three days were very bad (each with a score of 20), the fourth day was fantastic (score of 90), and the last three days were very bad (each with a score of 20). If you were to add up the total happiness of each of the three scenarios, they would be: 160, 560, and 210. Clearly, from an aggregate perspective, scenario two is the one that should be remembered as the best. But Nobel laureate Daniel Kahneman has shown with his "peak-end" model that most people will judge an overall experience by its peak,[46] meaning that many people will remember the first or third scenario as the better vacation because they reached higher peaks (and especially the first scenario because the peak was at the end).

As an evolutionary behavioral scientist, I'm always interested in examining the Darwinian reasons that explain the architecture of the human mind. So the obvious question is, why do people assess their happiness in the ways predicted by the peak-end rule? Kahneman nailed it when he stated: "Memory wasn't designed, you know, to measure ongoing happiness or to measure total suffering. For survival, you really don't need to put a lot of weight on duration—on the duration of experiences. It's how bad they are and whether they end well. I mean, that is really the information that you need for an organism. And so there are very good evolutionary reasons for the peak and end rule and for the neglect of duration. It leads to, you know, in some cases, to absurd results."[47] But those are the results, nevertheless.

The Mismatch Hypothesis as an Impediment to Happiness

Much modern unhappiness stems from evolutionary adaptations that were beneficial in the past but that are a mismatch with our modern-day environments. Our gustatory preferences, as coded by our taste buds, are a telling manifestation of this point. These evolved to solve a recurring and endemic evolutionary problem—namely, our ancestors faced environments that were defined by caloric uncertainty and scarcity. From this perspective, it is natural for us to prefer high caloric foods, such as a fatty steak or a rich chocolate mousse or potato chips, to raw carrots or celery. But now, in societies where caloric scarcity is largely a thing of the past, and where we live more sedentary lives, this evolutionary adaptation that has us favor high caloric foods is no longer aligned with the current reality. In the science of evolutionary medicine, this is known as the mismatch hypothesis, and it captures the global epidemiology of the lifestyle diseases that plague us in the modern world; in short, to understand some of our current health ailments (physical and mental), we need to appreciate the incongruity between how our brains and bodies have evolved and modern environments.[48] The pursuit of happiness can be analyzed with a similar evolutionary lens, looking at modern environments, how they conform or depart from traits we have acquired through evolution, and how we respond to them.[49] For example, why is it that so many people who live in major metropolitan areas feel lonely? They are surrounded by literally millions of people, yet they feel all alone. This is because there is a mismatch between contemporary urban living and the evolutionary environments in which our ancestors evolved, typically consisting of small bands of up to 150 people (known as Dunbar's number).[50] Such environments allow for the formation of deep emotive and affiliative bonds that cater to our evolved need for meaningful social interaction. You might cross paths with a thousand or more people on your way to or from work and yet feel alone in an endless sea of strangers: innumerable people, alone together.

As parents, we raise our children with the "stranger danger" maxim. Of course, it makes perfect evolutionary sense to be wary of strangers on occasion, but strangers also present many new opportunities for future friendships. After all, a stranger today might become your best friend eventually. And it is clear that deep, meaningful friendships constitute a central feature of a happy life, an insight that Aristotle made long ago.[51] Several papers and one recent book have documented how connecting with strangers can contribute to our happiness and well-being, be it when sitting on a plane, taking the subway, or interacting with the barista.[52] We can take the impersonal nature of the big city and turn it into an environment that mimics the past, the reality in which we evolved, creating de facto tribes or small communities within giant cities.

In writing this book, I often went to a local café. There is a table at the back of the establishment that has become "my" table. On one visit to the café, my son accompanied me and, scouting ahead, informed me that "my" table was occupied. What? Given my routinized behavior, it took me a moment to recover from the indignity of having to find a new table. The gentleman occupying my table, who had noticed my surprised reaction, approached me and asked if I wanted to have "my" table back. We introduced ourselves and then I realized that he was the new owner of the café. He asked me if he could offer my son and me something on the house (I got an espresso and my son a pistachio cookie), and I invited him to join us at "my" table. We started to chat, at which point I found out that he was half Pakistani and half Persian, and I shared with him a bit about my background (Lebanese Jewish). He was excited to find out that I was the author of *The Parasitic Mind* because the previous owner of the café had purchased a copy of my book and placed it up front on the café's bookshelf. His dad's wife (his parents are divorced) had previously remarked to him that she had purchased a copy of my book. He then found out that I had been a frequent guest on Joe Rogan's show and that I hosted my own popular show (*The Saad Truth*). In those few minutes, we bonded by an act of hospitality and friendship. As he got up to leave "my" table, he said, "You're so low-key." This meeting took place the day prior to my travelling to Florida to deliver a lecture at an event organized by Hillsdale College, as well as my appearing on Tucker Carlson's podcast. I had a million things to do prior to travelling the next day, and yet I was more than happy to seize the moment and connect with someone who appeared to be a lovely, warm, and generous individual. I did not allow my situational stress and time pressure to derail me from this otherwise lovely encounter. This is a parable of how to live an enriching life. Be open to the endless opportunities that life throws at you. When serendipity comes knocking, answer the call. Also, be generous, not only with your time but in your hospitality. When guests come to our home, I expect them to put on weight given the tsunami of food that they are about to consume. Short of that, I have failed as a host. An openness of one's spirit opens you to countless enriching moments, the totality of which makes a quilt amounting to a good life. As a side note, the owner just came up to me to pick up the empty dishes from "my" table. I advised him that I was writing a passage about our encounter, at which point he unleashed a radiant smile and said, "Thank you. That's very flattering."

Ideological Impediments to Happiness

I teach at a business school, so my teaching must have real-world applications. In all my courses, be they on evolutionary consumption, the psychology of decision-making, or consumer behavior, I always begin by laying the foundations of how evolutionary biology and evolutionary psychology are necessary to fully understand the human mind. When I first ask my students to explain how this knowledge might be relevant to marketers, they are oftentimes unsure what to answer. I quickly remind them that a great marketer or an effective advertiser is one who has a deep understanding of human nature. If you create advertising messages or design products that are congruent with our evolved expectations, you increase your odds of success. If you choose to target consumers whilst ignoring the biologically based preferences that shape our minds and bodies, you do so at your peril. Take for example romance novels. The readership for this genre is almost exclusively female. It is a form of fantasy escapism for women centered around a desirable male who fits an ideal archetype: he is tall; socially dominant or successful (a prince or a neurosurgeon); he has an impressive abdomen, including six-pack abs; and he's a little dangerous and reckless and can only be tamed by the love of the female protagonist. From a marketing perspective, this is not difficult to understand. Women do not fantasize about pear-shaped men with high-pitched, nasal voices who suck their thumbs in a fetal position whilst having a good cry watching *Bridget Jones's Diary*, when taking a break from playing video games all day in mom's basement. That is not part of the repertoire of female fantasies. But for a moment, let us suppose that an ultra-progressive publisher of romance novels decided to break free from the shackles of "toxic masculinity" and boldly created a new line of books with a wimpy and sensitive male archetype, called the Brian Stelter line. This would impart unhappiness on all, both the female readers, since none of them likely fantasizes about Stelter types, and ultimately the company's executives (and their bottom line). Commercial happiness (success) would only be restored when the company released the Gad Saad line.

What about socioeconomic and political systems? How are these related to human flourishing? To answer this question, I return to one of my favorite quotes, offered by the late Harvard entomologist E. O. Wilson. When asked about the failings of Marxism, he replied: "Good ideology. Wrong species."[53] As an expert on the social organization of ants, he knew that what might work in the largely egalitarian ant society (one reproductive queen, a few drones, and many workers) would not work in human societies. Humans are not as interchangeable as most ants are. We are far more differentiated in our talents, our personalities, our drives, and our abilities, and this natural heterogeneity leads to natural hierarchies. Humans thrive—in every way: economically and in their pursuit of happiness—when given the freedom to instantiate their individuality. This is precisely why East Germany had walls meant to stop its citizens from fleeing to the West. Too many East Germans knew that if they could escape from the "utopian egalitarianism" of communism, they would flourish and be happy in the capitalist West. It is the same reason that for more than six decades Cubans have risked shark-infested waters to seek freedom and happiness on the shores of the United States. Political and economic systems that are antithetical to human nature inevitably produce unhappiness. On the other side of the ledger, the economic freedom, competition, and prosperity produced by capitalism is a leading cause of Western happiness, including in the so-called social welfare states of Scandinavia, which are still capitalist societies.[54] The real-world experiments of comparing socialist-communist countries and capitalist ones have been repeated on countless occasions, and the data could not be any clearer that socialist-communist societies produce poverty and misery and capitalist societies produce prosperity and happiness. And yet, Alexandria Ocasio-Cortez and Bernie Sanders persist in their ideological delusions, unencumbered by the corrective historical evidence to the contrary.

Militant feminism (which, like socialism and communism, is something that I would call an "idea pathogen," a bad idea that gets transmitted virally, largely by universities) is an ideology that has imparted immeasurable misery on millions of women, because it denies human nature and the reality of sexual differences. That men and women should be treated equally under the law (equity feminism) is a veridical position. But militant feminism has pursued the idea of sexual equality to the point of lunacy, arguing that any differences in behaviors between the sexes are manifestations of an evil patriarchy that must be eradicated. Take, for example, the old alleged double standard regarding human sexuality—namely, that promiscuous men are admired whereas promiscuous women are reviled. According to feminist ideology, this is a means by which the patriarchy keeps women in check. Say no to the patriarchy! Burn your bras, engage in meaningless one-night stands, and refrain from having children. Hey ladies, you are no different from men; and if they are promiscuous, you should be too! Millions of women answered that call, and yet the longitudinal data tracking women's happiness levels have shown that the trends are going in the wrong direction. Specifically, over a thirty-five-year period, women's levels of subjective well-being in the United States have declined both in an absolute sense as well as relative to men.[55] This is perhaps not too difficult to explain: Convincing women about the virtues of one-night stands is certain to make men happier than women, at least in the short term. Unencumbered sex is seldom a path to happiness for women; it is marriage (which relies on commitment and trust), not promiscuity, that is positively correlated with happiness.[56] This does not imply that women do not at times enjoy the pursuit of unencumbered sexual variety, but they certainly do not do so to the same extent as men.[57] To recognize this obvious evolutionary fact does not make one a patriarchal misogynist but someone rooted in reality. It is incontestable that many postulates of militant feminism have been detrimental to women's senses of happiness and well-being.

Larry Elder is a highly successful nationally syndicated radio host who espouses wise and commonsensical positions on politics and economics, and because these positions are designated dangerously "conservative" by the media elite, Elder (a black man) has even been referred to as the "black face of white supremacy" by apocalyptic progressives.[58] Progressives are fully committed to diversity, inclusion, and equity (the DIE religion, as I coined it in *The Parasitic Mind*) and the advancement of people of color as long as such folks do not commit the unforgivable act of exhibiting personal agency and freedom of thought. When people of color violate edicts of progressive orthodoxy, they become white supremacists. Obviously.

Elder has long weighed in on the ills of the black community. Rather than blaming systemic racism, he argues that black people, like anyone else, can be successful in a free society like the United States. The reason for high rates of black poverty and crime is not "systemic racism," but the absence of fathers in the lives of so many black families. The research showing that this is true is vast and has been known for decades, even if progressives prefer to ignore it or deny it or blame "systemic racism."[59] Elder, however, rightly recognizes that if we want to maximize people's opportunities to live a good life, then we need to be honest and properly identify the real impediments rather than indulge in politically correct, "blame others," faux causality.

Is one's political orientation related to happiness and well-being? Numerous studies have established that conservatives report being happier than liberals, exhibit greater well-being, and possess a greater sense of meaning and purpose in life.[60] Anecdotally, my public engagement in the culture wars seems to support this general premise, especially when you compare conservatives to the super-woke progressives, or, as I call them, the blue-haired Taliban, who are always angry, cantankerous, and miserable, and dedicated to radically altering society to create utopia (or, in fact, dystopia). Conservatives, on the other hand, tend to be happy and content because they are grounded in the eternal truths of humanity and human nature, have a much stronger sense of family and nurturing traditions, and have an appreciation for the order and ancient wisdom that has brought us Western democracy and capitalism. Progressives seek to eradicate the past—knocking down statues, rewriting textbooks, banning old books of which they disapprove—and start anew. Alexandria Ocasio-Cortez, whom I refer to as Occasional Cortex (apparently so does Michael Savage[61]), even wishes to dismantle existing buildings and refit them in a way that is consistent with the so-called Green New Deal. Those who have a burning desire to destroy the past—and the present—are unlikely to be happy. And their promise—or belief—that utopia is just around the corner is false and can never be fulfilled, which leads to further unhappiness.

Happiness without God?

If conservatives are happier than liberals, and conservatives are more religious than liberals, does that mean that religion makes people happier? For many people, life cannot have full purpose and meaning without a religious or spiritual component. I have long argued, though, that there are endless ways by which we can achieve a "spiritual" connection with nature, with others, and within ourselves without requiring that such connections be rooted in a supernatural ethos. While conducting my research for this book, I had to engage the thoughts of innumerable brilliant thinkers spanning several millennia. In doing so, I am intellectually connected to their ideas in a deeply meaningful and, one could say, spiritual manner. When I sit on a beach watching the sunset, I experience a deep reverence for the awe-inspiring beauty of nature without needing to root such a satisfying experience within a divine framework. That said, I fully understand that for most people, life is simply unsatisfying without a reverence for the divinely sacred, for God. Hence, even though I am a nonbeliever when it comes to the religious elements of my religion of birth, I am fully anchored in my Jewish identity and understand that religious belief is the rule when it comes to humanity, and I am part of a minority of unbelievers. Several years ago, I was asked to explain my ability to live a purposeful and meaningful life void of a guiding god. Here is what I wrote:

> It is an affront to human dignity to suggest that purpose and meaning in one's life can only be garnered via the belief in a deity. To lead a rich and righteous life is more laudable when pursued void of the "guiding" edicts of a dictatorial higher power. My life is fulfilling in endless earthly ways be it via my intellectual and scientific pursuits; my university teaching; the love that I share with my family members, beloved canine companions, and close friends; traveling to new lands to immerse myself in new cultures and awe-inspiring land-scapes; nourishing my being with knowledge, music, art, and films; and innumerable other daily quests, each of which reminds me of the magic of life.
>
> Carpe Diem (seize the day) is best instantiated when one recognizes the ephemeral and finite nature of our existence. There are no supernatural do-overs or eternal afterlives. My lack of religiosity makes it easier for me to appreciate the importance of every second, every minute, and every hour. You get one shot to experience life fully and hopefully make a difference. To assuage the existential angst inherent to our ever-looming mortality, I say: Fear not, immortality can be achieved but not via a religious-based afterlife. As a loving father to my children, I am effectively propagating my genes

while as an author and professor I am disseminating my memes onto future generations. To recognize the evolutionary roots of our lifelong pursuits does not render them any less awe-inspiring. Instead, science and reason liberate us from the shackles of superstition by offering us a framework for understanding our shared humanity. Ultimately, we all have the capacity to treasure life and enrich the world in incalculable ways, each of which does not require adherence to religious dogma.[62]

As an evolutionist, I am well aware of the tension between science and religion generally, and evolution and religion in particular. That said, the late paleontologist Stephen Jay Gould argued that religion and science ought to peacefully coexist via the NOMA principle (non-overlapping magisteria): namely, they each tackle separate, non-overlapping questions (such as science explaining the natural world, while religion works on establishing moral truths). I personally reject this dichotomy as false because I believe that morality does not reside outside the reach of science (and can be explained by our evolution as a social species). In any case, in several of my previous books, I have discussed the evolutionary roots of religion,[63] as well as the functional benefits reaped from religion.[64] While I may not be a religious person, I fully appreciate that the default value is for humans to be believers. If so, does being religious make people happier? Religiosity and happiness generally exhibit a small positive correlation, though the findings have been quite mixed with some studies yielding no correlation between the two constructs.[65] In other instances, the strength of the correlation has been shown to vary as a function of cultural settings.[66] Of interest, spirituality (but not the extent of religious practice) has been shown to be a strong predictor of happiness in children.[67]

There is no single path for achieving happiness. Some cannot imagine being happy without God, while others reject the need for the supernatural and find that rejection no impediment to experiencing the good life. Happiness has many causal elements, including our genes and personalities, the culture in which we grow up, the political and economic system in which we live, the mindsets we adopt, and the decisions that we make. In the next chapter, I turn to two of the most important decisions when it comes to happiness.

CHAPTER THREE

Key Life Decisions: The Right Life Partner and the Ideal Job

Of all forms of caution, caution in love is perhaps the most fatal to true happiness.[1]

—Bertrand Russell

Never continue in a job you don't enjoy. . . . If you're happy in what you're doing, you'll like yourself. And if you like yourself, you'll have inner peace. And if you have that, along with physical health, you will have had more success than you could possibly have imagined.[2]

—Johnny Carson

If I were to ask you to name your most frequent purposive act, what would you answer? You probably did not say "decision-making" (but if you did you get a gold star). Decision-making is something we do all the time, every day, and with tremendous consequences. Forget about René Descartes's *I think, therefore I am*; a more pointed and correct adage is *I decide, therefore I am*.[3] Life is an interminable sequence of decisions. The choices we make have downstream effects, and few, if any, will be as consequential as our choice of job and our choice of spouse.[4] These two choices are central to our happiness because they are where we spend our lives—at work and with our families.

Accordingly, we'd better make the optimal decisions when it comes to these two sources of potential happiness—or potential misery.

I wake up on most days feeling very happy for three key reasons. First, I am fortunate to have that disposition. Second, I get to wake up next to my wife. She makes me happy in countless ways. You cannot get up on the wrong side of the bed if the one sharing the bed with you makes you happy! Third, as I mentally go through my to-do checklist for the looming day, I am always gleeful and brimming with anticipatory excitement at the innumerable opportunities that lie ahead. I might be spending some time working on my next academic paper, writing a few hundred words on my next book, teaching a class filled with inquisitive and bright students, holding a chat with a fascinating guest on my show *The Saad Truth*, having a consulting meeting with a client or hearing a pitch from a company that wishes to make me a business proposition, perhaps meeting with some of my graduate students whose theses and dissertations I am supervising, or making one or more media appearances. These are some of the recurring tasks of my daily professional life, and they each provide me with a deep sense of purpose and meaning. A life devoid of purpose is an unhealthy life. I mean that literally. It turns out that people over fifty who possess life purpose have greater protection against all-cause mortality.[5] And for most of us our life's purpose is deeply wrapped up with our work and family.

Aristotle argued that to live a good life requires *phronesis* (practical wisdom).[6] At times, longitudinal scientific studies merely confirm that which your grandmother taught you (*phronesis*); and if your grandmother ever told you that there was wealth in having friends, she was absolutely right. Deep and meaningful relationships offer a direct path to happiness. Psychiatrist George Vaillant, former director of the multigenerational Harvard Study of Adult Development that has run for more than eight decades, noted that "when the study began, nobody cared about empathy or attachment. But the key to healthy aging is relationships, relationships,

relationships."[7] He has also stated that "warm, intimate relationships are the most important prologue to a good life."[8] Psychiatrist Robert Waldinger, current director of the study, echoed Vaillant's conclusions: "And when we gathered together everything we knew about them about at age 50, it wasn't their middle-age cholesterol levels that predicted how they were going to grow old. It was how satisfied they were in their relationships. The people who were the most satisfied in their relationships at age 50 were the healthiest at age 80."[9] This insight was corroborated in a meta-analysis of 148 studies involving 308,849 people. The strength of one's social relationships yielded a 50 percent increase in survival rates.[10] Warm relationships offer a protective benefit, and none is more important to your happiness than your relationship with your spouse. It might be yet another cliché uttered by your grandmother, but a successful marriage makes for a happy life; and one of the keys to a successful marriage is open, honest, friendly, respectful communication. My wife and I never go to bed mad at one another, and we are much more likely to praise or appreciate each other than to criticize each other. Psychologist John Gottman has spent many decades studying marital patterns that lead to divorce. Not surprisingly, he found that spouses who act contemptuous of each other, or who are critical, defensive, or evasive in communicating with each other, are much more likely to get divorced.[11]

Mate Choice Is a Compensatory Process—You Can Make Up for Your Shortcomings

The One is a 2021 Netflix series based on the biological determinant premise that you can find your ideal marital match—namely, the one—by submitting your DNA to a central database where it can be matched with others'. But in reality, this is not how life works, largely because mate selection is what we might call a multi-attribute compensatory choice. Let me explain. If a tall man is generally considered more desirable than a short man, how is it that millions of shorter men attract beautiful women as sexual partners? The answer is that mate choice is compensatory, meaning that we can compensate for a shortcoming (forgive the pun) by scoring highly on other desirable traits. A tall man who opens his mouth and signals to the world that he is dumber than Occasional Cortex (Alexandria Ocasio-Cortez), a nearly impossible reality to achieve, might be less attractive to most women than a somewhat shorter man who is highly intelligent, charming, and socially dominant. How else do you think that I was able to marry my immeasurably lovely and beautiful wife? If you are unhappy with your romantic life, please realize that you can alter it. We have the power to improve our prospects in the mating market, and in doing so increase our chances at happiness. For instance, a young unemployed man living in mom's basement playing video games is unlikely to find an orderly line of beautiful women wanting to marry him. But if he were to get a job, exhibit assertiveness and ambition, cut his greasy hair, wear attractive clothes, go to the gym regularly, and involve himself in active social circles, he would have a much better chance of finding an attractive mate. Similarly, a five-hundred-pound woman who attends body positivity seminars and rails against the patriarchy is unlikely to find an orderly line of studly, high-status men waiting to court her. But if she were to get off the proverbial couch, lose those excess 350 pounds or more, adopt a sunnier disposition, and travel in social circles that don't hate men, she will certainly have a broader range of prospective suitors. And by the way, before my reader takes offense, I live my advice. I have lost a lot of weight myself; I consciously strive to be friendly and ambitious; and I have a very happy marriage.

Beware of Matchmakers!

I returned to my home city of Montreal in 1994 to start my career as a young and single assistant professor with a newly minted Ph.D.

from Cornell University. Gleeful matchmakers abounded. After all, in some Jewish circles, it is a *mitzah* (a divinely prescribed good deed) to play the role of a matchmaker. Not surprisingly, not all matchmaking efforts prove successful. In my case, perhaps the most memorable failed attempt occurred when a couple who had been long-standing friends of my parents dropped by while I was visiting. The male friend asked if I'd be interested in meeting some beautiful Lebanese-Jewish and Syrian-Jewish women from the New York–New Jersey area. I shrugged, gave him a tepid affirmative, and he summoned me closer for a more intimate conversation. He said, "This professor thing you are doing, is this something that you are going to stick with? Because these girls are very wealthy, you know. Their families are very wealthy." I mimicked his tone of confidentiality and replied: "You tell those girls that if they would be ashamed to marry a professor, and if their parents would be ashamed to have their daughters marry a professor, I'm unlikely to be interested in meeting them," and I dismissed him with a hand gesture. Once the couple left and I was alone with my parents, how do you think they responded? The answer is: with exasperation! My mother (with my father's approval) admonished me: "Why do you have such a sharp, venomous tongue? Why must you answer in this manner?" Apparently, my parents were not angered by the disrespectful idiocy of their friend but rather were annoyed by my sarcastic reaction to said idiocy. I share this story because there is a truly important life lesson here. When you get married, you are not merely marrying an individual with whom you might share great short-term chemistry. You are marrying their values, their beliefs, their mindset, and that of their family. If any of these additional layers show fissures of incompatibility, run away quickly.

I faced another dating disaster around the same time. I was introduced to a beautiful Syrian woman through a childhood acquaintance. Her parents were very keen on the match because on paper I was an ideal candidate (her dad was also a professor). I met with the parents alone (old-school) at a Lebanese sweets store. As we were leaving, the mother turned to me and said in Arabic: "You know, our daughter, she has not been opened up by a man [a euphemism for being a virgin]." While I am also from the Middle East, this struck me as rather vulgar. I did not think that one should discuss such deeply personal facts in public—a clear proof that acculturation matters, and that you might want to ensure that your family and that of your prospective mate exhibit cultural homophily. In any case, I responded awkwardly, "Ah, thanks for letting me know" (or something to that effect), and they gave me their blessing to go out with their daughter. My subsequent failed interaction with the daughter perfectly captures the tribalism of the Middle East. The family in question were Syrian Christians, and they were desperate to know whether I was a Christian or a Muslim (no other option seemed possible to them). With that in mind, the daughter spent 95 percent of her time trying to find out my religion without directly asking the question (as this might be considered gauche). I quickly recognized the pattern and decided to take her on a joyride of obfuscation (part of my ethos of viewing life as a playground). Once I had tired of her charade, I looked at her and coldly stated: "I'm your parents' worst nightmare." She asked what I meant by that comment. I called her out on her repeated attempts to find out whether I was Christian or Muslim. And I reiterated: "I'm your parents' worst night-mare." At that point, she answered with disdain: "What, you are Muslim?" I responded, "No. Much, much, worse." She was utterly confused. She probably did not even imagine that Lebanese Jews and Syrian Jews existed. Once I advised her of my religious heritage, our date was essentially over. In the car ride back to her home, she leaned against the passenger door in order to maintain maximal distance from the Jew. Once we arrived at her apartment building, she almost jumped out of the moving car and furtively uttered, "Good luck to you," to which I answered, "You mean with my disease? Say hello to your parents. I miss them." Again, I share this story because it highlights the familial context in which mate choices are made. You are marrying not merely an individual but their values and those of their parents. If these do not match yours, the likelihood of a happy, long-lasting union is negligible. Love does not conquer all trials and tribulations. Some obstacles cannot be overcome.

The Ubiquity of the Matching Process

Many decisions that we make in life involve a matching process. For example, you might have heard that dog owners choose dogs that look like them, that there is a matching process between an individual's morphological features and those of his dog. Science has indeed documented this phenomenon cross-culturally in the United States, Venezuela, and Japan.[12] Of note, there is also a matching process between an owner's personality and that of his dog, a link that was found using samples from Hungary and Austria.[13] Anecdotally, I could have vouched for these findings from personal experience. Belgian Shepherds are regal, majestic, aristocratic, beautiful, athletic, and courageous. Is it any surprise that we own Belgian Shepherds? Another form of canine matching takes place at confirmation shows wherein judges choose a specific dog as the best in show. Perhaps the most famous confirmation show in the world is the Westminster Kennel Club Dog Show, which has been held since 1877. The key question is establishing what is meant by "best." It seems rather awkward to compare an English Mastiff (that can weigh up to 230 pounds) to a Pomeranian (that can weigh up to 7 pounds). The height, weight, and other morphological features of these two dogs could not be any more different, and yet judges arrive to a final rating as to which of the two is best. How is this possible? They do so by a matching process. Specifically, they compare each dog against the standards of its breed, and the one that comes closest in matching these is chosen as the winner. Dog shows are a matching process. And so is much else.

For example, the matching process is also applied when consumers choose between a wide assortment of products. Self-congruity theory posits that consumers prefer products that best match important elements of their personhoods, be it their personalities or their values.[14] Car purchases, for instance, can be matched, in the aggregate, to certain demographic groups, which show a preference for certain types of cars, as well as matched to people's faces.[15] When individuals (salesmen) recommend a product, they do so using a matching process, which can include a customer's physical appearance (heavy or thin, round or angular).[16]

The matching process takes places in countless other important settings. High school counselors suggest student career paths on the basis of student academic and personality profiles. A similar matching process takes place when prospective employers administer personality tests to job applicants. The objective is to identify the optimal match between a company's culture and an individual's personality. JPMorgan Chase & Co. has a very different organizational culture than Google—even though both organizations are supremely woke—and the same individual, doing similar work, might flourish in the former and flounder in the latter based on personality. This is precisely why I do not recommend that people choose their professions in response to market conditions; that is not a good prescription for long-term happiness. The proper fit is between you and your chosen profession, not between you and hot job opportunities. Choosing the job that is the best for you will increase your chances for long-term happiness. Choosing a job that is in demand but is a bad fit makes it much more likely that you will experience an existential midlife crisis.

Birds of a Feather Flock Together

In popular culture, we often hear two opposing truisms when it comes to mate choice: *Birds of a feather flock together* and *Opposites attract.* Which is the veridical one when it comes to predicting a couple's long-term success? Generally speaking, people who share similar values are much more likely to have successful long-term unions.[17] It is important to note, though, that there are many variables on which people might assort, not all of which are equally likely to augment a couple's future happiness together. Incidentally, the one factor on which people choose people who are dissimilar to them is sampled via our noses and our sense of smell.[18]

On one of my recent appearances on Joe Rogan's podcast, I offered a theory regarding the likely trajectory of a marriage's success or failure. I first explained that people assort with one another based on their overall mating value.[19] Let us suppose that there are ten key attributes on which men and women are evaluated. Once the entire basket of attributes is summed up for an individual, this yields an overall mate desirability score on a 0 to 100 scale (least desirable to most desirable). People will assort along their overall mating value scores such that a woman who scores a 90 is unlikely to choose a mate who scores a 45 (or vice versa). People choose others that are of roughly equal overall mate value. Next, I expanded this idea using a longitudinal lens. If two people get married straight out of high school, they might have had at that point equal mate values (for example, he is the star quarterback and she is the beautiful valedictorian). It is befitting that the king and queen of prom night would end up together. Now fast-forward ten years. The former high school football player reached his apex when he was eighteen; he has been on a steady downhill trajectory since. He works at a menial job, makes very little money, and shows little ambition or drive. On the other hand, his wife has completed medical school and is now starting a neurosurgery residency. I posited on Joe's show that this divergence in their longitudinal mating value would cause nearly insurmountable stressors on their marriage. Put formally, if a couple's mating value diverges beyond a certain level, the marriage is unlikely to survive. Hence, when seeking a life partner, it is worth bearing in mind whether you might be marrying up or down or sidewise (it is advisable to marry someone of equal overall mate value), and in which directions you and your potential mate might go in the future in terms of your respective mate values. While it is not easy to predict your life trajectories, you should at least be aware of the stresses they could put on your marriage. If your potential partner is always growing personally and professionally, it might be a good idea if you match his or her journey, in your own way, rather than wallowing in an apathetic, self-contented status quo. Of especial note, if the divergence in mate value is such that the woman's mate value is longitudinally increasing whilst that of her male partner is decreasing, this puts additional strain on a marriage, as a man's testosterone levels will fall if he has endemic lower status than his wife.

How I Met My Wife

I met my wife nearly twenty-three years ago through the magic of life's serendipity. I was at the gym doing some weight training when an individual greeted me with a "Hey, professor." Another gentleman within earshot asked if I was truly a professor, and if so in what field. He told me that he was the founder and CEO of a direct marketing firm and was looking for business-related in-house education for his executives. He asked if I would develop a six-week course covering topics like advertising, decision-making, consumer behavior, and so on. We came to an agreement, and shortly thereafter I arrived at his company's headquarters. A beautiful woman with a radiant smile met me at the elevator and asked if I was Professor Saad, and then she led me to the room where my seminars would be held. The second or third week of the course, I was stricken with a nasty bout of bronchitis. During a break, the woman who had greeted me at the elevator (and who was one of my students) brought me a cup of hot tea. Now I thought she was not only beautiful but caring and considerate. She also was eager to continue discussing my lecture topics outside the classroom. I later found out that she was more interested in the professor than the taught material!

Shortly after the course was over, we went to see a movie together (*The Insider* starring Al Pacino) accompanied by one of her friends. My dad had experienced a recent health scare, and so I had acquired a pager (younger readers might have to look that up) so that I could be reached in case of an emergency. My future wife and I also used the pager. We had agreed on the meaning of a set of paged codes so that we could communicate with each other when we were separated and not near a phone. One of these codes was "222," meaning "I'm thinking of you." Well, as I left her that evening, and had hardly walked 100 yards, my pager rang with "222." That experience, coupled with her showing up a few days later at my university office with a picnic basket of epicurean goodies, sealed the deal for me.

One of my all-time favorite movies is the 1993 film *A Bronx Tale*, starring Chazz Palminteri and Robert De Niro. Unlike other classic movies where De Niro portrayed a mobster (like in *The Godfather Part II*, *Once Upon a Time in America*, and *Goodfellas*), in this movie he assumed the role of a hardworking bus driver (Lorenzo) seeking to keep his young son (Calogero, nicknamed C) away from the neighborhood mobsters. Palminteri's character (Sonny), the neighborhood's Mafia boss, befriends C, to the father's dismay, and takes him under his wing. Sonny serves as a mentor to the young man, dispensing a broad range of wisdom (answering such questions as "Is it better to be loved or feared?"). But of relevance to the current context, the mobster turns into a relationship expert when the young man tells him of a looming date with a beautiful girl. Sonny teaches C about the door test; namely, he instructs him to open the passenger door for his date and come around the back of the car. If the girl scooches over to the driver's side to unlock the door, then she is a considerate person. If she fails to do so, in the infamous words of Sonny: "Listen to me kid. If she doesn't reach over and lift up that button for you so you could get in, that means she is a selfish broad and all you've seen is the tip of the iceberg. You dump her and you dump her fast." The positive lesson from the door test is precisely what I gleaned from my future wife when she brought me the tea to soothe my cough (considerate and kind).

Many marriages fail because couples did not heed problematic signals early on (like the door test, among many other cues). Oftentimes, individuals succumb to the exhilaration of their early lust, thinking that this will suffice in building a successful long-term union. But lust will only get you so far. A long-term romantic union has three distinct emotional phases, lust, attraction, and attachment, each of which is associated with a set of endocrinological and neural responses.[20] One needs to navigate all three phases successfully to ensure the long-term viability of a marriage.

Seek a Spouse Who Can Be Your Best Friend

On most weekday mornings, my wife and I see the kids off to school and then we head off for a 65-minute round-trip walk to one of our local cafés. Beyond the obvious health benefits of starting off the day with a long walk, doing so outdoors rather than on a treadmill engenders what Andrew Huberman, associate professor of neurobiology and ophthalmology at Stanford University and popular podcaster, refers to as *optic flow*.[21] Huberman explains this phenomenon as follows: "When [you] look at a horizon or at a broad vista, you don't look at one thing for very long. If you keep your head still, you can dilate your gaze so you can see far into the periphery—above, below and to the sides of you. That mode of vision releases a mechanism in the brain stem involved in vigilance and arousal. We can actually turn off the stress response by changing the way that we are viewing our environment, regardless of what's in that environment."[22] In other words, a long walk triggers the visual system in a manner that yields a reduction of stress. Our long walk also allows us to have leisurely, meaningful conversations. On one recent walk we met the father of one of our daughter's friends. He looked at us and said: "How do you do it?" I replied: "Do what?" He explained that he always sees us walking in the neighborhood hand in hand, smiling, blissfully chatting with one another, and he wondered how we are able to maintain such happiness. My answer was simple: my wife and I love to be around one another. We trust one another. We laugh together. We play together. She is my wife but also my best friend. We have our respective friends, of course, but I have no need for "man cave evenings," and she does not require "girls' nights out." Our union, in short, is all-encompassing. As political scientist Charles Murray of *The Bell Curve* fame once said on my show, the happiest marriages occur when you "marry someone who is your very best friend to whom you are also sexually attracted."[23] That is indeed a good recipe for a happy marriage.

Love Is Humble

I know a couple who were married in 1950, were together for well over sixty years, and then finally separated late in their lives. Throughout their long marriage, there was an underlying tension because both suffered from pathological pride. In English, the word *pride* does not differentiate between its positive connotations (I'm proud of my accomplishments) and its negative counterpart (the primary deadly sin of excessive self-love). In French, though, that distinction exists. *Fierté* refers to the positive connotation, whereas *orgueil* refers to its negative counterpart. If you are too proud, you never admit to your mistakes.

You never apologize for your mistakes. Hence, imagine a marriage wherein one partner does something wrong and should correct it by admitting it and apologizing for it. The mistake need not be something as consequential as infidelity. Even a curt and impatient reply might necessitate an apology. But now let us assume that both parties have gone on record stating that they have never made a mistake. Well, this places them in a difficult spot. The reality is that we all make mistakes, but if we are so prideful as to presume that we are perfect and mistake-free, we can never resolve our conflicts. The dynamics in such a marriage become an avalanche of unresolved negativity and unaddressed violations, none of which have ever been resolved positively. In Corinthians 13:4, one finds the following: "Love is patient, love is kind. It does not envy, it does not boast, it is not proud."[24] That is an excellent definition of love. And the old adage is true: if you want a happy marriage, you should never go to bed angry at one another. Imagine though if you have never apologized for any transgression because you are too prideful. Every night becomes another tally in the "going to bed angry" column. Do this for years and you will eventually separate.

But if you approach your marriage with humility, if you recognize that we all make mistakes, if you immediately apologize for your mistakes, you have established the basis for forgiveness, honesty, and integrity in your marriage. It is important to note, though, that the science tells us that when apologizing for a mistake, the apology must be sincere, contrite, and at times it must serve as a "costly signal."[25] That is, in order for a "signal," a communication, to be construed as honest, it sometimes must be costly; this is how the recipient knows that it is not the work of a schemer or a scammer. The 2006 film *The Last Kiss* starring Zach Braff and Jacinda Barrett highlights this important lesson. They are a young couple in love and expecting their first child. Their idyllic romance is shattered by a moment of weakness when Zach's character (Michael) has a sexual liaison with another woman (played by Rachel Bilson). With great remorse, he eventually admits his infidelity to his wife-to-be, who is unwilling to forgive him. An exchange between Michael and his fiancée's father (Stephen), played by Tom Wilkinson, highlights the importance of an apology serving as a "costly signal."

> **Michael:** I'm in love with your daughter, Stephen. Maybe that doesn't mean anything to you but I'm standing here. You are her father. I am looking you in the eyes and I'm telling you I will do anything in the world to get your daughter back.
> **Stephen:** Anything?
> **Michael:** I'll do anything.
> **Stephen:** People say that; they don't mean it.
> **Michael:** But I mean it!
> **Stephen:** Well, it's very simple, just do whatever it takes.
> **Michael:** It's that simple?
> **Stephen:** Yes. You can't fail if you don't give up.

True to his word, Michael plants himself outside the entrance to their home for a few days and nights, not eating, drinking, or shielding himself from the weather. At first his unforgiving fiancée ignores the remorseful and diminished Michael, but slowly she relents. Finally, she opens the front door and invites him in. His willingness to suffer was a "costly signal" of his commitment to her. He realized he had made a terrible mistake, but through his contriteness and humility he was able to win back the woman he really loved. Love is humble. Always apologize to your spouse when you have genuinely erred. You need to get this right, because having a great relationship with your spouse is one of the two most important secrets to being happy. The other is finding purpose and meaning in your work, your career, to which I turn next.

Find the Right Job

In 2007, I authored a paper in a medical journal on an evolutionarily relevant variable that might explain male-to-female suicide rates around the globe.[26] Globally, men are three times more likely than women to commit suicide, even though women are more likely to make an unsuccessful attempt (perhaps because, with women, it is often meant as a call for help). Beyond suicides, men are much more likely than women to be the victims of a murder, to be incarcerated, and to be homeless;[27] one wonders why the patriarchy has yet to resolve those disparities in men's favor. I am sure that the Wellesley College Women's Studies department is assiduously working on explaining how these epidemiological facts make women the primary victims in all of these situations. It is interesting too that male-to-female suicide ratios can differ sharply between countries. What explains the difference? I argued and found that a country's economic conditions serve as a strong predictor of suicide ratios between men and women. Specifically, the lower a country's average per capita gross national income, the more pronounced the male-to-female suicide ratio. While poor economic conditions affect both sexes, there is a pronounced strain that attacks a man's psyche if he is unable to achieve a desired level of economic prosperity. For example, the link between unemployment and suicide has been documented in several studies and is much more pronounced in men than in women.[28] Moreover, a 1 percent increase in the unemployment rate has five times the negative effect on well-being as a 1 percent increase of the inflation rate.[29] While many economic variables matter, when it comes to happiness employment is much more important than purchasing power. Having a job provides people with some measure of purpose and meaning. Of course, not all jobs are created equal in their capacity to garner happiness or misery. Prior to exploring some of the relevant job characteristics, a quick comment about forced retirement, a type of induced unemployment.

At many universities, full-time faculty members face a mandatory retirement age (often at age sixty-five). In some instances, this might make sense in that you often have professors who become deadwood after obtaining tenure. While there are several important reasons for tenure, it can engender a slacker mentality among some members of the professoriate. That said, many professors have remained extraordinarily productive well into their golden years. Take, for example, my former doctoral supervisor, the cognitive psychologist J. Edward Russo. He is currently in his late seventies and his productivity remains exemplary. He continues to be a very active researcher despite the fact that he has no extrinsic reasons for retaining his high productivity standards. (I recently attended his retirement party at Cornell.) He is simply a scientist at heart. Donald Trump stepped down as president when he was seventy-four. Bernie Sanders ran for president when he was in his late seventies. These are hardly spring chickens, and yet we do not place them—or even the current, and cognitively impaired, president of the United States, Joe Biden—under forced retirement. Why should individuals who might have access to the nuclear codes be allowed to assume arguably the most stressful job in the world, and yet innumerable productive and experienced people are put out to pasture at an earlier age? Whether you enter the retirement stage in your life voluntarily or mandatorily, it is crucial that you find ways to retain purpose and meaning in your life. Several studies have documented the physical and mental health benefits that stem from delaying retirement, having "bridge" employment (engaging in paid work after retiring from one's main career), or doing volunteer work after retirement.[30] I have often heard anecdotal evidence that someone's parent was hit with a *coup de vieux* [a hit of old age] shortly upon retiring; and as a social scientist I can confirm that there is compelling research demonstrating that refraining from retirement serves as a protective measure against cognitive decline, notwithstanding the problematic case of Joe Biden.

Temporal Freedom, Job Control, and Justice at Work

Many laypeople wrongly presume that a professor's main responsibility is to teach, whereas the reality is that this constitutes a small, albeit important, part of the job. Between my research, teaching, and administrative duties, coupled with my external professional activities (such as media appearances and consulting), it is typical for me to work very long hours. That said, I'm seldom stressed by the amount of work that I face. Rather, my greatest occupational stressor is when my week includes multiple meetings. Meetings constitute an infringement on my temporal freedom and as such serve as a form of scheduling asphyxia. The pursuit of truth and freedom are the guiding values in my life. I may end up working for fourteen hours on a portion of a book or an academic paper, but so long as I have personal agency to decide what I am working on and for how long, I am happy. Contrast this with the reality faced by some employees who possess little to no freedom in terms of their tasks or their schedule. At work, a person's sense of happiness, satisfaction, and meaningfulness can be tied both to personal autonomy and to the *variety* of tasks and skills required by a job.[31]

Early in my professorial career, parents or siblings would often scoff when I said I was heading off to work: "Oh right, off to 'work' at the café again?" It was difficult for them to conceive that someone might use a public space such as a coffee shop to sit down and read academic studies, work on a scientific paper, draft a book, or prepare a lecture. For them, work had to be defined by an identifiable physical space (like a retail store, a physician's office, or a manufacturing plant). My life was apparently that of a café *flâneur* skipping through life with a happy gait of insouciance. If you can be a café vagabond as an integral part of your job, take it!

Speaking of cafés, I recently ran into a lovely Tunisian man whom I had originally met whilst watching the unfolding of the 2018 men's soccer World Cup at the neighborhood's Italian coffee shop. He was excited to share the good news with me that his partner (who was with him) was pregnant. After congratulating them both, I turned to the woman and asked her if she was planning to eventually return to work, and in the process I inquired about her profession. Upon hearing that she was a flight attendant, I blurted: "I don't know how you do it." I assumed she might think I was referring to a fear of flying, so I quickly added that I simply could not understand how someone could enjoy being so physically and temporally constrained once those airplane doors were locked. Your fate is sealed for the duration of the flight. I could never do that. Nor could I imagine enjoying the restrictions placed on a sailor in a submarine. Personally, I need freedom to schedule myself and to involve myself in a variety of activities. It turns out, according to social science, that my own preferences are a formula for happiness and good health.

Studies show definite negative health consequences to those who hold jobs that offer them low intellectual discretion (a measure of how repetitive a job is) and little freedom of schedule (such as the ability to take a break at one's discretion). Those holding such jobs are at significantly higher risk for coronary heart disease.[32] A more recent meta-analysis revealed that the risks go beyond coronary heart disease to include significantly higher rates of all-cause mortality for workers with low job control.[33] Lack of occupational freedom kills!

The social epidemiologist Sir Michael Marmot has been a leading researcher at the intersection of how our health is affected by the types of jobs that we hold.[34] Generally speaking, jobs can affect our health via several proximate pathways including our blood pressure, cortisol levels, and inflammation markers.[35] Not surprisingly, job strain has a profound effect on our health.[36] Not only do jobs affect our well-being, but our psychological well-being has a positive effect on our job performance. From an organizational perspective, happy and optimistic employees perform well on the job, as was shown by a data set comprised of more than 900,000 soldiers. Those who received performance or heroism awards (12.6 percent of the sample size) scored higher on well-being measures as well as on optimism.[37] Jobs affect individuals' well-being, and their well-being affects their job performance.

Another key contributor to employees' job satisfaction is whether they perceive their workplaces as just environments. Are employees treated fairly? Are their accomplishments properly valued and appreciated by their bosses and more generally by their companies? I'll share a few examples from my own career. Back in 1998, I had been invited to speak at the business school of another local university. During my visit, I held a chat with the then chair of the department, who was exploring the possibility of making me a job offer. When I asked him about the likely salary that I might be offered, he took out a salary grid and inquired about the number of years it had been since I obtained my master's degree (this posed a problem since I have both MBA and MS degrees, and I thought it rather strange that he didn't ask about my doctorate). I asked why this mattered, and he said that it was the metric they used to set salaries. So I asked him: "Would my salary be the same if, after my master's degree, I had been flipping burgers [as a short-order cook] or won the Nobel Prize?" He paused and answered, "Yes." I knew then (I had other reasons too) that this was not the place for me, as its ethos was antithetical to a meritocratic system.

My own university is hardly different. First, it is in Quebec, and Quebec is a haven of socialist thinking and aggressive mediocrity, because meritocracy is undoubtedly a form of white supremacy. The key purpose of the faculty's union is to ensure "equity" across its members. Hence, if you are an overachiever, this places great strain on the ethos of equal non-productivity: "Hey overachiever, stop showing off your accolades. You are making the rest of your colleagues look bad." Several years ago, our then department chair encouraged faculty members to send their recent relevant achievements so that they could be announced publicly. True to the request, I sent along such a list, but the chair announced only a small fraction of it. When I inquired why, the chair said the list in its entirety would have made others feel bad. This non-meritocratic ethos is pervasive in academia, and I have often been its target. In late January 2022, I was humbled and honored to receive a personal letter from the prime minister of India, the Honorable Narendra Modi, commending me on my work (as part of the celebration of Republic Day). I asked the relevant senior administrators and communications officers at my university if they would like to announce this wonderful accolade. No such announcement has taken place. I should also add that the international success of *The Parasitic Mind* has gone largely unnoticed by the university. Universities are a lot more interested in what I call "Stories of First." Congratulations to the first transgender Indigenous Muslima who self-identifies as disabled (but is not) for being valedictorian of the Intersectional Feminism bachelor's program, or kudos to the first nonbinary transracial Latinx for having been interviewed by a local magazine on the need to dismantle the heteronormative patriarchal economic system known as capitalism. "Sorry, Dr. Saad. Your accomplishments are not worthy of further promotion." Hence, I exist in two realms. In one, the world at large, there is appreciation of my work, both as an academic and as a public intellectual. In the other, my own place of employment, I am practically an invisible man when it comes to recognition of my accomplishments. This lack of justice at work has been shown to be detrimental to one's heart health.[38] I can only hope that my genes, good eating habits, exercise routine, and the fact that I have never smoked a cigarette protect me from the occupational injustices that I face. Both my personal advice and the data from social science should encourage you to try to find a job where your talents and contributions are fully appreciated. Life is too short to be willfully ignored by those who should bask in your reflected glory.

Finding Purpose and Meaning through the Creative Process

There are endless ways that an individual can contribute to improving and enriching the world, from a small gesture of kindness to a grand act of philanthropy. From a very early age, I taught my children the old adage that they should leave a place better than they found it. My children were first inculcated with this ethos at the beach, where we would scour the sand picking up bags of litter. Once we had amassed some psychologically satisfying number of objects, we would return to our beach play in the knowledge that we had improved this small swath of public space. It captures the "think locally" mindset when it comes to finding purpose and meaning and satisfaction in one's daily life. Within the time and space constraints of a particular day at the beach, we managed to make a small difference for the greater good. But what of a grander pursuit of meaning and purpose? Could people find such an elusive goal via their chosen jobs or professions? Are there particular occupations that are more amenable to finding such existential bliss? Of course, some professions, by their very nature, can impart huge impact. Think of the physician who saves you from a dreadful disease, the religious leader to whom one turns for advice, or the teacher who educates your young children (not, one hopes, in the faux allure of critical race theory). Practiced properly, these professions are inherently noble, and accordingly they can offer purpose and meaning to their practitioners.

Notwithstanding such occupational callings, it is my contention that the most effective way to live an enriched professional life is via the magic of the creative process. Take, for example, a chef who practices the culinary arts. The term is apt in that a chef is creating a gustatory tapestry that will enrich your life even if only for a fleeting moment. The same could be said of the painter who uses a combination of colors to create a visual tapestry that enriches your visual cortex. Or the architect who uses a combination of scientific principles and aesthetic acumen to create structures that enrich our lives every day. The romantic allure of many European cities stems in part from their architectural beauty. In my case, the need to create is a visceral need not unlike thirst or hunger. I create new scientific knowledge via the peer-reviewed academic articles and books that I publish; I create new bridges between academia and the general public via my engagement on social media and my media appearances; I create publicly consumable content via my YouTube channel and podcast; I author articles for the general public via my *Psychology Today* column and popular books like this one and *The Parasitic Mind*. Many of my waking hours are spent creating. This gives me great psychological satisfaction. I could never be fully happy and content had I not chosen a profession that allows me to be creative.

There are two ways to leave a legacy: one is through genetic propagation, begetting children and investing in one's kin (such as nieces and nephews), and the other is through memetic proliferation.[39] Genetic propagation is known as inclusive fitness in evolutionary biology. Using the currency of evolutionary theory, an individual who has had ten children has greater reproductive fitness than a celibate monk who forsakes the joys and challenges of having children. There is a second non-genetic way by which each of us can achieve a semblance of immortality. In his 1976 book *The Selfish Gene*, zoologist Richard Dawkins argued that a meme is the cultural equivalent of the gene. Memes refer to packets of information (ideas, beliefs, fads, jingles) that can spread from one brain to another in a process akin to genetic propagation. Viewed from this perspective, a library is a gigantic repository of memes that are stored and catalogued in individual books. As such, when we read a great Shakespearean play, the playwright may be dead, but his words, ideas, and creative imagination live on to be consumed by millions of people around the world. Shakespeare has achieved memetic immortality through the creation of his many plays that poignantly capture key features of the human condition. Through my creative output—the online content that I have created, the students that I have taught, the papers and books that I have written—I have secured my memetic legacy. I strongly suggest that you seek a profession that allows you to be creative and that grants you the opportunity to attain memetic immortality, realizing that creativity can be expressed in innumerable ways. It is an assured path to finding meaning and purpose in one's daily activities.

What if an individual does not possess any creative talents that might be channeled into a fulfilling career outlet? One can still contribute to creative pursuits via a broad assortment of supporting roles. You may not have the creative genius of filmmaker Steven Spielberg or the creative writing abilities of Ernest Hemingway, but if the film or publishing industries are alluring, you might consider a career as a talent agent or acquisitions editor. I don't mean to imply that other career paths outside of the creative realm are unimportant or uninteresting. Clearly, accountants, business managers, and insurance adjusters serve vital roles in our economy, but I'm unsure that such jobs offer existential purpose and meaning to those who hold them; perhaps these people can find their creative outlet via hobbies or volunteer work, outside of their normal careers. But it is an advantage if you can find a profession that allows you to instantiate the "work as play" motto rather than the "work to live" adage. Whenever creativity is involved, work becomes an act of play, and that makes it much more amenable to the pursuit of happiness.

Business owners, too, can create—not only by creating a new business and new jobs but by creating dual-purpose spaces. For example, my wife once celebrated my birthday by booking us for a special evening at the back of a cookbook store. One of the owners, who was a chef, held short cooking tutorials in a beautiful industrial-grade kitchen in the back of the bookstore. The paid guests learned how to make four broths and then got a chance to sample the finished products. Similar spaces exist for workshops on glass blowing, ceramics, painting, and knitting, among other creative activities. The owners of such spaces—whether they are creative themselves in these specific arts and crafts or not—offer a conduit for such creative endeavors. Small-business entrepreneurs can find additional purpose and meaning in owning and operating retail artisanal spaces precisely because the commercial interaction there is not purely transactional.

Many people who are lucky enough to land jobs or professions that provide them with purpose and meaning end up succumbing to workaholism.[40] They are unable to strike the right balance between their passion for work and other important pursuits in life. This serves as a segue to perhaps the most universal of all prescriptions for the good life, namely that all good things should be pursued in moderation, the topic of the next chapter.

CHAPTER FOUR

The Sweet Spot: All Good Things in Moderation

We all think and assume that more is better, but unintended consequences can arise in a complex system. However, in our complex world, everything of consequence follows an inverted U curve.[1]

—Daniel M. Fatovich

Nothing in excess.[2]

—Delphic maxim 38

The straight path: This [involves discovering] the midpoint temperament of each and every trait that man possesses [within his personality]. This refers to the trait which is equidistant from either of the extremes, without being close to either of them. . . . This path is the path of the wise. Every man whose traits are intermediate and equally balanced can be called a "wise man."[3]

—Maimonides

When I was a mathematics student, I was fascinated by the equations that might explain the curves and shapes found in nature. Take a very simple example, a line in two-dimensional space. All you need to know are the coordinates of two points in a plane, and this suffices to then identify the function that will join these two points (a line). Of course, not all curves and shapes in nature are as simple and regular as a line or a circle. Imagine the contours of a country's borders on a map or the structure of a Romanesco cauliflower. What are the functional forms that might generate such complex and irregular patterns? This was solved by Benoit Mandelbrot, a French-American mathematician who pioneered the field of fractals and fractal geometry.[4] A fractal is a self-replicating algorithm that produces the same pattern across different scales, which can then model countless phenomena in nature. The beauty of fractals is that a simple process of self-replication yields such complex patterns. Furthermore, fractals can be used to explain countless phenomena, be it in cell biology, botany, medicine, geography, graphic design, computer graphics, image compression, climate science, architecture, or art, among many other disciplines. I love fractals because they cater to the way my mind operates: I am always seeking to unify knowledge across disparate domains.

This is perhaps why I was astonished when I recently heard of "Benford's law" on a Netflix documentary series titled *Connected* (hosted by Latif Nasser). The premise of the show is identifying connections between otherwise seemingly unrelated phenomena, or, as the late Harvard biologist E. O. Wilson would say, finding *consilience*![5] Benford's law stipulates that if you look at a numerical data set, the distribution of leading digits (the first digit of a given number) will follow a very specific non-uniform distribution. Positive numbers can start with one of 9 digits (1 through 9), so a uniform distribution would suggest that all 9 digits have an equal probability of occurring (11.1 percent). But it turns out that the probability (expressed as percentages) for 1 through 9 are respectively: 30.1, 17.6, 12.5, 9.7, 7.9, 6.7, 5.8, 5.1, and 4.6 (these add up to 100).[6] Not only is this a mind-blowing set of percentages but it replicates across a dizzyingly broad and unrelated number of areas. For example, if you list your Facebook friends with the number of friends they have, the first digit of that data set will follow Benford's law![7] It is a form of mathematical sorcery. Benford's law has been applied in many disparate contexts, including to detect financial fraud (such as tax evasion) and anomalies in electoral data.

Both Mandelbrot's fractal geometry and Benford's law speak to how elegantly simple algorithms can explain complex phenomena. Is there an equally elegant equation, or rule or law, to explain how human beings can experience optimal living, flourishing, and happiness? In the wisdom of the ancients, there are several worthy contenders, including the Golden Rule, which states: "Do unto others as you would have them do unto you." But for me, Aristotle hit the mark squarely on the head when he established the rule of the golden mean in Book II of *The Nicomachean Ethics*.

The golden mean is the sweet spot between two extremes. Take for example the virtue of courage. It is the mean between cowardice (deficiency of courage) and recklessness (excess of courage). The golden mean can be applied to a great many things and is captured by the maxim "All good things in moderation," or what has more recently been dubbed as the "too much of a good thing effect." Mathematically, this is known as an inverted-U curve since it captures pictorially this powerful insight (see Figure 1).

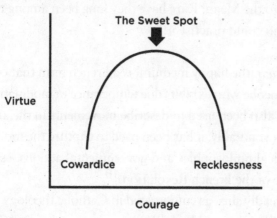

Figure 1. The inverted-U relationship between courage and virtue.

Aristotle's insight has been espoused by other historical thinkers in widely disparate cultures. Buddha's Middle Way is about striking the right balance between self-denial and self-indulgence. It also applies to an ontological middle ground regarding what happens to individuals once they are deceased, something between eternalism (an individual has an eternal and invariant essence) and annihilationism (an individual ceases to exist).[8]

In Confucius's *The Doctrine of the Mean*, one finds the following passage:

> II. 1. Chung-ne said, "The superior man *embodies* [emphasis in original] the course of the Mean; the mean man acts contrary to the course of the Mean."
>
> 2. "The superior man's embodying the course of the Mean is because he is a superior man, and so always maintains the Mean. The mean man's acting contrary to the course of the Mean is because he is a mean man, and has no caution."
>
> III. The Master said, "Perfect is the virtue which is according to the Mean! Rare have they long been among the people, who could practise it!"[9]

Le juste milieu [the happy medium] is a French term that colloquially refers to someone who exhibits due temperance in modulating their behavior. It has also been used to describe movements in the arts or in architecture. Most notably, it has been used to capture the moderation of centrist political philosophies and governmental actions, especially around the time of the French Revolution.[10]

The seven deadly sins, as enumerated in Catholic theology for well more than a millennium and a half, serve as a warning against our proclivity to stray from the sweet spot either by succumbing to apathy (sloth) or intemperance (greed, lust, gluttony). Somewhere between these two extremes lies the sweet spot, where we can live a life in accordance with the four cardinal virtues of prudence, justice, fortitude, and temperance. Individual sins could also be construed via the prism of the inverted-U curve. Take for example lust. It is the hyperactivation of the mating drive. For a married couple, lust can lead to infidelity. But a hypoactivation of the mating drive is clearly suboptimal as well. A sexually loveless marriage is not a happy medium. Empirical science tells us that people in relationships enjoy the maximal well-being benefits of sexual intercourse if they engage in it once a week. In other words, there is a curvilinear relationship between sexual frequency and well-being.[11]

The inverted-U curve is arguably one of the most prevalent patterns in well-being. Its explanatory power extends to phenomena at the macro, individual, and neuronal levels. It is operational in countless domains, including in defining one's optimal personality traits. Take for example perfectionism. If one is lacking any perfectionist bent, one will lack the necessary attention to details that constitutes an important element of the creative process. On the other hand, if one is too perfectionist (I suffer from maladaptive perfectionism), one will spend an inordinate amount of time rechecking one's work rather than advancing it. Somewhere between apathetic nonchalance and maladaptive perfectionism lies the sweet spot. That I recognize that I possess a frailty in my personality (maladaptive perfectionism) speaks to the importance of having self-awareness, including the capacity to engage in self-criticism. But as should be evident by now, the inverted U captures the optimal level of healthy self-criticism, be it at the individual or collective levels. Somewhere between self-loathing and egotistical grandiosity lies the optimal sweet spot. You can be self-reflective about your failings as an individual without presuming that you are a vile manifestation of human filth. You can be self-reflective as a society about past or current injustices without proclaiming that you are loathsome by virtue of your skin's hue (white). The progressive civilizational self-flagellation that is condoned by the woke is in the diminishing part of the self-criticism curve.

To reiterate, the inverted-U curve is prevalent in a broad range of domains, including in peak performance (at work or in athletic training), advertising, psychology, economics, politics, management, consumer behavior, and parenting, among others. The optimal functioning of human brains and bodies, companies, economic systems, and political systems are all under the purview of the inverted-U curve. The maxim "All good things in moderation" is truly a universal law of life.

Peak Performance

The Yerkes-Dodson law has been around since 1908.[12] It posits an inverted-U relationship between individuals' arousal states (such as feelings of stress or pressure) and their performance on a given task. Too little stress will result in too little focus on the task at hand, whereas too much stress can be stultifying. There is a sweet spot of arousal that allows an individual to maximize his performance. This is a law that has become enshrined in sports psychology for obvious reasons. There is some optimal arousal sweet spot that will yield maximal athletic performance. Beyond peak athletic performance, the inverted-U shape explains the maximal health, cognitive, and affective benefits reaped as a function of exercise intensity (this is known as a dose-response curve). For example, health guidelines from medical associations recommend a moderate level of exercise intensity for maximal benefits.[13] Peter Warr, who specializes in the study of work psychology, has introduced the vitamin metaphor in explaining the effect of various predictors of happiness. Some vitamins, such as vitamins C and E, follow an asymptotic relationship whereby consuming a greater dosage is beneficial up to a point, with any additional dosage yielding no additional benefits (but no detrimental effects). On the other hand, vitamins A and D follow the inverted-U model, whereby increased dosage is good up to a point and then one enters the detrimental region of the curve at very high doses.[14] More generally, hormesis is a concept that captures the relationship between drug dosage and its reward value, and it turns out that in many pharmacological settings, the dose-response curve follows the inverted-U pattern.[15]

Robert Sapolsky is a brilliant neuroendocrinologist whose online Stanford lectures are some of the most viewed of any professor.[16] I first became acquainted with his work via his 1994 book *Why Zebras Don't Get Ulcers.* Sapolsky argued that zebras (and other prey animals) experience momentary stress, which triggers a flight mechanism. In other words, the zebra does not suffer from prolonged bouts of long-lasting stress. A zebra realizes that it is permanently surrounded by endless dangerous predators. But it goes about its life void of existential angst. Only when it needs to flee from predators does its stress response kick in. Humans, on the other hand, do experience persistent and enduring stress levels. This has many negative health consequences. The optimal response curve of stress, not surprisingly, is an inverted-U curve. Too little stress or too much stress is not good for us, a finding confirmed by Sapolsky in a 2015 paper.[17] I recently explained this principle to my very young son when he approached me with an enduring level of stress regarding an upcoming quiz. I explained to him that a moderate level of stress is good because if you experience no stress at the thought of the looming quiz, you are likely to forgo studying. On the other hand, if you suffer from prolonged and paralyzing fear, this could affect your ability to perform well on the test. A sweet spot of stress is indeed what the doctor ordered. The inverted-U curve has been documented across many brain studies, including the relationship between brain activity and behavioral performance (moderate activity is optimal); a broad range of dose-effect curves in learning, memory, and cognitive control (for example, moderate dopamine levels yield optimal cognitive function); and the relationship between neural mechanisms (activity patterns in specific regions of the brain) and the optimal functionality of specific mental features (such as self-awareness).[18] The "average is good" maxim applies to our brains.

La maladie créatrice [the creativity-inducing malady] refers to mental psychopathologies that can actually engender creative output. Think of the mad genius archetype, namely the painter, novelist, musical composer, or scientist who produces great works of creativity during a bout of mental illness or mania. That said, the research on finding links between creativity and psychopathology has yielded mixed results, and some have argued that the conflicting findings might stem from an inverted-U relationship between the two constructs.[19] In other words, an extremely reasonable, sane person might lack the out-of-the-box thinking that is required for bold creativity, whereas severe mental illness becomes too debilitating for any creativity whatsoever and is simply self-destructive. There is a sweet spot where one's creative juices are maximized without sacrificing one's sanity! On a related note, researchers have uncovered a so-called intermediate effect in the clinical practice of medicine. Junior medical students, senior medical students, and neurologists were asked to read clinical cases, offer a diagnosis, and then recall the details of the case, as well as the pathophysiological explanations. Whereas the diagnostic accuracy was greatest for the neurologists, the senior medical students exhibited the so-called intermediate effect. They recalled more of the information and offered richer explanations than the two other groups.[20] In the case of the novice students, they did not have enough knowledge to recall and generate rich clinical information, whereas for the neurologists, their knowledge was encapsulated into organized schemas (a form of informational pruning).

When it comes to tracking scientists' most important works throughout their careers, what is the general pattern? Does their best work take place during their early years, when they possess the greatest amount of vigor and energy, or perhaps late in their careers, when they have had a chance to build many decades of cumulative knowledge? It turns out that across several biomedical fields, the relationship between a scientist's best work and his age follows the now expected inverted-U shape.[21]

Repetition Effects and Optimal Fear

One of the most powerful findings in advertising is the so-called repetition effect. How many times should an advertiser repeat a message as part of an advertising campaign? Not surprisingly, this effect is best described via an inverted-U curve.[22] If you show the advertisement too few times, the target audience will not learn all that is required about your message. On the other hand, if the advertisement is shown too many times, consumers will react negatively toward the ad, if not the advertised brand. There is a sweet spot, which when exceeded leads to diminishing returns. To spend more money on an advertising campaign beyond the sweet spot is counterproductive both monetarily and in terms of other measures of efficacy. This inverted-U curve has even been documented in the way that people evaluate risk. Warning someone about risk over and over again can be counterproductive.[23] More is not always better, because repeated warnings can sometimes sound like the boy who cried wolf. So, if you are trying to scare someone into corrective behavior—say, with a public service announcement about the dangers of smoking or leading a sedentary lifestyle or drinking and driving—how much fear is maximally persuasive? Advertising and communication researchers refer to these types of messages as fear appeals. Some researchers have argued that the inverted-U curve applies here; if you do not sufficiently scare someone, they might not pay attention to the message, and if you scare them too much, it might lead them to a fatalistic acceptance of their fate.[24] There is a moderate amount of fear that is maximally persuasive in leading to behavioral change.

During the COVID-19 pandemic we again saw the utility of the inverted-U curve. To take no precautions at all was a mistake in the face of a highly contagious novel virus. But to become a shut-in, fearful of appearing in public, clinging to a mask as a safety blanket, was also clearly not conducive to one's mental or physical well-being. Fear can prompt beneficial adaptive behaviors, but only within a modulated range.

Psychology

The ubiquity of the inverted-U curve is found in many areas of psychology. The psychologists Adam Grant and Barry Schwartz reviewed some surprising contexts wherein the inverted U occurs, including between optimism and well-being, self-esteem and health, volunteering and well-being, organizational commitment and whis-tleblowing, and empathy and distress.[25] The last example is one that I have personally witnessed with my eldest child. Her empathy is so extreme that it will often cause her debilitating distress. Whenever we come across a depiction of hardship as experienced by a third party, she will repeatedly ask: "Is he/she sad?" The only response that we can offer to end the ruminative question is "No." Any other answer will send her into an infinite abyss of angst. Whenever I wish to tease her, I will say something to the effect of, "Oh look at that [individual, animal, inanimate object]. I'm sure that they are sad." The rest of the family will usually crack up laughing and brace for the same one-question onslaught!

While my daughter's stress is relatively easily assuaged, most people cannot as easily brush off their daily stressors. The fast pace of modern life is a source of great stress to millions of people. One remedy to address this corrosive reality is to engage in a broad range of mindfulness practices (meditation, breathing techniques, and so on) that have been shown to have many psychological and physical benefits. However, even something as beneficial as mindfulness obeys the inverted-U curve. Too much mindfulness can lead to negative outcomes, including increased anxiety, depression, social avoidance, disassociation, and depersonalization, among other unfavorable downstream effects.[26] Going for a weekend silent retreat might be a wonderful idea. Doing so for a decade might be a terrible idea, as humans flourish in communicative sociality. Too much of anything, even a good thing, can become detrimental.

The humanist psychologist Abraham Maslow proposed five levels of hierarchical needs to explain the key drivers of human motivation, the third of which is the "love and belongingness" need. An individual who succeeds in meeting this need is likely to be popular within key social circles. Being popular usually implies that you possess certain desirable qualities, be it that you are fun, good-looking, or extroverted. Hence, all other things being equal, someone with a large network of friends might be viewed more favorably than one with a small network. But is there an inflection point where having too many friends becomes detrimental to how people perceive you? A study sought to examine how a person's number of Facebook friends affected their perceived social attractiveness. Researchers created five Facebook profiles that varied in the number of friends that were associated to each profile (102, 302, 502, 702, or 902 friends).[27] The relationship between number of Facebook friends and perceived social attractiveness follows the inverted-U curve such that the profile with 302 friends yielded the highest ratings. I definitely need to go back and cull some of my friends from my personal Facebook page, as my current total stands at a "suboptimal" 719 friends!

The inverted-U shape is also operative within key relationship dynamics. Suppose that you are out on a first date. Your date is wearing a beautiful dress that accentuates her beauty. If you fail to sufficiently compliment her, it might come across as inattentive. On the other hand, if you spend much of the night gushing about how beautiful your date is, she will likely be turned off by your incessant complimenting, reading it as either inauthentic or desperate. Somewhere between lack of interest and obsessive groveling lies the sweet spot.

There is also the question of romantic jealousy, a ubiquitous emotion. Even the most secure and self-confident individuals in a marriage might occasionally experience feelings of jealousy, worried about a spouse's other friendships. Naturally, however, romantic jealousy follows the inverted-U curve. If you never express any jealousy, this might serve as a diagnostic signal that you do not care enough about your partner. This is precisely why some individuals will willfully seek to trigger a jealous response from their partners as a means of feeling loved and desired. On the other hand, too much jealously is deeply destructive. It is a telltale sign of mistrust in the relationship, or insecurity in one's self-worth, and will on many occasions result in the dissolution of a marriage because, for instance, the pathologically jealous individual becomes too controlling or even abusive. Somewhere between no jealousy and obsessive jealousy lies the sweet spot of how to express one's caring for his or her spouse.

I end this section with an exploration of the psychology of aesthetic appreciation. The Wundt curve, named after the father of experimental psychology, Wilhelm Wundt, is a psychophysics phenomenon that postulates that the extent to which we enjoy a stimulus depends on its intensity, with a moderate intensity level being the preferred modality. This inverted-U curve has subsequently been used in a variety of psychological contexts, including by Daniel Berlyne's psychobiological theory of aesthetic preferences, which posits an inverted-U curve between the familiarity of a stimulus and the complexity of a stimulus and how much it is liked. There is a moderate level of familiarity or complexity that is optimal when it comes to aesthetic preferences. This theory has been tested for varied aesthetic judgments, including musical preferences. An analysis of fifty-seven studies from 1901 to 2015 that have examined the inverted-U curve of musical preferences found that it held true in 87.7 percent of the studies (fifty out of fifty-seven).[28]

Parenting and Mentoring

I recently held a chat on my show with Yale law school professor Amy Chua, whose book *Battle Hymn of the Tiger Mother* was a *New York Times* bestseller back in 2011.[29] In it, Amy espouses a strict parenting style to ensure children's success. Many Asian parents follow this model, as do Jewish parents, regarding their children's pursuit of academic excellence. But as you might guess by now, the scientific data show that an intermediate style—somewhere between being an overbearing, obsessive "helicopter" parent on the one hand and being a laissez-faire "kids deserve their independence" parent on the other—is in many cases the best approach, as was documented in a study exploring children's academic achievement (in terms of the grades they achieved) and the extent of parents' supervision over their children. The highest grade point averages corresponded to the children who received an intermediate level of supervision.[30]

As a professor, one of my responsibilities is to train the next generation of academics within my areas of expertise. As part of this, I supervise graduate students' theses and dissertations. The mentorship can be a very rewarding part of my job, but it is also extraordinarily time-consuming. One of the challenges of a good supervisor is to know how to strike the right balance in terms of the amount of independence to grant one's students. If you grant too much independence, they are often sucked into a black hole of unproductivity, as they can get lost in unorganized or misdirected research. Many students become rudderless because they have never been expected to exhibit intellectual entrepreneurship on this scale. On the other hand, if you grant the students little to no independence, they never learn to fend for themselves. They become dependent on you to serve as the driving engine of their progress. The sweet spot lies between disengaged non-guidance and overbearing mentorship.

Economics and Politics

To reiterate, the inverted-U curve is found across a very broad range of economic phenomena. Simon Kuznets, the 1971 laureate of the Nobel Memorial Prize in Economic Sciences, proposed an inverted-U curve to explain the relationship between a nation's level of economic growth (as measured by income per capita) and its income inequality.[31] In this case, the peak income inequality takes places at a moderate level of economic growth. Hence, one needs to avoid that sweet spot. Interestingly, the relationship between income inequality and happiness follows an inverted-U shape as well.[32] Specifically, people are happiest in countries where there is an intermediate level of income inequality. The environmental Kuznets curve posits that the relationship between economic growth and environmental degradation also follows an inverted-U relationship.[33] As a nation first expands its economic activity, there is a negative effect on the environment, but eventually an inflection point is reached whereby greater economic growth leads to reduced environmental deterioration.

The relationship between competition and innovation also adheres to an inverted-U shape.[34] Think of a monopolistic industry ruled by a single firm: the lack of competition reduces incentives to innovate. A highly competitive environment, however, might also reduce innovation because it is seen as too risky. The relationship between intellectual property protection and innovation also follows an inverted-U curve.[35]

As with economics, so too with politics. It turns out that the extent to which people involve themselves in politics is highly dependent on the extent to which people have confidence in the political and economic system. Across data from fifty countries, an inverted-U relationship was found between confidence in the system and political engagement. If you have no confidence in the system, there is no point in your political involvement. But similarly, if you have very high confidence in the system, you might assume it will take care of itself and that it will autocorrect any flaws or mistakes without your involvement. There is some intermediate level of confidence in the system that yields the maximal level of political engagement in terms of voting and other political activity.[36]

It might be no surprise that moderate temperatures have their advantages, but studies comparing crime rates to ambient temperature have found that there are more violent crimes at intermediate temperatures than at cooler or hotter ones.[37] At the same time, our ability to learn and retain information is optimal when it is neither too cold nor too warm. Male participants' performance on a paired association task (learning and recalling a list of word–number pairs) was evaluated at one of five room temperatures (52°F, 62°F, 72°F, 82°F, or 92°F). Exactly in line with the inverted-U effect, the best performance occurred at the moderate temperature of 72°F.[38]

I am typing these words from a neighborhood café. For the first time, I had to produce an electronic COVID vaccination passport on my iPhone in order to sit inside. Of course, there are pros and cons to this issue, but it speaks to the optimal level of governmental intrusion that citizens should tolerate. Too little government intervention in the affairs of society (such as restricting law enforcement from arresting violent criminals) leads to anarchy; too much government intervention results in

centrally planned dictatorships like communism. In government regulation of the economy, there is a great deal of difference between intrusive
regulations that dictate when you can open your restaurant's outdoor
dining facilities and regulations that prevent corporate fraud. Most of us
want a society governed by law and good order (safe streets and efficient
public services) that still maintains a large degree of personal freedom.
The pursuit of life, liberty, and happiness cannot be achieved if Big
Government is constantly intruding into the minutiae of our daily lives.
Good governance is about finding that sweet spot.

Management

This raises the question, of course, of how corporate management
affects our happiness as workers and managers, consumers and citizens, in a capitalist society. The scope of corporate responsibility has
radically changed over the past century.[39] Originally, the near-sole
focus of a corporation was to create products, and in the early stages
of mass production that could lead to adages like Henry Ford's: "Any
customer can have a car painted any colour that he wants so long as
it is black." As corporations grew and became more efficient and could
diversify their operations and assembly lines, the production-centric
model of the corporation gave way to the marketing-centric model,
where customization and differentiation to target markets and consumer demand were key. The third stage of corporate development
established an expansive model of corporate social responsibility.
Companies were now expected to create products, innovate to meet
specialized consumer markets and popular demand, *and* prove that
they were solicitous of the needs of their employees and the environment, setting aside a portion of corporate profits for charitable activities. Finally, we are now in the fourth stage, known as *woke capitalism*,
wherein companies must go beyond "social responsibility" and adhere

to *social activism* and show their commitment to work on behalf of "social justice" as defined in part by leftist Ivy League executives and enforced by placard-wielding blue-haired activists who graduated with women's studies degrees from Wellesley College. Perhaps needless to say, not only do these protestors—noxious propagators of idea pathogens—make many people annoyed and unhappy, but their efforts are in large part counterproductive, at least to the well-being of the corporations they afflict.

Several studies in widely different cultures, from France to Japan, have yielded the expected inverted-U relationship between corporate environmental investments and economic performance.[40] The same is true of corporate ideological propaganda. Disney and Netflix recently found themselves on the wrong side of the inverted-U curve when it came to woke politics, and their stock prices took a hit accordingly.[41] Elon Musk referred to these woke companies as having been infected by a "woke mind virus." Many people have suggested to me that Musk must have read *The Parasitic Mind*. I hope so. In any event, the preliminary data (with admittedly small sample sizes) show that, generally speaking, woke capitalism is less successful than apolitical capitalism, as measured by a recent study of the stock prices of woke companies.[42] Somewhere between the amoral organizational culture depicted in the television series *Mad Men* and the wokeism of Disney and Netflix lies the optimal sweet spot of being socially responsible (taking care of the environment in which a business operates) without alienating the great majority of your consumers with blue-haired progressive nonsense.

In a 2013 study, researchers examined the inverted-U curve in eight areas of corporate management, including organizational behavior, human resource management, entrepreneurship, and strategic management.[43] The inverted-U curve held true, whether it was measuring the relationship between a leader's assertiveness and effectiveness or an employee's conscientiousness and job performance.[44] It would seem that as both workers and managers, we would all enjoy our work more if we followed the golden mean.

Consumer Behavior

But we are more than workers or managers; we are consumers. Does the inverted-U effect have relevance here as well? The answer is: of course! Moderation in eating and drinking, for example, has been recognized as wise for millennia. Now we can support the adages of the past with scientific studies. For example, moderate alcohol consumption is associated with improved cardiorespiratory fitness, reduced cardiovascular disease, and reduced mortality from all causes.[45] Moderate fish consumption has been linked with improved cognitive and academic performance.[46] In some instances, however, the middle ground is not the best ground. Moderate enjoyment of spicy foods, for instance, has been linked to abdominal fat.[47]

We often think that greater consumer choice brings happiness. But this is not always the case. I can illustrate this principle by the trauma that confronts me whenever I am about to head off on a trip. I always face the same daunting decision of which book to pick from my sizeable personal library to bring along on my voyage. My wife often teases me about the agonizing choice paralysis that I experience as I stare at hundreds of alluring contenders. So much knowledge to consume, and so little time! This decisional angst is precisely what the psychologist Barry Schwartz referred to in his book *The Paradox of Choice*. Contrary to the classical economic presumption that more choices are always better than fewer, people can become overwhelmed with a deluge of alternatives and thus experience choice overload and increased post-decisional regret.[48] Choice overload can be detrimental, as demonstrated in a set of three studies that explored people's behaviors and responses when choosing between six or twenty-four jams, six or thirty chocolates, and writing an essay for extra credit where the choice of possible topics was six or thirty. People were more likely to purchase the two products and were more satisfied with their final choice when facing fewer alternatives to choose from; and when it came to extra credit, they were likelier to write the essay—and performed better on the assignment—when given fewer choices among essay topics.[49] When it comes to consumer choices, the inverted-U curve strikes again, showing that most consumers prefer a midpoint between having no choice and a plethora of choices.[50] A broad range of happiness researchers, including economists, neuroscientists, philosophers, and psychologists, have recognized that even when it comes to things we presume to be good—like money, fame, and status—more is not always better when it comes to personal happiness.[51]

All Things in Moderation—Including the Pursuit of Happiness

Science tells us that even happiness should be pursued in moderation, and that the optimal level of happiness follows, at least in certain contexts, the logic of the inverted-U curve.[52] Contrary to one's naïve intuition, seeking more happiness is not always better. A constant striving for greater happiness can lead to such detrimental behaviors as excessive risk-taking. Beyond demonstrating that more happiness is not always better, psychologists have demonstrated that there are contexts where too much happiness can increase one's gullibility, and that an excessive, willful pursuit of happiness can result in greater loneliness.[53] As is true for most things in life, temperance and moderation, even in the pursuit of something as positive as happiness, is ideal.

I end this chapter by quoting Aristotle from *The Nicomachean Ethics*: "For instance, it is possible to feel fear, confidence, desire, anger, pity, and generally to be affected pleasantly and painfully, either too much or too little, in either case wrongly; but to be thus affected at the right times, and on the right occasions, and towards the right persons, and with the right object, and in the right fashion, is the mean course and the best course, and these are characteristics of virtue."[54] If I were to add to Aristotle's brilliant edict, I would posit that life requires the proper modulation of our personality traits, drives, and pursuits, as well as of our cognitive and emotional responses. The degree and type of moderation we should pursue will depend on our age, circumstances, and personality, and the desire to achieve moderation varies across individuals, as captured by the "preference for moderation scale."[55] But what is unequivocally clear is that in almost every aspect of our lives, there exists a golden mean. If you fail to find it, you will misappropriate your time, your efforts, your funds, and your potential for maximal well-being. Everything in moderation is a universal maxim of optimal functioning across all units of analyses, be it the neuronal, individual, organizational, economic, or political levels. The place to find your maximal happiness is in the exercise of virtuous moderation.

CHAPTER FIVE

Life as a Playground

Of all animal species, humans are the biggest players of all. We are built to play and built through play. When we play, we are engaged in the purest expression of our humanity, the truest expression of our individuality. Is it any wonder that often the times we feel most alive, those that make up our best memories, are moments of play?[1]

—Stuart Brown

Stay playful.[2]

—OREO commercial tagline

It is not only possible to say a great deal in praise of play; it is really possible to say the highest things in praise of it. It might reasonably be maintained that the true object of all human life is play.[3]

—G. K. Chesterton

People often ask me why I always seem happy and good-natured. In part this is my disposition. However, I also tackle life in a way that allows me to maximize the hedonic benefits of every situation. If we go on a vacation, within the first three days, every single person at our hotel has already shared with me their deepest secrets! Because I listen. Because I care. Because I take an interest. Because I can be playful even as I tackle deeply serious issues. I can be funny when critiquing idea pathogens (at the root of the mental illness of political correctness and wokeness); I can have fun when conducting a research study; I play with my children; I play with my wife. Hence, it is a way of living life that is rooted in play. The Strong Museum (National Museum of Play) has culled quotes about play stemming from some of the most influential thinkers of the twentieth century.[4] Here are a few wonderful examples: "Almost all creativity involves purposeful play" (Abraham Maslow, humanist psychologist); "If you want to be creative, stay in part a child, with the creativity and invention that characterizes children before they are deformed by adult society" (Jean Piaget, developmental psychologist); "Play is hard to maintain as you get older. You get less playful. You shouldn't, of course" (Richard Feynman, physicist and Nobel laureate). There are countless other leading thinkers who have weighed in on the importance of play, including the psychoanalyst Carl Jung ("The creation of something new is not accomplished by the intellect but by the play instinct acting from inner necessity") and the developmental psychologist David Elkind ("Combining ideas from Sigmund Freud and Jean Piaget, the author views play as one of three necessary elements of a full life, the others being work and love").[5]

The 1988 movie *Big*, starring Tom Hanks, is a heartwarming and lovely film. I first watched it as a young man when it was originally released and again more recently when I introduced it to my children. It is part of a genre of body-swap movies where a person is transformed into another version of himself (like *17 Again* starring Zac Efron and Matthew Perry) or when two individuals switch bodies (as in *The Change-Up* starring Ryan Reynolds and Jason Bateman). In *Big* a young boy (Josh) makes a wish to be a grown-up in front of a Zoltar machine (often seen at fairs and amusement parks). His wish is granted and he metamorphosizes into an adult. In his new grown-up body, the transformed kid heads off to New York City seeking a job and lands one at a toy company. While Josh has the body of an adult, his mind and behavioral patterns are those of a twelve-year-old boy. Josh accepts a data entry job at the toy company but is quickly noticed by the owner of the firm (played by Robert Loggia) precisely because of Josh's apparent youthful exuberance and quirky ways. Unlike the stuffy MBA types, Josh is spontaneous and free. During a company meeting to discuss various toy prototypes, Josh distinguishes himself from the conventional MBA-type analyses with his childlike enthusiasm. His peculiar attitude and behaviors even attract the romantic interest of an otherwise uptight female coworker (played by Elizabeth Perkins). His playfulness is refreshingly unique precisely because it is so rare to see in an adult.

The idea that the workplace should be construed as a playground (to unlock one's creative juices) has received increased attention in the academic literature.[6] Henry Ford was perfectly incorrect when he famously stated, "When we are at work we ought to be at work. When we are at play we ought to be at play. There is no use trying to mix the two. The sole object ought to be to get the work done and to get paid for it. When the work is done, then the play can come, but not before."[7]

Evolutionary Roots of Play

Evolutionary psychology distinguishes between two levels of scientific explanations, proximate and ultimate.[8] Much of science operates within the proximate realm, which deals with an elucidation of the *how* and *what* of a phenomenon. *How* does diabetes work? *What* are the factors that augment your chances of being diagnosed with diabetes? Ultimate explanations, on the other hand, refer to the Darwinian *why* of a phenomenon. Hence, evolutionary theory augments the explanatory power of proximate scientific conclusions by adding ultimate ones that allow us to fully understand anything involving biological beings. An example that I often like to use to explain this distinction is pregnancy sickness. There are innumerable proximate explanations that one might explore when studying this phenomenon. One might investigate how hormone levels are associated with the symptoms or how to relieve the severity of the symptoms, and so on. Of equal importance, though, is to consider why this condition exists—that is, why did it evolve in human beings? It turns out that it is an adaptive mechanism that has evolved to protect the fetus from exposure to teratogens (foodborne pathogens) during the crucial period of organogenesis.[9] Hence, the attractions (to foods like pickles) or repulsions (to foods like eggs) that pregnant women experience are adaptive strategies for protecting the fetus from foods that are more likely to carry foodborne pathogens. Women who experience greater pregnancy sickness during the first trimester often have better outcomes on measures of a successful pregnancy (including a lesser likelihood of having a miscarriage). Thus, from an evolutionary perspective, when a pregnant woman's gynecologist provides her with a treatment to shut off her pregnancy sickness, this is the perfectly incorrect thing to do!

If we apply evolutionary theory to the study of play, what do we find? Many people intuitively construe play as a product of childhood, a form of useless and purposeless frolicking that we eventually outgrow as we enter adulthood. In other words, in the same way that our appendix or our wisdom teeth have been construed as vestigial (it is assumed they no longer confer an evolutionary function), is play a vestigial pattern of behaviors? Hardly. The reality is that play is an integral element of our human nature. Play has evolved precisely because it has conferred an adaptive advantage, and that continues to be the case. Peter Gray is a psychologist who specializes in applying evolutionary theory to the study of play. In a recent summary article, he posits that play has evolved to achieve one of four functions. Play teaches: 1) skills and behaviors that are germane for survival and mating (play fighting, engaging in predator-prey chasing); 2) how to respond appropriately to uncertain negative events (building emotional and physical resilience); 3) creativity (which can include problem-solving and innovation); 4) and friendly cooperation (a central feature of human sociality).[10]

Play is found in all human societies, and across many mammalian species. The play instinct is so powerful that even during wartime, children find a way to play.[11] During the Lebanese civil war, two of the many ways to die were at the hands of the ubiquitous, indiscriminate snipers and via the relentless shelling. (We quickly learned from the "whistle signature" of the incoming bombs which were the most or least dangerous.) I recall being told to play in a particular area but not to stray—otherwise I would be in the snipers' visual field. I also remember on one occasion going out to play with my then closest friend (my second cousin) and accidentally but severely cutting the middle finger on my left hand with a pocketknife I had brought for "protection." (I still bear the scar today.) My memories include those of war, but also those of play that helped me escape the war's daily horrors. I fully understand the reaction of two young boys from Damascus who responded to their experiences in the Syrian civil war by saying, "We want to play every day. . . . We love to play in the neighborhood. We don't play anymore because of snipers and shelling in our neighborhood."[12] I lived a similar experience: *plus ça change, plus c'est la même chose* (the more things change, the more they stay the same).

As a sidenote, my second cousin, with whom I used to play amidst the brutality of war, was "horrified" by my favorable disposition toward Tucker Carlson. I had posted a photo of Tucker and me, after having taped a conversation on his podcast. My caption was: "What a fantastic conversation with the immeasurably charming @TuckerCarlson. Thank you!" I didn't know my cousin monitored my Twitter account, but he replied: "really, shame on you. how low can you go?"[13] Here is a life lesson regarding the good life: Don't be my cousin. Our shared child-hood experiences did not instill within him broad sympathies or toler-ance and understanding or deepened friendship. Instead, he remained the same narrow-minded and judgmental person I remembered. My cousin's action proves that personality traits are rather stable throughout one's lifetime.

The urge to play can be found in numerous contexts that might otherwise seem grim. Patch Adams is a physician who has spent five decades promoting the healing power of laughter.[14] His medical school training was depicted in the 1998 movie *Patch Adams* (starring Robin Williams). Two exchanges capture the tension of using play and laughter in the medical context, the first between Adams and the dean of the medical school (Dean Walcott, played by Bob Gunton) and the second between Adams and one of his classmates (Mitch Roman, played by Philip Seymour Hoffman).

> **Dean Walcott:** Do you wanna tell me what it is you think you're doing? [Patch is clowning around in a patient's room.]
> **Patch:** Oh. Uh. Just getting a few laughs, sir. The *American Journal of Medicine* has found that laughter increases secre-tion of catecholamines and endorphins which in turn increases oxygenation of the blood, relaxes the arteries, speeds up the heart, decreases blood pressure, which has a positive effect on all cardiovascular and respiratory ailments as well as overall increasing the immune system response.

And now the exchange between Patch and Roman:

> **Patch:** If you don't like me, just say it.
> **Mitch Roman:** I don't like you!

Patch: Why don't you like me? You're a prick, and I like you.

Mitch: Because you make my effort a joke! I want to be a doctor! This isn't a game to me! This isn't playtime! This is serious business!

But all serious business, all parts of life, can be made better by certain aspects of play. Perhaps nothing is as serious a topic as the Holocaust, which led to the systematic genocide of six million Jews among countless other innocent victims. And yet, the 1997 movie *Life Is Beautiful* sought to strike a delicate balance in demonstrating that, even within the horrors of this gargantuan tragedy, a father's love might take the form of play to distract his son from the terrible realities around them. Of note, the historian George Eisen wrote a book about how children engaged in play behavior in the extermination camps.[15] Play is such a fundamental feature of the human spirit that it is used as a tool in psychotherapy, an area that typically involves an exploration of the roots of mental suffering.[16] Hence, even in the darkest of circumstances, the desire to play manifests itself.

Developmental psychologists and pediatricians have long demonstrated the benefits reaped when children play.[17] Not only is play a fundamental feature of a child's healthy physical and psychological development, lack of play is often associated with a state of reduced physical and psychological health. In other words, play is both an antecedent to good health (we play more when we are in a positive state) and an outcome of good health (we feel better when we play).[18] But of course, play should not be an activity restricted to children. Individuals who score higher on an adult playfulness scale exhibit greater psychological and physical well-being on a broad range of variables, and they also possess greater life satisfaction.[19] In other words, a playful mindset into adulthood protects our bodies and minds in a myriad of ways and gives us a more positive outlook regarding our lives. In a study of the twenty-four character strengths that are best correlated with life satis-faction, hope, zest, gratitude, curiosity, and love came out on top.[20] Note that curiosity and zest are both linked to a playful mindset.

When the humanist psychologist Abraham Maslow proposed his hierarchy of needs, he put self-actualization at the apex. Some elements of self-actualization serve as ultimate forms of play, such as when we actively seek to explore new landscapes, interests, and activities for the sheer pleasure of doing so (enrolling in a cooking course, taking up crossword puzzles as a hobby, or travelling to an exotic location). The path to happiness is paved through the magic of play.

On the Importance of Laughter

Dave Chappelle is one of the most successful comedians of all time. He does not succumb to the soft bigotry of low expectations (as coined by Michael Gerson, George W. Bush's speechwriter). He does not put on kid gloves when writing jokes about particular groups.[21] He is an equal opportunity offender in that he will make fun of the LGBTQ activists, blacks, whites, Jews, Asians, and, most tellingly, himself. And yet in today's grand game of Victimology Poker, it is simply unaccept-able to make fun of some groups because they are allegedly marginal-ized (when in fact many of them are endlessly celebrated by the media and the institutions of the liberal West). As I explained in my book *The Parasitic Mind*, ideas that cannot be mocked cannot be true. Truth is anti-fragile. It is not brittle. It does not shatter into a million pieces because of an "offensive and hurtful" joke. An individual with a strong personhood can laugh at others (in a playful manner) and laugh at himself. Humor is a test of anti-fragility and non-brittleness in a person and in a society. A society that can't laugh at others and at itself in a good-humored way is on its way out. If you can laugh at yourself (as I often do), this is the ultimate symbol of your confidence (self-deprecating humor is thus what we would call a "costly signal," made, it appears, at the expense of one's self-esteem). Not surprisingly, historically speaking, dictators have always despised the use of humor, precisely because they recognize that their hold over people is ultimately fragile, based on force and lies, and humor undermines their rule.[22]

In fall 2021, I hosted the journalist and attorney Megyn Kelly on my show. While introducing her, I admitted to being a big fan of hers, to which she replied as follows (slightly edited for expository clarity): "I'll return the compliment. Last night at our house we had over two very powerful law enforcement types and, we, Doug [Megyn's husband] and I, were imitating different Gad Saad acts—you know, how you do your funny bits. We each had our favorite; I was doing mine; he was doing his; and so you have two new, big fans; one is a CIA guy, and one is a cop guy."[23] On my show, I have several lines of satirical sketches that are meant to mock various elements of the current zeitgeist. For example, I have a series of satirical clips that utilize the Aslan-Uygur Decoder 5000 (named after Reza Aslan and Cenk Uygur, two hopelessly lobotomized progressives). The prop in question is a toy phone, which I use to "decode" various progressive nonsense. I have also posted many self-flagellation clips wherein I utilize three types of whips of self-loathing (a belt, a swatter, and a flogger sent to me by a fan). I will literally whip myself on camera whilst satirically apologizing for past "transgressions," such as having been friends with Jordan Peterson.[24] My "hiding under the desk" series has also become a global favorite. Each episode involves my speaking to the camera whilst feigning excessive fear and literally hiding under my study's desk. The inaugural episode was a satirical take on the hysterical faux fear that all progressives were expressing at the inauguration of Donald Trump.[25] Other persons or things that have since sent me into hiding include the successful podcaster Joe Rogan, the Freedom Convoy (in Canada), voter ID laws, the acquittal of Kyle Rittenhouse, the Pronoun Taliban, the

January 6 "insurrectionists," Donald Trump's impeachment acquittals, the appointments of Amy Coney Barrett and Brett Kavanaugh to the United States Supreme Court, Jussie Smollett, Brexit, and climate change. I have also satirized Elizabeth Warren's "slice of life" interaction with her husband in her kitchen, the cackling of Kamala Harris, the bizarre interaction of Kamala Harris with several child actors (in promoting space research), Hillary Clinton having "raped" me, Jussie Smollett and his friends having attacked me in a hate crime, and Ketanji Brown Jackson having assaulted me at Camp B'Nai Brith (possibly in 1977). It takes sizeable self-confidence to produce such content precisely because most professors are severely constrained by their stiffness. They wrongly presume that to be a serious professor requires that they present themselves to the world in all circumstances in a solemn manner. Hogwash. I can publish a very rigorous scientific paper in a leading academic journal, author a bestselling book, accept speaking engagements at leading universities, and be funny, playful, and irreverent. In February 2022, I spoke at a national event organized by Hillsdale College. The next day, Larry Arnn, the president of this wonderful anti-woke institution, ran into me at breakfast. After complimenting my work, he added, "And you're a hoot." My life is greatly enriched by having a playful and humorous personality. It does not diminish the seriousness of the issues that I tackle. Rather, it offers some much-needed levity from the doom and gloom inherent to some of the topics that I address. My ability to be playful serves as a pressure relief valve from the otherwise unbearable, ugly realities that I deal with on a daily basis. It is part of the homeostatic mechanism for retaining my sanity.

Researchers have argued for the evolutionary roots of laughter and humor. They've done so using several disciplines, including cognitive neuroscience, primatology, developmental psychology, positive psychology, and play research.[26] The reality is that laughter and humor constitute indelible elements of our human nature, and not

surprisingly laughter yields many mental and physical health benefits.[27] In one recent study in Norway with more than fifty-three
thousand participants, humor (the cognitive component) was protective against specific forms of mortality in men (infections) and women
(cardiovascular diseases and infections).[28] The old adage "laughter
is the best medicine" appears to be empirically true.

Playing Outside, Biophilia, and Well-Being

My wife and I are only too familiar with the addictive nature of
electronics, be it iPads or iPhones. It has proven nearly impossible to
modulate the amount of time that our children spend on these devices.
The ill consequences on one's health and well-being with increased
usage of these devices is unequivocal. With increased usage comes a
greater likelihood for obesity and depressive symptoms, poorer dietary
choices, decreased quality of life, greater anxiety, decreased metabolic
and cardiovascular health, worsened psychosocial health, reduced
cognitive development and educational achievement, and worsening
sleep patterns, among other negative consequences.[29] Instead of being
stuck interacting with electronics, children benefit greatly from interacting with the natural world. The lack of time that children now spend
outdoors immersed in the restorative benefits of nature was coined
"nature-deficit disorder" by bestselling author Richard Louv.[30] While
an obsession with electronics is a tragic reality for many children, the
ill effects apply to adults as well. I have experienced firsthand the negative consequences of being endlessly accessible online. I'm more stressed
out, more agitated, and more short-tempered. Whenever I take an
enforced break from social media, I see an immediate improvement in
my general well-being. Children and adults alike reap great psychological and physical benefits from playing outside. The forms of play
might vary depending on your age, but the need to engage in "green

play" is universally beneficial whether you are seven or seventy-seven years old.

The lockdowns associated with the COVID pandemic have been disastrous on many levels. To be stuck indoors, isolated from others, for long time periods is a tough reality to bear. Fortunately for my family, our backyard proved to be an oasis that has offered us an inoculation against pandemic-related cabin fever. I suspect that urban apartment dwellers who did not have daily access to a green space had more difficulty coping with the lockdowns, because there is plenty of research that supports the importance of interacting with nature.[31] The evolutionary biologist E. O. Wilson coined this term "biophilia," recognizing the innate need humans have to interact with nature. Such interactions have clear positive consequences on one's mental and physical health.[32] Biophilic architecture recognizes this basal human need by creating living spaces that are congruent with it. For example, post-surgery patients placed in rooms with views of nature do far better than those placed in rooms facing a brick wall. Those with a window to nature had shorter stays in the hospital, fewer negative comments from attending nurses, were administered fewer analgesics, and experienced fewer postsurgical complications.[33] The restorative effects of having access to a window to nature are not restricted to hospital settings. Employees in offices with views of a forest have greater job satisfaction and less job stress than those who don't.[34]

Over the past year or so, a friend and I have instituted walk-and-talk sessions. He is a clinical psychologist and colleague who shares many of my broad intellectual interests, and hence our conversations are always fun, intense, and engaging. Rather than simply meeting at a café to catch up with one another, we go on long walks and use the opportunity to engage in a free-flowing exchange of ideas (a form of intellectual play). The German philosopher Friedrich Nietzsche famously opined that "only thoughts that come by *walking* have any value" [emphasis in original].[35] While this might be an overstatement on his part, it is incontestably true that to be in movement can trigger one's intellectual juices.[36] It is perhaps not surprising to know that two of the greatest thinkers of the twentieth century, the physicist Albert Einstein and the mathematician Kurt Gödel, took long walks when they worked at Princeton University's Institute for Advanced Study.[37] When in doubt, go for a walk!

Science as Play

Close to a decade ago, I was approached by a Canadian rapper named Baba Brinkman, who asked me to appear in a rap video titled "I'm A African."[38] Brinkman uses rap music to inspire young children about the beauty of science in general and evolution in particular. I was more than happy to oblige, and in the true spirit of play, I put out a call on social media asking people to suggest a stage name for my "new career" as a rap star. Although I received many worthy suggestions, none seemed to stick. One day I mentioned this to the owner of a local café. He looked at me and said, "Oh, that's easy. You're The GadFather." Bingo! The moniker has so taken off that I now often receive professional letters with the salutation "Dear GadFather." This nickname stems from a desire to have fun and play. Other professors would never dare take this step of adopting a playful stage name, because it is a testament of humility. As Joe Rogan kindly remarked on one of my appearances on his show, I can be a very serious professor whilst not always taking myself too seriously.

Many people have mental images of what different professionals should look like. Accountants, for example, should be buttoned-down bean counters with glasses. Interior designers should be "flamboyant." And professors should be serious, measured, and sullen—because these qualities give an aura of profundity. Nonsense. Richard Feynman, the

Nobel Prize–winning physicist, was known to be a partier who had an exuberance for life. He partied hard and worked hard. The desire to play need not be a separate realm from the austere pursuit of science. On the contrary, science is the epitome of intellectual play. It requires many of the same elements of play, namely imagination, curiosity, and creativity. People purchase elaborate one-thousand-piece puzzles as a form of play. They pay money to be locked up in a room from which they must escape using clues available in that room (known as an escape room). They go on treasure (or scavenger) hunts where they must interpret the meaning of various clues in order to collect a set list of items. Each of these forms of play contains many of the same elements found in scientific pursuits, including identifying patterns or clues that permit for a solution to be found.

Several years ago, as the COVID pandemic was about to be unleashed globally, my daughter was embarking on her fifth grade science project. She decided to explore whether two odorless and tasteless food colorants (red and blue) placed in a clear soda drink would alter people's perceptions of the drink on three key metrics: sweetness, refreshment, and flavor. The entire family used this as a wonderful opportunity to engage in intellectual play! First, we had to purchase the relevant colorants, soda drink, and cups. We also had to develop and print out the questionnaire. Finally, we had to find a venue to set up our drink stand for the experiment. We ended up using the indoor dome at my university, where we intercepted people and encouraged them to take part in the experiment. Twenty-nine participants tasted each of the two drinks and rated them. Later that day my daughter and I excitedly tabulated the results in an Excel spreadsheet. Upon going through these various steps, my daughter, in an ebullient and effusive gasp of excitement, advised me that "this was so much fun!" I told her that this is what I did for a living. I could see in her eyes that I had inspired her. This personal anecdote reminds me of Emily Rosa, who likely remains the youngest person to have ever published a paper in a peer-reviewed medical journal, let alone one as prestigious as the *Journal of the American Medical Association.*[39] For her grade four science project, she designed an experiment to test the validity of therapeutic touch (a New Age form of medical quackery based on the idea that human energy fields can cure disease). Not surprisingly, practitioners of this "therapy" were shown to possess a less than random chance at being able to detect such fields. This is the beauty of the scientific method. It is democratic in that there are no institutional barriers to entry. If a nine-year-old child is able to identify a worthy research question, apply the scientific method, and arrive at valid conclusions, she is just as worthy to publish a scientific paper as anyone else.

At the 2014 annual Society for Consumer Psychology conference, consumer researcher Darren Dahl (who has been a guest on my show)[40] delivered a presidential address on the importance of play as an integral part of the research process. The talk greatly resonated with me because I have always tried to impart to my students that the pursuit of science is a form of intellectual play. Dahl concluded his talk by saying, "We all want to publish lots of papers. We all want to do great things. But don't get so caught up in that end goal that you lose the process. Because, in my mind, discovery, creativity, and play will make you happier and hopefully will help you produce better work."[41] Several scholars have made this exact point, namely that scientific research is a form of play:

"Play in scientific research is seldom discussed in print. Perhaps we scientists take it for granted. Or maybe we are a little self-conscious and try to hide it from others. After all, we don't want taxpayers to think they are subsidizing adults who are acting like a bunch of kids, thereby squandering hefty amounts of public money."[42]

"When we set up encounters between various chemicals, our expectations extend those of the child who has been given a paint box and tries mixing various colors just to see what comes out. In the same mood, the chemist asks himself what would happen were he to change the proportions or modify the sequence of the operations in a complex synthesis. Such a playful, childlike attitude can be extremely fruitful. Let us not be too embarrassed to acknowledge that play is often what motivates us."[43]

"Real science has the potential to not only amaze, but also transform the way one thinks of the world and oneself. This is because the process of science is little different from the deeply resonant, natural processes of play. Play enables humans (and other mammals) to discover (and create) relationships and patterns. When one adds rules to play, a game is created. This is science: *the process of playing with rules that enables one to reveal previously unseen patterns of relationships that extend our collective understanding of nature and human nature*" [emphasis in original].[44]

"Science, like religion, is a form of sacred *play*. It creates a world that transcends the world of our senses, a world of make-believe that we may enter if we choose to play. Like all play it offers a confrontation with important truths about ourselves and the world beyond us" [emphasis in original].[45]

"It is widely held that the objectivity of the language of scientific communication has served science well. It is less clear that it has served to open the *game* of science to the broader society of which the scientific community is a part. Possibly ways could be found to *play* science as a more public game in which the purely intellectual play that characterizes science at its best is more visible and readily accessible" [emphasis in original].[46]

The reality is that most academics *play* the publication game (publish or perish),[47] and in so doing they lose the creativity and spontaneity of engaging in intellectual play. They become constrained by a rigid reward structure. I believe that scientists and other academics should ignore the careerist considerations of publish or perish and instead become more intellectually inquisitive—a form of mental play that in the long term will make them better scientists and scholars. The Dutch historian Johan Huizinga referred to human beings as *Homo Ludens*, "man the player."[48] Well, there is no higher form of play than the discovery of new knowledge, using an ethos of childlike wonder.

In my nearly thirty-year career as a professor, I have had countless opportunities to evaluate scientific projects whilst wearing numerous hats, be it as a grant reviewer, a reviewer for many leading academic journals, a supervisor, or a researcher. Perhaps the leading weakness of most academic research is that it is profoundly uninteresting. Granted, this might be a somewhat subjective judgment. But are there universal markers of interestingness that one might use? In a classic paper published in 1971, the sociologist Murray S. Davis offered a set of twelve criteria that might adjudicate between interesting and non-interesting research, and called for the development of a new field, which he called the "sociology of the interesting."[49] In general, his criteria correspond to counterintuitive and surprising features of a finding (for instance, that variable A was thought to cause variable B but in reality it turns out to be the opposite). Many forms of play have a similar bottom-up emergent feature where the trajectory of the play session unfolds in unexpected ways, as occurs, say, in a comedy improvisation theater.[50] Ultimately, the scientific enterprise is nothing short of a form of cerebral adult play governed by a singular governing rule: the strict and unbiased adherence to the scientific method.

Find a Life Partner with Whom to Play and Laugh

Many years ago, one of my cousins was engaged to a woman who seemed, on paper, to be an ideal prospective wife. All was progressing nicely toward an eventual marriage until they went away on a beach vacation. It turned out that the fiancée did not like the feeling of sand on her toes. This proved an impediment to their beach vacation and ultimately was one of several reasons why they split up. My family is from Lebanon. We live and play at the beach. It is no surprise that Southern California is my second home. If I have to face a Sophie's choice between the beach (and my capacity to play there) and a prospective wife who hates the beach, the latter better be as intelligent as two-time Nobel laureate Marie Curie and as beautiful as the actress Blake Lively, otherwise it's beach time!

Earlier I discussed the importance of assortative human mating, namely the idea that birds of a feather flock together when it comes to a broad range of attributes. Does this apply to adult playfulness? Are people who score similarly on such a disposition more likely to be attracted to one another? Intuitively speaking, this would make perfect sense in that it is difficult to imagine a long-lasting marriage wherein one spouse is sullen and humorless whilst the other is playful and hilarious. Not surprisingly, individuals who are humorous, fun-loving, and playful tend to be attracted to those who exhibit a similar sunny mindset on life.[51]

Of the many reasons that my wife and I have a successful marriage, one is our ability to have fun with one another, to play with one another, and to make fun of ourselves and each other in a loving manner. I have often shared some of the funny quips between us on social media. Here is an example from Twitter:

> Me to my wife: "Come see this gorgeous body. Look at it! If I lose another 10 lbs, I'll be impossible to live with."
> Wife to me: "I'm starting a 'please help me page.' My husband's ego is too large for this house now that he is thin."
> Life as a playground. See my next book.[52]

In a cross-cultural study involving five countries (China, Russia, Turkey, the United Kingdom, and the United States), marital satisfaction was positively correlated with a spouse's level of humorousness.[53] A meta-analysis showed that humor shared by spouses (relational humor) had a greater positive effect on marital satisfaction than humor that expressed itself in other ways.[54] Couples who laugh together are more likely to have successful unions. This makes perfect evolutionary sense in that humor is a sexually selected trait that serves as a proxy measure for such desirable qualities as intelligence or extroversion.[55] The ability to foster a fun and playful family environment will also help to bring out these qualities in one's children. I have seen this with my own children, who are becoming ever more adept at satire and commenting about serious issues with complete playfulness.[56]

Having a playful mindset can help parents bond with their children, and I have created numerous play-related creative pursuits, all of which serve to strengthen our familial bonds. One such game is a photography competition in which all of the family members have to take a photo of anything that they can find in the house as their official contest "submission." We then send the photos to my in-laws, who judge the winning photo without knowing the identity of each photographer. A second game, which I have played with my daughter, is one I call "rapid-fire poetry."[57] One of us suggests a word (say, "brain") and then we have twenty minutes to generate a poem about it, using the following rules: the poem must consist of three verses, four lines per verse, and up to seven words per sentence. Through various creative games, I have been able to carve out quality family time via the magic of play.

When the Mossad Calls, Play!

I'm about to recount a deeply personal story that I did not share with anyone for more than two decades after the events had taken place, and I have only told it to a few individuals since (including my wife), but never in a public forum. So here we go. Let us hope that the unofficial statute of limitations on the story's confidentiality has passed, as the parties in question are not folks that you would want to upset. Back in the early 1980s, when I was in my late teens, I was approached by a relative who wanted me to meet a male friend of hers. I agreed to the meeting with some trepidation—it seemed an odd request—and my interest was soon piqued even further. The friend told me some Israeli men wanted to meet me, possibly to work on projects of theirs. I met the men, and they told me they worked for Israeli security. They wanted me to help them test possible weaknesses in their security operations. I was all in. I was going to be James Bond in real life!

For my first mission, they wanted me to visit an El Al travel bureau in downtown Montreal. I was to enter the office, sit in the waiting room, leave a bag under one of the chairs, ask a question at the reception desk, and then leave without taking the bag. I headed off to the El Al offices, followed my instructions, and the office security forces (unaware that they were being tested) immediately took steps to ensure that the bag I had left behind wasn't a bomb. They passed the test easily.

A few weeks later, I was given another, more challenging, assignment. I was to enter the Israeli consulate with a (fake) gun hidden in my winter gloves. The cover story was that I was a university student studying political science who wanted to interview the Israeli consul for a paper I was writing. The script for this operation was elaborate because the security procedures were tighter, and I had to know how to act at each step of the way. At the final layer of security, there would be a more invasive check of my person to establish that I was not carrying any weapons. As you might imagine, I was very concerned that the Israeli agents would discover the gun and harm me, if not kill me. I was assured that my handlers would be there, monitoring the situation, and would intervene before anything grave happened. Not very comforting, but I decided to accept the mission. On that fateful day, I arrived at the consulate and passed through the initial security layers until I arrived at a room where I was alone with a security agent who patted me down. I could feel my heart racing, but I remained cool. He made his way to my winter gloves, and just as he realized what I was hiding, a shout came from my handlers, who were hidden nearby, advising the security agent that this was a test.

Several weeks later I was approached for a third mission to test El Al's security readiness at the airport (specific details withheld). I had truly graduated to becoming an international man of mystery—and it was exhilarating that no one, not even my parents, knew what I was up to. But then someone—I suppose my relative—spilled the beans to my mother, and she went absolutely hysterical. Apparently, the Mossad (or perhaps Shin Bet)[58] does not wish to mess with an angry Lebanese-Jewish mother. My mother made me swear on everything under the sun that I would never accept another mission from the men in question, which I honored (and they never reached out to me again).

Later that summer, I was travelling to Israel for the first time to spend several months with my extended family (many of whom I had never met). As I made my way to the El Al queue, who do I see coming towards me but one of the secretive security men! He was an older gentleman, the leader of the group that had employed me. We looked at one another. He nodded. I reciprocated the nod. And he disappeared into the crowd. For me, as serious as the security tests were, this was all about play. I was playing a role, and the incidents remain vividly entrenched in my memory as an amazing example of *life as a playground*.

Get a Dog!

As far back as I can remember, I have always been in love with Belgian Shepherds. I was never able to convince my parents to let me have one; so, I made getting one a top item on my to-do list when I'd be on my own. But when I was a graduate student at Cornell University, I thought I was too busy with my studies to bring a dog into my life. Similarly, when I became a young assistant professor, I was too busy establishing my academic career to get a dog. And then I met my wife. I had just gotten tenure, I lived in a beautiful apartment, and the stars seemed finally aligned, but I still somehow felt that acquiring one of these beautiful creatures was an unattainable dream. A few months into our union, I confessed to my wife my obsessive love for these dogs. She listened and then said, "Well, let's get one." Wait, what? It's that simple? I had placed countless imaginary obstacles in my mind for no apparent reason. As a young adult, I had attended numerous dog shows just to hang out with the Belgian Shepherd breeders. In the process, I had befriended one in particular. I contacted him, and he told me that while he had an available litter, he very much doubted I would ever acquire a dog. I proved him wrong! Our first Belgian was named Amar (which means "moon" in Arabic; it is also used as an adjective for "great beauty"). Several years later, we added a second Belgian named Samra (means "dark one" in Arabic). It is difficult to express the joy that these two beautiful beings brought to our lives. Our human children grew up knowing no other reality than being protected by two majestic domestic wolves.

Dogs are true marvels of nature. They possess many noble qualities that most people aspire to exhibit, and few of our faults. They serve as companions; they protect us; they find us under collapsed buildings and rescue us from avalanches; using their extraordinary olfactory ability, they can sniff out bombs and detect dangerous and illicit drugs, as well as a wide range of cancers even at a very early developing stage;[59] they serve as guide dogs; they detect an oncoming epileptic seizure or a change in a diabetic's blood sugar levels; they herd our sheep; but perhaps most important, they play with us. All that a dog asks in return is food, affection, and a chance to play. That is one fantastic deal. The American Kennel Club has drafted an exhaustive list of benefits that stem from having a dog as part of your family. They reduce our sense of isolation and loneliness; they improve our heart health in part by causing us to be more physically active; they reduce our stress levels; they augment our oxytocin levels; they help us in the mating market by making us appear more attractive to prospective mates, as well as facilitating our ability to interact with others (think of the 2005 movie *Must Love Dogs* starring Diane Lane and John Cusack); and they force us to play.[60] The urge to play is so strong in dogs that many K-9 police units use play as the fundamental reward to motivate their dogs to perform well on the job. Not unlike humans, dogs have evolved a strong drive to play, thus explaining why they are our best friends in the animal world.[61] When you return home from a hard day's work, and your dog greets you as though you were the Messiah and immediately begins to solicit you to play, it becomes easy to destress. Your dog lives in the moment, while most of us wallow in the past and worry about the future. Your dog looks at you and communicates the following: "Here we are, just the two of us. We only have this moment. Forget about your worries. The past is gone. Don't fret about tomorrow. Let's play now!" There are few decisions that you will ever make that will augment your happiness and well-being as much as when you choose to share your life with dogs. Dogs are so special that even the act of spending money on them increases our happiness![62] Forget about Prozac; get a dog and immerse yourself in play.

Life is fleeting. Every moment is immeasurably precious. One of the ways by which we can honor our wondrous and improbable existence is to adopt a playful mindset as we navigate through the trials and tribulations that life throws at us. Being playful does not imply that you are not a serious person. To the contrary, many of the most austere moments in our lives are deeply enriched by having an open spirit that permits us to tap into our inner child with wide-eyed excitement. To be a maximally happy human is to immerse oneself in perpetual play across countless life domains. Life is too serious not to play.

CHAPTER SIX

Variety as the Spice of Life (Sometimes)

No pleasure endures unseasoned by variety.[1]

—Publius Syrus

Sameness is the mother of disgust, variety the cure.[2]

—Francesco Petrarch

*Having a thousand different ladies is pretty cool, I've
learned in my life. I've (also) found out that having one
woman a thousand different times is more satisfying.*[3]

—Wilt Chamberlain

*The secret of happiness is this: Let your interests be as
wide as possible. . . .*[4]

—Bertrand Russell

The pursuit of variety is one of the fundamental ways human beings forestall existential monotony. But while the "variety effect" yields many benefits, it is not always the preferred path to take, and more is not always better.

Let me give you an example. I love Vietnamese food, and at my favorite Vietnamese restaurant I almost always get the same dish, beef pho. At my favorite Mexican restaurant in Laguna Beach, California, I almost always get the calamari burrito. When it comes to these two restaurants, I seem to have found a dish that brings me great gustatory satisfaction, and accordingly I fail to activate my otherwise enthusiastic taste for food variety. I am a bit of a germophobe, too, but I do not shy away from trying novel and exotic foods, to the point of buying snake soup from a street vendor in Hong Kong. The reality is that both variety and routine have their benefits when it comes to our happiness. At any given point, an individual faces multiple Darwinian pulls. The challenge is to know how to navigate the potential minefields into which our instincts guide us. Behavioral scientists have explored many motives and factors that drive human beings to seek variety. A typical argument, especially in consumer psychology, is that introducing novelty into our normal range of choices thwarts the risks of psychological or physiological satiation.[5] Another thing to remember is that the evolutionary reasons that promote variety-seeking differ when we are talking about different domains, whether it be food, intellectual stimulation, or sexual activity.

So, what are some of the contexts in which variety leads to greater happiness? Using both correlational and experimental studies, we know, generally, that having a variety of activities and goals is linked to well-being.[6] For example, researchers found that users of the Live Happy app who engaged in a wider variety of happiness-inducing exercises were happier than those who employed a more limited selection.[7] But there has also been a documented *negative* relationship between pursuing too many presumed positive activities and happiness.[8] As is true of most things in life, the challenge is to find the right balance and understand the right conditions so that the pursuit of variety is beneficial and not detrimental. At times we may seek the solace of a familiar routine, whereas on other occasions we benefit from an infusion of novelty.

Variety-seeking is, in part, a personality trait. Some people are inherently greater variety seekers than others, and this might correlate to a wide range of personality traits.[9] Aside from variety-seeking as a personality trait, there are situational variables that have a profound effect on the extent to which we seek variety. For instance, researchers have found that we are less likely to seek variety in the morning as compared to later in the day.[10] They propose that this is linked to changes in physiological arousal associated with our diurnal circadian rhythms. We know too that it is unwise to go grocery shopping when you are hungry, as you are more likely to buy more of everything.[11] Other situational variables that alter people's desire for variety include hunger, thirst, sleepiness, and the weather. People who are hungry or thirsty exhibit an increased penchant for food variety and drink variety, respectively.[12] Drowsy people seek food variety because it is a form of psychological arousal that helps in wakefulness.[13] When weather worsens our mood, human beings are apt to seek more variety as an arousal-inducing pursuit.[14] The COVID-19 lockdowns also prompted people to seek more variety when they were finally able to travel.[15]

The "Diversity Is Our Strength" Mantra versus Optimal Variety

In addition to his job as the prime minister of Canada, Justin Trudeau also acts as commissar of the Bureau of Diversity, Inclusion, and Equity (DIE), where we are all obliged to repeat the party slogan, "Diversity is our strength"—no matter the social, political, and economic realities and problems around us. Inflation is rampant. No worries, "Diversity is our strength." Crime is up. Easily solvable with more diversity. Islamic terrorism a threat? Canada needs more diversity. Do you suffer from diabetes? Perhaps you need a more diverse collection of doctors who are less interested in body-shaming you. Needless to say, the single-minded focus on DIE is wrongheaded on many levels. First, the pursuit of diversity is utterly irrelevant to many issues. For example, a research group's ability to solve a problem in pure mathematics does not depend on the ethnic, racial, or gender identities or sexual orientations of its members. Apparently, if only transgender women of color had tackled Fermat's Last Theorem, the world would not have needed to wait more than 350 years to have a heterosexual white male, Sir Andrew Wiles, prove it in 1995. Could you imagine how much quicker the double helix structure of DNA could have been identified had we not relied on two white men (Francis Crick and James Watson) to resolve this issue in 1953? Imagine if nonbinary Latinx people had not been marginalized by the scientific establishment, the mysteries of DNA could have been elucidated long ago. And do not get me started on the mapping of the human genome. Too much reliance on the scientific method (also known as "white science") has clearly held us back. The second problem with the DIE cult is that it focuses on all the wrong metrics of diversity. There are contexts where a greater diversity of political orientations or personality traits is important. In other words, greater variety in some instances does yield optimal performance. It has been demonstrated, for instance, that there is an inverted-U curve on how many highly extroverted individuals there should be in task-performing groups.[16]

The concept of diversity (as a proxy for variety) has clearly become a politically laden term. Progressives love all forms of diversity except when they don't—intellectually, politically, or culturally. Indeed, they are Talibanic in their desire to cancel, ban, obliterate, and destroy speech, ideas, and statues of which they disapprove. That being said, does one's political orientation affect one's general penchant for variety-seeking? The answer is yes, but perhaps not in the way that you might expect. People who scored higher on political conservatism, or who were primed to be in a conservative mindset, were more likely to be engaged in greater food variety-seeking.[17] In a quest to explain this otherwise counterintuitive finding, the researchers argued that to the extent that seeking product variety is a social norm in individualistic societies, and conservatives in Western societies are more likely to adhere to individualistic social norms, this might be at the root of the conservative variety-seeking effect.

Whereas universities are now bastions of ideological homogeneity (lack of variety) due to the overwhelming number of professors who are left-leaning and progressive in their political bent—and who mostly, if not exclusively, hire like-minded candidates—how well do these institutions fare in promoting intellectual variety-seeking? Colleges and universities often tout to parents the importance of a broad liberal arts education. But does this merely sound good as part of a university's mission statement to parents? Is it otherwise ignored? I turn next to how the pursuit of intellectual variety-seeking can lead to cerebral happiness.

Intellectual Variety-Seeking vs. Specialization

Intellectual variety-seeking is a fundamental feature of a psychologically rich life.[18] Indeed, a psychologically rich life is one "best characterized by a variety of interesting and perspective-changing experiences."[19] When I was pursuing my undergraduate degree, the start of each semester was a uniquely exciting time for me. I would spend the first few weeks sitting in on countless courses prior to deciding on my final choice of electives for that semester (courses outside of my specialization in mathematics and computer science). It was akin to an all-you-can-eat buffet, albeit the offerings were food for thought and not for your belly. I ended up taking courses in ceramics, the history of French cinema, anthropology, consumer behavior, linguistics, accounting, marketing, economics, and astronomy, among other topics.

In other words, I was instantiating the ethos of seeking a broad and well-rounded education even though I was majoring in very technical disciplines. Unlike some of my undergraduate cohorts who were quantitative jocks (so to speak), my interests spanned the natural sciences, the social sciences, and the humanities. This has always been the case, as evidenced by the fact that I won the chemistry and history awards when graduating from high school in 1982. As far back as I can remember, I have always been drawn to a very broad range of intellectual interests.

Back in 2008, I was invited to the University of Arizona to deliver lectures on three separate topics. One of the lectures was titled "To Strategize or Not to Strategize: That Is the Question—Musings of an Interdisciplinarian and Iconoclastic Evolutionary Consumer Scholar." The theme was to explore the pros and cons of two distinct research strategies when pursuing an academic career. The first and most accepted approach is to operate within a very narrow academic area of expertise and develop research streams that probe deeply within this tightly defined knowledge base. A key benefit of this in-depth strategy is that it affords academics economies of scale in terms of staying abreast of the relevant academic literature, the appropriate methodologies to use, and the accepted theoretical frameworks. There is no need to constantly revamp one's areas of research expertise if you are a "stay in your lane" professor. An example of such an academic was the late Alice Isen, a professor of psychology and marketing at Cornell University during my time there as a doctoral student. Much of her scientific career was spent studying the relationship between positive affect and various phenomena (such as word association, memory tasks, intertemporal choice, creativity, and variety-seeking). The second and less accepted strategy is to pursue broad research interests unencumbered by topical constraints, disciplinary boundaries, or methodological confines. My scientific career has been defined by this second, broader approach. I have published papers in medicine, psychology, consumer behavior, economics, politics, advertising, marketing, evolutionary theory, and bibliometrics, to name some of the intellectual disciplines, on an extraordinarily wide range of topics within them. The driving reason for doing so stems from my need for intellectual variety-seeking. I am unwilling to remain within a tightly defined intellectual landscape. Rather, I view my role as a professor as one where I seek to advance knowledge whilst being an intellectual hedonist. Life is simply too short to be a one-trick pony.

In 2016, I was invited to speak at the psychology department of a Californian university. More than a speaking engagement, it was a second attempt by that university to hire me. In 2011, the president and chancellor at the time wanted me to become a professor at their institution. The deal was nearly done when in all likelihood "progressive" faculty members protested and succeeded in blocking my appointment (albeit I was told that it was due to budgetary constraints). The full story is an extraordinary tale of academic cowardice and institutional rot, but I will leave the details for another time and place. For my 2016 visit, I prepared a lecture covering several of my published and ongoing projects, most of which shared the application of evolutionary theory to a broad variety of phenomena, including the behavioral genetics of decision-making, the effects of conspicuous consumption on men's testosterone levels, the effects of the menstrual cycle on women's beautification choices, the universal hourglass figure as advertised by online female escorts, the different ways men and women approach mate selection, and the genetic factors that affect gift-giving at Israeli weddings.[20] My point was to highlight precisely how evolutionary theory allows me to bring theoretical coherence under a unifying framework to many subjects. I assumed that my wide-ranging talk—a form of intellectual variety-seeking—would entertain and instruct. Boy, was I wrong! The feedback that I received was that my work was too scattered and unfocused. I should have instead presented a set of studies in a very narrow research area. (For me, this would be a quick cure for insomnia.) Hyper-specialization is the hill where big ideas and disruptive innovations go to die.

I will accept, however, that a hyper-generalist might be insufficiently well-versed to make a significant contribution in a particular field. Think of the adage "jack of all trades, master of none." As in most things in life, the optimal point lies between these two extremes.

In an otherwise bleak landscape of DIE insanity, today's universities at least recognize that many of the most pressing scientific and practical problems that involve academic research require an interdisciplinary approach.[21] Needless to say, interdisciplinarity requires a mindset rooted in intellectual variety-seeking. Take, for example, the mapping of the human genome. It utilized knowledge from a broad range of disciplines including biology, chemistry, physics, bioinformatics, genetics, mathematics, and computer science.[22] Twenty-five years ago, Moti Nissani, an interdisciplinary professor, provided a list of ten reasons to explain the importance of interdisciplinarity, including:

> 5. Many intellectual, social, and practical problems require interdisciplinary approaches. 6. Interdisciplinary knowledge and research serve to remind us of the unity-of-knowledge ideal. 7. Interdisciplinarians enjoy greater flexibility in their research. 8. More so than narrow disciplinarians, interdisciplinarians often treat themselves to the intellectual equivalent of traveling in new lands.[23]

Reason 5 speaks to the importance of interdisciplinarity to cracking problems that no single area of expertise can. Reason 6 is a recognition of the importance of consilience as espoused by the late Harvard biologist E. O. Wilson. Reason 7 acknowledges that a penchant for intellectual variety-seeking engenders cognitive flexibility, whereas reason 8 is in line with my view that life is too short to refrain from visiting a broad range of intellectual landscapes. Cerebral variety-seeking, as instantiated via an ethos of interdisciplinarity, yields the good life by helping us address important societal and scientific challenges. An analysis of papers published in 2000 across a very broad range of disciplines revealed that the top 1 percent of most cited papers also happen to be more interdisciplinary than all other papers.[24] Not surprisingly, interdisciplinarity yields scientific works that have more impact on society.[25] Of note, two measures of interdisciplinarity (the diversity and variety of cited references) have a positive effect on being cited by other scholars in the long term (but not so over the short term).[26]

Most universities proclaim that the pursuit of interdisciplinarity is one of their central missions, and yet when it comes to actually supporting such endeavors, they quickly revert to disciplinary tribalism. Case in point, back in 2009 I had hosted the eminent evolutionary biologist David Sloan Wilson at Concordia University. David pioneered the evolutionary studies program at Binghamton University, where students are now able to obtain an interdisciplinary minor in evolutionary studies. I tried to establish a similar program at my university, but when I pitched the idea to the various deans I received less than enthusiastic responses. The program would have been an important first for a Canadian university, but bureaucratic inertia, lack of vision, and disciplinary tribalism killed it. Professors are ultimately human beings, and as such they exhibit the standard traps of the us-versus-them mindset. The reality is that academics are trained to think within disciplinary and functional silos. It is no surprise that I hardly interact with my business school colleagues in other disciplines. We may share a building, but we seldom collaborate with one another. Ultimately, the ethos of interdisciplinarity will only be fully instantiated when universities create reward structures that explicitly encourage intellectual variety-seeking. In the meantime, however, there is no reason why you, the reader, should not seek variety in your own intellectual pursuits, such as in your book choices for a quiet evening at home—as long as your home includes a copy of this book and *The Parasitic Mind*!

Analogical Reasoning, Generalists, and Polymaths

In my public engagement, I often use analogical reasoning to demonstrate the fallacy of a given position. The power of analogies comes from our human desire to compare and contrast experiences and data. Or to put it in the context of this chapter, analogies apply intellectual variety-seeking and interdisciplinary interests to the commonsense application of logic.

Some of the great scientific insights in human history were arrived at via analogical reasoning, perhaps none as famously as Johannes Kepler's use of extensive analogies in developing his cosmological work on planetary motion.[27] We know this because Kepler kept a detailed account of his cognitive processes of reasoning and discovery. Kepler's cognitive detailing would be referred to in today's parlance as concurrent verbal protocols (verbalizing what a decision maker is doing as he engages a task) or retrospective verbal protocols (verbalizing what a decision maker did after having completed a task). Verbal protocols are very laborious to analyze because they generate hugely detailed transcripts, but they are incredibly rich in terms of the cognitive details that are being described. In any case, the ability to generate incisive and illuminating analogies often requires that one be well-versed across intellectual domains. This is precisely what the psychologist Kevin Dunbar sought to establish with his research on the inner workings of molecular biology labs.[28] Specifically, Dunbar highlighted how scientists use analogical reasoning and showed that labs with members coming from a greater variety of disciplines yielded greater analogical reasoning. The bottom line is that to be an intellectual variety-seeker enriches one's life on a personal level and enhances scientists' ability to come up with breakthrough discoveries.

An analysis of U.S. patents (a measure of innovation) filed between 1975 and 1999 in the electronics industry found that in technological environments defined by high uncertainty, having a generalist on the team yielded positive effects in terms of the economic relevance of the patent.[29] Interestingly, in slow-paced scientific domains, generalists fare better than specialists.[30] Generalists and specialists assess information differently, and an examination of patents filed by 3M inventors revealed that both are needed. In terms of the raw number of filed patents, generalists performed better, but, not surprisingly, sophisticated technical inventions came from specialists.[31]

The ability to harness the creative power of a variety of people with radically different backgrounds to solve problems that otherwise have stymied specialists is at the root of InnoCentive, where people get together to "solve the world's greatest challenges."[32] The company has proclaimed an 80 percent success rate in generating crowdsourced solutions. On a related note, the Arrowsmith bibliometric project, founded by Don R. Swanson, is a systematized platform that uses algorithmic formulas to identify links in scientific research papers that are otherwise in disconnected disciplines.[33] Many important discoveries have been made by identifying links between otherwise disparate scholarly endeavors.[34]

Highly accomplished academics often exhibit broad interests outside of their areas of expertise. The late Nobel laureate physicist Richard Feynman was an ardent bongo drummer. The economist Thomas Sowell, one of the original slayers of woke ideas, has been an avid photographer for many decades. The classicist Victor Davis Hanson has been a farmer for many years. A study that contrasted five groups, namely Nobel laureates in the sciences, National Academy of Sciences (NAS) members, British Royal Society (BRS) members, Sigma Xi members (scientists in general), and the general public, found that Nobel Prize winners were the most likely to have arts and crafts avocations, followed by the two other groupings of eminent scientists (NAS and BRS), which had roughly equal avocations, and coming in last were Sigma Xi members and the general public, who had roughly the same number of avocations.[35] Hence, the more eminent a scientist is, the more likely he is to exhibit broad interests outside his area of scientific expertise. On a related note, an analysis of the academic background of Nobel Prize winners in medicine or physiology found that many had a multidisciplinary education as part of their academic training.[36] A mind trained in intellectual variety can unlock important scientific mysteries that elude others.

Back in 2014, I wrote a *Psychology Today* column listing the ten historical figures I would invite to a party, and I asked people on social media to offer their own lists.[37] The two most popular responses were Albert Einstein and Charles Darwin. Here are mine (in no particular order): Charles Darwin, Albert Einstein, Isaac Newton, Galileo Galilei, Socrates, Plato, Aristotle, Leonardo da Vinci, Maimonides, and King Solomon. If I had to put one guest above the others, it would be da Vinci, because he was the ultimate Renaissance man: a polymath extraordinaire interested in anatomy, botany, and cartography who made astounding contributions as a painter, engineer, scientist, sculptor, and architect. Some of his sketches were prophetic of future inventions—like the machine gun and the helicopter. A copy of da Vinci's famous drawing *The Vitruvian Man* hangs in our bedroom in honor of this great man's intellectual and artistic achievements.

While it is increasingly rare in today's academic ecosystem to be a polymath, the benefits are incontestable. As Michael Araki, a researcher in the fields of innovation and entrepreneurship, has stated:

> Polymathic breadth, rather than detrimental to rigorous
> inquiry, provides the resources necessary for critical thinking

and sheds light on previously unseen gaps in our understanding. It helps us identify common foundations among
disciplines, offering solid grounds for future inquiry. It fosters
development of rich collections of ideas, experiences, and skills
that enable novel and surprising combinations, which can lead
to powerful, otherwise unreachable, insights. Unsurprisingly,
humanity's most celebrated discoveries came from people who
engaged with a variety of interests and integrated them into
synergistic networks of enterprise. Clearly, whenever critical
thinking or innovation are necessary, it pays to encourage the
development of the rich, examined, and integrated repertoire
that is the hallmark of polymathy.[38]

When I established my show *The Saad Truth* in 2014, my objective
was to hold conversations with interesting people irrespective of their
professions or areas of specialization. Unlike many podcasts that focus
on a singular theme (whether it be crime, psychology, fitness, or happiness), I could not bear to restrict myself in this manner. I'm an intellectual variety-seeker! As in most other pursuits in my life, my show
would be defined by the broad variety of my guests. I've held chats with
psychologists, physicians, philosophers, physicists, chemists, biologists,
primatologists, anthropologists, economists, political scientists, histo-
rians, a bioethicist, a geneticist, a sociologist, a geophysicist, a statistician, porn stars, media personalities, athletes, literature professors,
politicians, an ex–Islamic extremist, an imam, the founder of Twitter,
a legendary soul singer, a cartoonist, a satirist, journalists, lawyers, a
wrongly jailed prisoner who spent twenty-nine years in prison for a
murder that he did not commit, activists, a film director, actors, comedians, the Navy SEAL who killed Osama bin Laden, and the niece of
Osama bin Laden.[39] It is not easy to carry on meaningful and engaging
conversations with such a varied guest list. It requires intellectual

curiosity, epistemic humility, and open-mindedness, all of which are ultimately linked to a desire to sample from a heterogeneous intellectual buffet. I am infinitely richer for having met these brilliant people and engaged them in long-form conversations.

Engaging your mind in a variety of intellectual tasks is absolutely necessary for living the good life. As Socrates reputedly said, "The unexamined life is not worth living"; he and his greatest pupils showed an interest in everything. This made them fully human. It did not necessarily make them *happy*—there is a distinction between "the good life" and being happy—but for many of us, exercising our reason across broad fields of endeavor, and finding links between those fields, certainly *helps* us find happiness.

Sexual Variety

Question: Are humans happiest when they seek sexual variety or when they accept monogamous bonds of marriage? As an evolutionary scientist, my first step to answering this question is to examine mating systems across the animal kingdom. Sexually reproducing species organize their mating systems in several ways. One way is polygyny, as practiced by mountain gorillas and elephant seals, where one male maintains a harem of multiple females. There is also polyandry, practiced by cassowaries and jacanas, where one female has multiple male mates. And there is monogamy, notably practiced by prairie voles and sandhill cranes, where one male mates with one female. Depending on the mating system, sex differences are either exaggerated or eliminated. For example, in polygynous species, the sexual dimorphism is sizeable, as evidenced by the size differential between a male elephant seal and its female counterpart. In the human context, men are roughly 15 percent larger than women. Where do humans fall when it comes to this particular taxonomy? Are we naturally monogamous, or do we seek sexual variety? The truth is that we seek both, to have the cake and eat it too, meaning that we have a desire for long-term pair bonding as well as an instinct to stray from our monogamous unions. The quest for forging monogamous relationships is rooted in the evolutionary recognition that human babies require tremendous investment from both parents. We are a "biparental species," which is a rarity among mammals. From the research that has been conducted on mammals, birds, and fish, we know that 90 percent of mammalian species have female-only parental care. Ten percent have biparental care. None have male-only parental care. Ninety percent of bird species are biparental. Eight percent have female-only parental care and 2 percent have male-only parental care. Most fish species offer no parental care, but of those that do, 50 percent are male only, 30 percent are female only, and 20 percent are biparental.[40]

What is often forgotten, given the dominance of Western culture, is that monogamy is not a given for human beings. Anthropological records suggest that, historically, 85 percent of cultures have permitted polygynous marriages (parts of the African and Islamic worlds still do); while monogamy is the marital system of nearly all of the remaining 15 percent of cultures.[41] There are very few cases of human polyandry, the most famous of which might be Tibetan fraternal polyandry,[42] which can, in rare circumstances, make evolutionary sense.[43]

Men and women thus face an existential sexual conundrum. We have evolved a desire for sexual variety in order to augment our mating success, concomitant with a desire to form monogamous long-term unions in order to raise children. The wedding jitters or proverbial wedding-day cold feet that many people experience as they are about to get married likely stem from two questions: 1) Am I marrying the right person? 2) Even if this is the right person, am I willing and able to remain sexually faithful to one person for the rest of my life? Hence, one's wedding day is both a cause for great celebration (I found my soulmate) and deep mourning (the death of sexual variety, as I'm denying all future sexual opportunities). Variety-seeking is nature's Viagra pill, and it has been documented across many species that sexual variety increases sexual interest. It has been given the term "the Coolidge effect," because of an anecdote from when United States president Calvin Coolidge and his wife were visiting a farm. Mrs. Coolidge, strolling separately from her husband, was told that a certain rooster mated multiple times a day. She was impressed, and told the farmworker to tell her husband. When President Coolidge was informed, he asked whether the rooster was mating with the same hen. He was told no, the rooster mated with multiple hens. President Coolidge supposedly quipped: "Tell that to Mrs. Coolidge." The Coolidge effect has been documented within the human context.[44] This penchant has been commercialized by Ashley Madison, a company that specializes in organizing sexual dalliances outside of marriage with such slogans as "When Monogamy Becomes Monotony" and "Life Is Short. Have an Affair."

Evolutionary psychology, and other scientific research, has shown that it is an incontestable fact that men desire sexual variety more than women do; this finding has been demonstrated in nations around the globe.[45] That notwithstanding, it is unequivocally true that women too have evolved a desire for sexual variety. Women are more likely to cheat when they are maximally fertile, are more likely to do so with males of superior genetic stock (as compared to the cuckolded partners), are more likely to orgasm when they cheat, and are less likely to insist on using contraception.[46] Taken together, this is known as the "shopping for good genes" mating strategy. A woman might marry Bill Gates for security but cheat on him with the brawny, sexy gardener.[47] Furthermore, as described by the evolutionary biologist Robin Baker in his 1996 book *Sperm Wars*, men's ejaculate contains three phenotypes of spermatozoa: the classic "swimmers" that look to fertilize a woman's ovum; the blockers that stand at the entrance of a woman's reproductive tract to block entry of another man's sperm; and the killers that seek to kill other men's sperm.[48] Given that sperm is viable for roughly seventy-two hours inside a woman's reproductive tract, the fact that men have evolved such chemical weaponry to thwart other men's sperm implies that evolutionarily speaking, it was highly likely that your female ancestors and mine had sex with at least two men within a three-day period. Finally, a comparison of the size of testes as a function of body size across primates is quite revealing regarding female promiscuity within a given species.[49] For example, gorillas have a polygynous mating arrangement wherein a singular dominant male monopolizes sexual access to many females (although extrapair copulations can occur). Hence, since the likelihood of sperm wars is minimal, male gorillas have relatively small testes. Male chimpanzees, on the other hand, are walking testicles. They have gigantic testes precisely because of intense female promiscuity. Would you like to venture where human males fit on that continuum? Are we closer to gorillas or chimpanzees? Gentlemen, please brace yourselves. Human males tend to have relatively larger testicles than gorillas' but smaller than chimpanzees', suggesting that evolutionarily speaking, human females are likely to seek sexual variety. Variety is a two-edged sword! What is good for the goose is good for the gander.

Since we have evolved both the desire to form long-term unions and a desire to seek sexual variety, how do these conflicting goals relate to happiness? Are those with fewer lifetime sexual partners happier than those with more? Does the single life or the married life lead to greater individual happiness? The data are quite messy, but it does seem that marriage improves one's well-being and that those with very few sexual partners prior to marriage are happiest.[50] That said, long-term couples who maintain a high level of sexual satisfaction with each other benefit from incorporating sexual variety within their relationships.[51] Of note, an examination of sexual frequency of American adults for a twenty-five-year period (1989–2014) revealed that married people have sex more often than unmarried people.[52] Is it better to have sex eighty times per year with one's spouse (no variety) or twenty times per year, one each with a different partner (high variety)? I suppose that the answer to this question will depend on a slew of personality traits but perhaps most notably on one's score on the Sociosexual Orientation Inventory, a measure of a person's desire for emotionally unfettered and hence noncommittal sexual contacts.[53]

A quick final note about women's drive for sexual variety. Whereas it is clear that women seek greater sexual variety when they are maximally fertile, this penchant is contingent on their perceived vulnerability to disease.[54] In other words, women's desire for sexual variety increases as a genetic insurance policy against increased disease threats. And women who are in the maximally fertile part of their ovulating cycles not only desire sexual variety, they desire a greater variety of consumer goods and hedonic foods.[55] The life lesson here is that if you are an ovulating woman, don't go shopping on the internet and avoid the all-you-can-eat buffet!

Food Variety

I am currently at my lightest weight since 1996. I have been able to achieve a dramatic weight loss in part because I have managed to redirect the variety effect, within the food domain, to my advantage. From an evolutionary perspective, it makes perfect sense to seek a multitude of varied food sources. After all, we are omnivores who crave a broad range of tastes, smells, and textures in our food offerings. It is perhaps not surprising then that the Mediterranean diet, which is defined by a heterogeneous set of food sources, is optimal for one's health, including for maintaining a healthy weight. The key, of course, is moderation in quantity while enjoying the diversity of offerings.

I should add here as a sidenote that I am a huge animal lover and I abhor the grotesque and diabolical cruelty that is endemic within the animal farming industry. As such, I am fully committed to a radical improvement in how we treat our sentient animal cousins. But humans have evolved a desire to consume animal protein, and they are not going to lose that desire. As such, it is wrong—and likely suboptimal to our well-being—to expect us all to become strict vegans.[56] That is simply a fact for which there is anatomical, physiological, morphological (cranial and dental), paleobiological, parasitological, archaeological, cross-cultural, anthropological, nutritional, genomic, genetical, medical, sexual, and psychological data to support my argument. But of all the many groups that come after me for stating plain evolutionary science, the three worst and most unreasonable are militant feminists (who dislike what evolution says about sex), the Pronoun Taliban (whose entire ideology denies science), and the Tofu Brigade (who cannot accept that humans are omnivores).

No amount of scientific evidence will ever make the Tofu Brigade happy. To them, I am a moral hypocrite because I often post photos attesting to my love of animals along with photos attesting to my love of food, including food that involves animal protein. Voilà! Therein lies the proof that I am a morally inconsistent degenerate Nazi who tortures puppies and kittens as a leisure activity. Nuanced thinking is never a strong suit of those parasitized by black-or-white ideologies.

I shall return to food variety shortly, but for the sake of completeness let me briefly mention my most harrowing ordeal with the immeasurably unhappy and angry Pronoun Taliban. It is only slightly hyperbolic to argue that ISIS militia are somewhat less scary than the Pronoun Taliban. Once they descend on you, it is best that you find a panic room or storm shelter in which to hide and weather their ire. I had posted a profoundly innocuous tweet recounting my wife's perplexity about how to address a barista who appeared to be a transgender individual. The tweet was meant to highlight my wife's sensitivity and kindness. Here is the full thread:

> My wife walked up to the server at our local cafe. The person was possibly transgender. She wanted to engage the individual but was frozen in fear that she might use a pronoun that might offend. Therein lies the problem with this language policing. It takes perfectly natural social situations and in the quest to not offend an extraordinarily small minority (who of course deserve to live fully dignified lives like anyone else), everyone is walking on [eggshells]. Fighting for a world free of bigotry does not imply that we must suppress perfectly natural categorization mechanisms that are built into our brains and our languages. I can be free of bigotry without being compelled to celebrate your unique personhood.[57]

The intellectual luminary and child actress Valerie Bertinelli weighed in as follows: "'Hi' 'Pardon me' 'How are you this morning?' 'May I please have' 'Thank you' Language you can use without worrying about someone's pronouns. But you don't really care about that, do you? You're just looking for targets, then you can cry victim when people come to their defense."[58] To which I replied: "She wanted to say to the server's colleague, 'he'll get the hang of it' (new server) but hesitated because of 'he'll.' Dial back the outrage. Read my tweet carefully. The interaction was otherwise very warm. Cheers."[59] Why do I share this exchange? Because it highlights many such exchanges that I have had with a variety of Twitter users. Those who act as the Pronoun Taliban (as well as the Tofu Brigade, the militant feminists, and many progressives) live their lives in a very agitated, unhappy, self-righteous, and perpetually offended state. Here is an important life lesson: Never be as ideologically angry as the Tofu Brigade or the Pronoun Taliban or the militant feminists, and avoid becoming a blue-checked, blue-haired, woke keyboard warrior. It is a pathway to venomous misery. Instead, pursue the reasoned calm that leads to happiness.

Returning to food variety, over the past two decades, my wife and I have gone to numerous all-inclusive vacation destinations, including several Club Med villages (Guadeloupe; Martinique; Turks and Caicos twice; San Salvador, Bahamas) and Sandals in Nassau, Bahamas. A key reason to go to any of these locations is, of course, to frolic on the beautiful beaches. But perhaps the main driver of any such vacation is best described by the Italian saying *La carne è debole* [The flesh is weak]. It is terribly alluring to know that you have unlimited access to delicious food buffets and innumerable drinks (albeit we are not avid drinkers). The gustatory pull is very strong, as per the anecdotal evidence that guests will typically return home having put on five pounds for each week spent at one of those all-inclusive waist-destroyers. It makes perfect evolutionary sense that we are attracted by food variety-seeking.[60] A recent meta-analysis has confirmed that food variety increases our food intake.[61] And of course, greater food intake will, all other things being equal, result in weight gain. The variety effect, though, is more nuanced. Using a *variety of varieties* model, researchers explained the conditions under which having greater food variety might actually yield weight loss.[62] Whereas food variety within a given sitting might cause weight gain, the variety of food offerings using a longer time period might result in weight loss. Hence, one cannot simply say that under all conditions, more variety implies weight gain. It depends on the type of variety that is being measured. Interestingly, greater variety of a given stimulus (for example, dots of one color versus dots of many colors) leads to reduced quantity estimates. When people are shown a bowl of M&M's candies consisting of one color and then asked to pour M&M's candies into a second bowl to equal the quantity found in the original bowl, they pour larger quantities when the bag that they are given is comprised of multicolored candies.[63] Hence, this perceptual bias coupled with our penchant for variety-seeking makes the all-you-can-eat buffet a severe impediment to our well-being (and waistlines). Note, though, that a greater variety of food colors on your plate is indicative of healthiness. Imagine a plate consisting of five colors versus one consisting solely of yellow-brown tones. The former likely consists of several colorful fruits and vegetables, whereas the latter is likely a mishmash of fried foods. The key takeaway is that there is no universal variety rule. At times, more variety benefits us; on other occasions it is detrimental to our well-being.

Variety of Activities and Geographic Locations

At my home, we have three cardio machines: an elliptical, a stationary bike, and a treadmill. Does the fact that we have three machines increase the amount of exercise that I do as compared to if we had only, say, one machine? Anecdotally, I would answer with an emphatic yes! In the same way that a food buffet induces greater eating, a buffet of exercise machines yields greater exercising. I often will do a "home biathlon" (using two of the machines in one session) and more rarely a "home triathlon" (all three machines in one session). This has certainly augmented the amount of time that I dedicate to my daily exercise routine. The science supports my anecdotal evidence. Incorporating a variety of exercise machines yields many benefits, including a greater number of completed repetitions, more cumulative weight lifted (on resistance machines), as well as greater liking of the exercise sessions.[64] The variety effect can make us fatter (greater food intake), but it can also make us thinner (greater amount of exercising)!

Of course, variety can also be challenging. At the beginning of my career as a professor, I was irked by the imposition of mundane errands that interrupted the flow of my work as an academic. If I was preparing lectures, I did not want to be bothered with anything else—and I was dedicated to completing one task before moving onto another. As my career progressed, I had to learn quickly how to multitask as my professional life took on a very hectic turn. I was soon juggling many assignments, from working on scientific papers to writing articles (for a lay audience) or books, teaching, supervising theses, applying for research grants, fielding media requests, hosting *The Saad Truth* online, answering fan emails, being a dad and a husband, and numerous other responsibilities and activities.

Does such a variety of activities lead to happiness? It turns out that it depends on a given time frame. Within a relatively short time frame (like an hour), greater variety leads to lesser happiness because it is usually regarded as a hindrance to productivity. But in longer time periods (say, over the course of a day), variety augments one's happiness because the variety of activities is more likely to be regarded as stimulating.[65] In today's era of social media interruptions, this finding resonates deeply with me. When I was working on my earlier books, prior to the era of hyperactive social media engagement, I never experienced a break of my writing flow stemming from this lure. Today, on the other hand, I detest the fact that I often experience the irresistible pull of scrolling through my Twitter feed. Twitter interruptions over a one-hour period are annoying, whereas tweeting during a dedicated thirty-minute block can be rewarding. Speaking of time management, using data from four countries (Canada, the United States, the Netherlands, and Denmark), researchers found that when individuals purchase time-saving products or services, their happiness increases.[66] In a world of endless time pressures, freeing up one's time is a pathway to well-being. I know of this firsthand, as it has become unbearably stressful to handle many of the logistical details of my daily life (such as booking guests on my show, arranging travel itineraries, and fielding the endless emails that I receive). Hiring a personal assistant would certainly add to my overall sense of well-being.

As I have previously explained, my wife and I frequently take one-hour morning walks. Is it best to repeat the same route, or do we benefit from incorporating a variety of settings? A recent study addressed this issue and found that individuals who experienced a diversity of locations experienced positive effects that could be seen in brain-image studies (including greater connectivity between the hippocampus and striatum regions of the brain).[67] It is clear that humans are creatures of habit, and as such we feel comfortable engaging in routinized behavior. However, the interjection of variety, in this case via an exploration of a heterogeneity of neighborhoods and environments, can serve as an elixir against the dangers of perceptual monotony.

CHAPTER SEVEN

On Persistence and the Anti-Fragility
of Failure

Gutta cavat lapidem, non vi sed saepe cadendo.
[The drop of rain maketh a hole in the stone, not by
violence, but by oft falling.][1]

—Hugh Latimer

No tree which the wind does not often blow against is
firm and strong; for it is stiffened by the very act of being
shaken, and plants its roots more securely: those which
grow in a sheltered valley are brittle: and so it is to the
advantage of good men, and causes them to be undis-
mayed, that they should live much amidst alarms, and
learn to bear with patience what is not evil save to him
who endures it ill.[2]

—Seneca

Success in life requires persistence and grit. Of course, one of the reasons that people do not persist is that they get smashed by rejection. Rejection in the mating market. Rejection as a starving musical band. Rejection from publishers. Rejection during the peer review process. Rejection when applying for jobs. Rejection is, clearly, an unhappy experience.[3] That said, as long as rejection does not kill you, it will indeed make you stronger, if you have the will to persist. Enduring failure, and coming back and persisting in your efforts, is how you become "anti-fragile."

You might think of wolves, lions, and tigers as some of the world's leading predators among land mammals. Their hunting skills have been honed by millions of years of evolution. Yet, it might surprise you to know that their kill rates are 14 percent for wolves, 25 percent for lions, and 5 percent for tigers.[4] Even the great white shark has only a 48 percent success rate when it comes to attacks on seals.[5] Not only is the predator-prey dynamic replete with failures (as we might expect, given that prey animals have evolved strategies of evasion), but failures define many intraspecies dynamics. Many courtship rituals across a broad range of species involve competition, typically between male suitors for a female. Failure is inevitable, especially for younger, smaller, less experienced males. But dogged persistence can also be rewarded, as these animals grow and adapt their fighting or courtship strategies.

The ability to overcome adversity and failure is an evolved capacity that is essential to countless organisms, including humans. The capacity to develop an anti-fragile response to repeated failures is a fundamental, necessary, and beneficial feature of life. No meaningful goal can ever be achieved without resilience and effort.

The Power of Anti-Fragility

In countless different settings in nature, stressors are at times necessary for optimal functioning. If you are a wine aficionado, you probably know that the best wines grow in harsh environments.[6] In the words of Jeff Cox, a wine expert, "The best wines are made from vines that have to struggle."[7] Staying within the botanical realm, trees benefit greatly from dealing with the stresses imposed by nature. Trees that were planted in the closed ecosystem of Biosphere 2 grew quickly but did not fully mature.[8] It turned out that the lack of stressors, most especially the lack of wind, actually impeded the growth of the trees. When trees are exposed to wind and thus allowed to sway, they grow stronger and develop larger trunks (among other properties).[9] This is part of the field known as seismomorphogenesis, namely the study of how movement affects plants' development and growth. This knowledge has been incorporated within the design of buildings where there is great seismological activity, like earthquakes. Buildings are now built with the capacity to sway and to have safeguards against becoming structurally brittle.[10]

So, too, do children need to be exposed to certain environmental stressors to learn adaptability and thrive—including stressors that strengthen their immune system. Children who grow up in allergen-poor environments are more likely to develop respiratory maladies precisely because their immune systems were not appropriately and adequately stressed when they were younger.[11] An allergen-free, sterile environment is actually detrimental to one's health. In my book *The Parasitic Mind*, I discussed how this could be analogized to ideological echo chambers; intellectual environments that do not contain a diversity of opinions yield suboptimal critical thinking (as human minds expect to be challenged).[12] Whether referring to wine, trees, human lungs, or human minds, among countless other biological systems, we benefit from being anti-fragile.[13] People can never be maximally happy if they navigate through life with a brittle, fragile personality or mindset (as progressives so often do).

In May 2022, I delivered two lectures at the Salem Center for Policy housed at the McCombs School of Business at the University of Texas at Austin. During the Q&A period following my lecture on *The Parasitic Mind*, a young man asked me:

> You have been through actual difficulty . . . in your life, and yet you've chosen to not identify as a victim, and you've

maintained a very high level of personal power seemingly throughout that. So, my question is, one, what do you think is the reason that you've continued to maintain that power even through those difficulties? And, for when people are going through actual difficult experiences, whether social justice topics or just generally in life, what advice would you have for people to maintain great personal power through that?

My response fully captures the anti-fragility mindset:

The adversity that I faced made me more desirous to succeed. So, for example, I even grew up with some difficulties in my nuclear family where for many years after we moved from Lebanon to Montreal, my parents were absent; they had returned to Lebanon. Actually, in 1980, they were kidnapped by Fatah, and I talk about this briefly in chapter one of *The Parasitic Mind*. And so many of these episodes that many of you may not have even heard of could have sent me straight into wallowing in victimology for the rest of my life. My unique combination of genes made it that I had this thing of "I'm going to shove it up everybody's ass," if you forgive the colloquialism. I'm going to succeed. . . . We grow by going through anti-fragility, right; that which doesn't kill you makes you stronger. Those sayings exist precisely because through anti-fragile mechanisms, it makes me stronger as long as it doesn't kill me. So there is no magic recipe. Look, I'm going to be very personal here regarding last week when I found out that the Quebec and Canadian government were going to literally steal more than 50 percent of my neuronal firings [my book royalties of *The Parasitic Mind*]. I went into a deep depressive existential crisis. I was wondering if I would have the moxie to come to give this talk here. . . . I'm still desperate about it but guess what? I'm gonna shove it up their ass. And so, you know, there's no exact magic recipe, but hopefully by me saying this it empowers others and so on goes the circle.[14]

My response received raucous applause from the audience.

Life can be tough, but adversity can drive us to succeed, and that very effort can make us happy. That is my own attitude, and this winning mindset has served me well.

A Mindset of Victimhood Breeds Misery—Be Resilient

In *The Parasitic Mind*, I discussed the psychological and societal processes that have made Victimology Poker the game of choice among Western progressives. The key currency of success is to possess the most compelling victimhood narrative, which can be ensured via the dual processes of Collective Munchausen (the manufacture of faux victimhood) and the homeostasis of victimology—redefine innocuous and banal "transgressions" as acts of "bigotry," "violence," "racism," "Islamophobia," or "transphobia" (or innumerable other alleged "phobias") so as to maintain a preestablished narrative regarding the evils of Western societies. When Oprah was told by a salesclerk in Switzerland that she could not afford a $38,000 handbag, this became her defining moment of victimhood.[15] Sure, she makes more money than entire countries, but she is shackled by white supremacy; and the unfortunate fact that a salesclerk in Switzerland failed to recognize her for the superstar that she is was obviously a hateful act of oppression. Move aside Nelson Mandela. Stop whining, Yazidi women. The gang rapes that you faced at the hands of sadistic ISIS fighters are nothing compared to the daily genocide that LeBron James must avoid when driving from Beverly Hills to the Staples Center for his basketball practice. He is a true victim. Dear Uyghur whiners, could you please stop complaining about your *séjour* in the concentration camps kindly organized for your reeducation by the noble Chinese government? When Oprah held a chat with Meghan Markle and Prince Harry, they confirmed that they are true victims. You see, Meghan said she had been told that her son would not be made a prince when Prince Charles ascended to the throne. The obvious reason, she said, was that of course the royal family is racist[16]—even though the awarding of titles is governed by set rules[17] and Prince Charles (now King Charles III) had long been trying to limit the number of royals.[18] Contrary facts can never displace a victimhood narrative. The courage that Oprah, Meghan Markle, and Prince Harry exhibit as entitled and pampered millionaires in the United States is exemplary. Only a fellow victim, like woman of color Senator Elizabeth Warren, could understand the full horrors of their plight. As I stated in *The Parasitic Mind*, the defining ethos is *I am a victim therefore I am.*[19]

The ethos of victimology is not restricted to individuals, but can become the defining feature of an entire people. World history is replete with endless tragic stories of conquest, murder, pillage, occupation, and renewal. Human history is forged by endless rivers of bloodshed and mayhem. My wife is Lebanese Armenian. Her ancestors fled the 1915–1917 genocide at the hands of the Ottomans. The birth of her parents in Lebanon stemmed from that original exodus. Of course, my wife's immediate family had to subsequently flee Lebanon in 1979 due to the brutal civil war there, and they settled in Canada. Between 1939 and 1945, six million Jews were systematically exterminated by the Nazis, and yet by 1948 the modern state of Israel was founded and has since flourished as an oasis of economic vitality and political freedom in a neighborhood of brutality and repression.

Some of my readers and listeners might remember the horrors that my family faced during the Lebanese civil war. There are no monopolies on narratives of genuine victimhood. There are no monopolies on human suffering. Armenians and Jews are quite similar in that they always constitute small minorities in their respective diasporas, yet they nonetheless end up overachieving. There are no magical recipes to explain this success other than a commitment to not wallow in their truly horrible stories of victimhood. They recognize their tragic histories of suffering, they remember the past, but they always look forward with optimism, pride, and personal agency. Not all peoples possess those coping mechanisms. Instead, they prefer to swim in a bottomless pool of resentment, grievance, and misery. Many of the idea pathogens that I covered in *The Parasitic Mind* are rooted in the politics of perpetual grievance, which is especially galling since those proclaiming to be victims are oftentimes "minorities" whose "victimhood" lies well in the past (in some cases, centuries ago). Successful, conservative black Americans like Candace Owens, Larry Elder, and Thomas Sowell are despised by leftist self-proclaimed leaders of the greater African American community precisely because these conservative stalwarts preach a message that rejects victimhood, that upholds the idea of personal agency, that recognizes the positives of living in a Western, democratic, capitalist land of opportunity like America. Happy people look to succeed in the business of life rather than flounder in a never-ending game of Victimology Poker.

If you were to visit a therapist to work through some childhood trauma, it is unlikely that the clinician would require you, or advise you, to be defined by those tragic moments. Instead, she would seek pathways to help you overcome the trauma and pursue a life of enrichment and happiness. While personal negative experiences need to be dealt with, no mental health professional will suggest that you wallow in a state of perpetual victimhood. And yet, this is exactly what the so-called progressive Western intelligentsia peddle to various identity groups. They tell them to shackle themselves to perpetual victimhood; they claim that only victimhood can bring them liberation! Progressives are like orchestra conductors, waving a baton so that every self-shackled identity group can whine on cue. Such orchestrated whining—whining of any kind—can never bring happiness. I offer a different message: Recognize that your past, which might include tragic elements, is a feature of your personhood. But you are not defined by past injustices. Rather, you should be invigorated by the promises of a better future. The only road to individual dignity and sustained existential happiness is to adopt an ethos of personal agency. *You* are the ultimate architect of your own happiness. So get to work!

Be Resilient in the Face of Rejections

Many years ago, my brother (an Olympian judoka) and I were hanging out at a nightclub in Southern California. While we are both extroverted characters, he has always been rather flamboyant in his social style. True to form, while standing around the dance floor, he turned to me and asked me to pinpoint the prettiest and most unattainable woman in the club. At first, I was hesitant to do so because I was reluctant to partake in some of his over-the-top antics. After his repeated insistence that I comply, I began to look around the dance floor for the most beautiful woman, who was hopefully accompanied by an ominous-looking boyfriend (hence rendering her even more unattainable). I zeroed in on a woman who was indeed very beautiful and dancing very intimately with her male partner. After my brother had confirmed with me that this was my final choice, he proceeded to the periphery of the dance floor and waited for the right opportunity to approach her. It took less than a few minutes for the intimidating-looking boyfriend to head off to the bathroom, at which point my brother approached the woman. My brother is short of stature, so the somewhat tall woman, who was wearing high heels, was towering over him. This was of no concern to my brother, who chatted with her for a minute or two and then returned to me and said, "She'll call me tomorrow," to which I retorted an incredulous, "No way!"

The next day, my brother summoned me to the answering machine (yes, the story is from many years ago) and said, "Listen." He played a message, which to my amazement was from the beautiful woman from the previous night. She was, essentially, asking for a date. How was he able to pull off this nearly impossible feat of getting a beautiful woman with an apparently serious boyfriend to take an interest in him? Well, there were two fundamental reasons for his success. First, he approached the woman with overflowing confidence. Women are very attracted to confident men; hence that which he may have lacked in terms of height, he made up for with self-assuredness. Second, he was utterly oblivious to the otherwise stifling fear of possible rejection. It is never easy to be rejected, but if one is truly able to demystify the negative emotions associated with ephemeral rejections, endless new opportunities appear. It is perhaps not surprising that early in his career, my brother was a very successful salesman in the software industry. An inherent reality in sales is the dreaded string of rejections that one is likely to face until a deal is finally signed. High-end sales constitutes an interminable sequence of "no, thank you" followed by an eventual lucrative "yes."

When men approach women for romantic purposes, the rejection rates are astoundingly high. In a classic study that examined the likelihood of a man or woman meeting a stranger and accepting an offer to have sex, many men accepted the invitation (as high as 75 percent) whereas not one woman did so.[20] Since the costs of making a bad mating choice are much graver for women, they are much more careful in the mating arena. For men, rejection is a central feature of the human courtship ritual. In many species, the courtship ritual involves a built-in test of persistence. This test is typically applied to males, and mating persistence is thus a sexually selected trait. This is not, however, an invitation to sexual harassment, but it also helps explain why it is common in human cultures for men to have to "win" a mate by proving their courage, wealth, intelligence, and other qualities. Competition is part of life, and with competition comes the constant reality that one might be rejected or defeated.

Jia Jiang is a man on a mission. He wants to demystify the paralyzing fear of rejection that most people suffer from. He created a blog titled "100 Days of Rejection Therapy" wherein he challenged himself to complete 100 tasks laden with rejection potential (walking up to a stranger and asking if he could borrow $100, knocking on someone's door and asking if he could plant a flower in his backyard, asking to be a greeter at Starbucks).[21] In a manner similar to how exposure therapy is used in clinical settings to overcome debilitating phobias, Jiang learned that we can attenuate the potentially crippling fear of rejection by forcing ourselves to deal with the repeated possibility of rejection. He also learned strategies to overcome rejection. As the old saying goes, experience can be a great teacher.

Stories of rejection are at the root of nearly every uplifting story of stratospheric excellence, be it in sports, the literary world, music, or filmmaking. Zinedine Zidane is one of the greatest soccer players of all time. He was largely responsible for France's lifting of its first World Cup trophy in 1998. He could have represented Algeria in terms of his national team (by ancestry), but the coach of the Algerian national team thought that he was too slow and accordingly rejected him.[22] Zidane was also rejected by Marseille, his boyhood club. Lionel Messi, the Argentine soccer player whom many experts consider the greatest soccer player of all time, was considered too small to succeed professionally even by his eventual club FC Barcelona, with whom he eventually broke every conceivable club record.[23] Michael Jordan, arguably the greatest basketball player of all time, was cut from his high school team during his sophomore year.[24] J. K. Rowling's Harry Potter franchise of seven books has sold more than 500 million copies, making it the all-time leading book series.[25] The first book of the series had been rejected by twelve publishers before Bloomsbury Publishing agreed to publish it.[26] The publisher's then eight-year-old daughter had read the submitted manuscript and loved it, which served as the impetus for Rowling receiving the contract.[27] She received a paltry £2,500 as an advance and five hundred copies were originally printed.[28] At the time, Rowling was an unemployed, financially destitute, depressed, single mother living on welfare. She admitted to having contemplated suicide. And yet, her persistence, self-belief, and the magic of happenstance (via the publisher's young daughter) have altered the literary and cinematic landscape forevermore. The Harry Potter series is one of innumerable astoundingly successful literary works that were originally repeatedly rejected. There is a website that keeps track of some of the most successful books of all time along with a count of the original number of rejections that their authors received.[29] These include *Chicken Soup for the Soul* (144 rejections),[30] *Zen and the Art of Motorcycle Maintenance* (121 rejections),[31] *Lord of the Flies* (21 rejections),[32] and Dr. Seuss's *And to Think That I Saw It on Mulberry Street* (27 rejections),[33] among many other literary classics. The Beatles, who are among the most successful musical acts of all time, were repeatedly rejected by music labels until they were eventually signed by George Martin.[34] Steven Spielberg was rejected not once, not twice, but three times from the USC film school,[35] and he went on to become one of the greatest film directors of all time, winning three Academy Awards. Imagine if these exceptional individuals had allowed a string of rejections to defeat them. The world would be a much poorer place.

While persistence is a central feature of eventual success, persistence, as a positive trait, follows the logic of the inverted-U curve. There comes a time when repeated failure is itself a lesson to do something else. If you are not in the least bit persistent, you will never achieve important goals in your life. But if you are inflexibly persistent, you might fail to walk away from a losing proposition and miss better opportunities. The capacity to walk away from unreachable goals is a crucial adaptive response for achieving optimal well-being and health (including reducing psychological and physical distress).[36]

Academia: Long String of Rejections Peppered with Occasional Successes

When I was applying to doctoral programs, I thought with complete self-assuredness that I would be accepted everywhere. After all, I had a stellar application dossier including rigorous degrees (B.Sc. in Mathematics and Computer Science and an MBA) from a leading university (McGill), top grades, very high scores on the standardized GMAT test, extensive experience as a research assistant, and strong letters of recommendation. I had to swallow a full serving of humble pie when the rejections started to trickle in. Eventually, though, I was accepted at several world-leading institutions and ended up enrolling at Cornell University (one of my top two choices), but the rejection letters served as a preparatory omen for the endless sequence of rejections to come throughout my academic career. I truly excelled in my doctoral studies at Cornell, so much so that the department's faculty chose me as their 1993 doctoral consortium fellow (top doctoral student) the year that I was going out on the academic job market. I was working on a very rigorous and exciting dissertation topic (the cognitive strategies that people use when deciding to stop acquiring additional information on two competing alternatives and commit to a winning choice), and I was supervised by a world-renowned and highly respected psychologist in the field.

I was considered one of the top candidates on the market that year and was offered many first-round interviews with leading universities (I believe that it was around twenty-five interviews). In the second round, five of the universities, including Harvard Business School, invited me for campus visits, each of which required that I present my doctoral dissertation work to the respective departments. Rumor had it that I had come close to landing the coveted Harvard position, but regrettably I was ultimately rejected (according to the grapevine, in part for reasons that had little to do with my dossier). This was a very disappointing outcome, but I did end up being offered an assistant professorship in my home city of Montréal. (A second offer was forthcoming, but there was a deadline to accept the standing offer, so I accepted it prior to hearing from the other university.) Several of my Cornell doctoral cohorts, most of whom were outstanding candidates, were unable to land assistant professorships, and they accordingly left academia. In my field, at that time, to land an academic job required that you obtain your doctorate from one of a few elite universities (with very low acceptance rates into their doctoral programs), be amongst the elite of your doctoral cohort (incredibly competitive, given the talent pool), whilst navigating through an endless sequence of heartbreaking rejections. One cannot navigate through such statistical realities without an anti-fragility mindset. Today, of course, universities do not even pretend to be interested in the ethos of meritocracy. Instead, they deploy DIE principles (Diversity, Inclusion, and Equity) to choose candidates based on immutable traits and other irrelevant factors that have nothing to do with intellectual or scholarly merit. Skin color, ethnic origin, and gender identity are at least as important as a candidate's talent in today's academic zeitgeist.

In my day (albeit this holds true today), once you had started out and landed the very rare and coveted academic position, the rejection rates only intensified moving forward. Grant applications to fund one's research were highly competitive, and it remains very difficult to land some of the more prestigious scientific grants. Once you secured the necessary funds to conduct your research, you then faced arguably the most daunting abyss of rejection, the prestigious academic journals, many of which have astonishingly high rejection rates. *Nature* has a 92 percent rejection rate, whereas the *New England Journal of Medicine* publishes only 5 percent of the research papers submitted to it.[37] Leading journals in psychology are also very competitive to crack. Data from 2017 lists the *Journal of Applied Psychology*, the *Journal of Personality and Social Psychology*, and *Psychological Review* as having rejection rates of 90 percent, 87 percent, and 86 percent respectively. The psychology journal with the highest rejection rate was the *Journal of Consumer Psychology* at 91 percent.[38] I am proud to have published five papers in that particular journal. My last paper of which involved the greatest number of rounds of revisions that I have ever faced prior to its being accepted.[39] It truly was an exercise in grit, determination, persistence, and unwavering discipline. A typical academic paper might take between one and three years from the conception of an idea to submitting it to a journal. It must then go through multiple rounds of peer review—and most papers will ultimately be rejected. Of course, when such a rejection occurs, the authors can then resubmit it elsewhere and the process starts all over again.

I have supervised many bright and talented graduate students. One day I met with one such student to discuss why there were delays in running our studies. I suspected he had succumbed to the fear of epistemological rejection. That is, he was worried that if we conducted the studies, the beautiful hypotheses might be rejected! He was honest enough to admit that my hunch was correct. I sought to assuage his fears by explaining to him that most worthy pursuits in life, including in science, are risky. We cannot continuously hide in the safety of beautiful albeit untested hypotheses. We must throw the proverbial dice and see what happens. Data can be messy and uncooperative, but this is what makes research the most fulfilling form of play, for scientists. Let us get our hands dirty and see what we get. The epilogue to this story is that key findings did not support some of our posited hypotheses, and yet we published the paper in a leading academic journal wherein we explained why that was so.

Do not be afraid to fail. Forge a path forward. Good things can happen when you try. They can even come from failure.

Attributing Failure to the Proper Causes

Scientists—in particular, psychologists—are well aware of a phenomenon known as "the fundamental attribution error." It occurs when people misattribute causality in their daily lives. For example, people often attribute their successes to themselves ("I did well on the exam because I'm smart") and their failures to someone else ("I did poorly on the exam because the professor is an unfair imbecile"). Depressives, interestingly, are one group that is less likely to engage in this sort of ego-protecting attribution of success and failure.[40]

The ability to learn beneficial lessons from a failure hinges on attributing failure to the right causes. Many entrepreneurs and small business owners are utterly impervious to their own contributions to their failures. Whenever confronted with a failing business, a failed pitch to venture capitalists, or a looming bankruptcy filing, they inevitably attribute blame to others. The culprits of their failures were the customers who had no taste to appreciate their product offerings, the venture capitalists who were too dumb to see their brilliant vision, or the creditors who were perhaps too shortsighted, myopic, and impatient in seeking to collect their due debts.

Entrepreneurs, by the very nature of their risky endeavors, need to be imbued with self-confidence. It is perhaps not surprising then that entrepreneurship is positively correlated with testosterone (a hormonal driver of risk-taking behavior).[41] It takes endocrinological fortitude to partake in a start-up venture when the failure rate of start-ups can be 90 percent, depending on the industry.[42] In other words, it is an inherent feature of the entrepreneur's reality that failure is the likely default value. Here is the description of the "Fail Faster" course at the Hasso Plattner Institute of Design at Stanford University:

> Fail Faster will dive deeply into one of design thinking's key tenets: Fail early, fail often. Students will explore ways to: [1] become comfortable with uncertainty, [2] develop tools to navigate situations of failure, and [3] learn to turn failures into opportunities. This exercised-based workshop will examine the physiological impact of failure and practice the psychological traits and the power of resilience through hands-on activities. Participants will acquire techniques to help them navigate, bounce back, grow and even flourish in the face of their failures.[43]

Failures can serve as valuable teachable moments, but only if we possess the humility to learn from our mistakes. Obstinate entrepreneurs who attribute all failures to external forces outside of their control are ignoring beneficial opportunities for self-growth.

Implementing a Successful Weight Loss Journey—a Lesson of Discipline and Grit

On a whim, I decided to run my first marathon in 1985. Prior to the event, I had attended a runner's convention where my body fat composition was calculated using two methods: skinfold measurements using a caliper, and a bioelectrical impedance analysis (using the principle that electric currents flow differently across muscle and fat). I had 4.3 percent body fat content. Some readers who follow me on social media might have seen some of the shirtless images that I have posted from that era wherein the chiseled eight-pack abs were on full display. Up to that point in my life (early twenties), I had always been extremely thin, seldom exceeding 130 pounds. Upon completing that first Montréal marathon, I had promised myself that I would attempt to complete one marathon a year and would complete the Ironman Triathlon by age thirty-five. Well, I kept the promise in 1986 when I ran my second Montréal marathon, so things were looking up, but then 1987 hit. I decided that I was not up for the punishment of another marathon, and in doing so, I set the grounds for a gargantuan weight gain over the next few decades. I hit many "first" milestones, including the first time over 150 pounds, the first time over 200 pounds, and the first time over 250 pounds. My heaviest recorded weight was 256 pounds. The weight gain was gradual but largely unabated, albeit there were periods of sizeable weight loss. (For instance, I became a vegetarian between 1996 and 1999 and dropped to 172 pounds.)

Despite my repeated attempts to permanently shed the weight, I was always unsuccessful at keeping it off. During the COVID pandemic, though, I managed to finally succeed at this nearly impossible feat, in part driven by the lockdown, which sharply curtailed my ability to indulge at my favorite restaurants. I have lost a total of 86 pounds. The scientific research is unequivocal regarding the small likelihood of long-term weight loss journeys,[44] and yet I have been successful thus far. How did I do it? Well, in terms of the general plan, I try to eat between 1,500 and 1,700 calories per day (largely chicken and fish with some vegetables) and clock between 15,000 and 20,000 daily steps (a combination of walking outside, treadmill, elliptical, and stationary bike). It requires extraordinary discipline, persistence, and grit never to deviate from the caloric and exercise goals day in and day out.

Of course, for all of us, there are days when you feel too tired after a long day at work to meet your exercise goals. Or perhaps it's your wife's birthday, and you'd like to have a piece of that alluring cake. And yet, at every moment, you face the choice: stick to your stated plan or violate it. If you make the correct choice on nearly every occasion for more than one year, you can wake up more than 80 pounds lighter.

A successful weight loss journey necessitates patience. You cannot hope to lose a sizeable chunk of weight and maintain the weight loss via crash starvation diets. Instead, the new regime must be internalized as part of your new default reality. Permanent behavioral changes must be instituted. Again, this requires discipline, persistence, and grit. In the past, whenever I hit a weight loss plateau, my commitment would falter, because I thought I had done enough. Instead of thinking that way, I reframed a plateau as a win, and used it as a motivational boost to keep going. While I am coding my current weight loss as a permanent victory, I am only too aware that it requires a daily commitment to make the optimal exercise and dietary choices, coupled with a weekly commitment to weigh myself.[45]

I'd like to briefly return to the two marathons, both of which I completed in respectable times of 4:07:42 and 4:29:36, respectively. To run a 26.2-mile race in less than four and a half hours requires you to be in very good shape. But much more important, one must possess an implacable mindset that compels you forward. Once a runner hits the proverbial wall, usually around the 18–20-mile mark, his muscles have been depleted of energy and he can experience a crushing fatigue, a sense of disorientation, and at times severe muscle cramping. At this point—and I can speak from personal experience—every fiber of your body is telling you to stop the pain, to lie down, to quit. The only thing stopping you from doing so is your mind. You activate your grit, your perseverance, and your resilience, and you go on one step at a time. In my first marathon, I did not hit the wall. But in my second, I hit it severely with symptoms that were sudden and seemingly debilitating. Yet, I made it across the finish line. As with that marathon, so with life. Life can be tough and painful, but if we persist, our incremental steps forward can lead us to a personal victory. Even today, more than thirty-five years later, I regret that I never attempted an Ironman Triathlon. Perhaps, though, it is never too late to try.

Meeting My Musical Hero—a Lesson of Persistence

What is your favorite music genre? Mine is known as the Philly Sound. It is a subgenre of soul music that was a contemporary of Motown Soul (The Temptations, Marvin Gaye, The Supremes, Smokey Robinson) and Memphis Soul (Otis Redding, Isaac Hayes, Al Green, Sam & Dave). Artists that fall within the Philly Sound include The Delfonics, The Intruders, and Harold Melvin and the Blue Notes. My all-time favorite group within this genre, though, is undoubtedly The Stylistics, who were fronted by Russell Thompkins Jr., with his astounding falsetto notes. Their music was seared in my brain, as I grew up listening to their melodic and hauntingly soulful songs. Whenever I would drive the Ithaca-Montréal route (my alma mater, Cornell University, is in Ithaca, New York), I would repeatedly play the same compilation cassettes of the greatest Philly Sound artists (the young readers might need to look up the term "cassette"). In 2001, I took a leave from my tenured professorship at Concordia University and joined the University of California at Irvine as a visiting associate professor for two years. I was now making a larger salary and decided that I was ready to explore the feasibility of pursuing a long-standing musical fantasy. How much would it cost me to invite The Stylistics to perform at a private concert? Bathing in self-delusional assuredness, I reached out to their management team and was quickly disabused of my plan. Apparently, professors, even business school professors, cannot afford

The Stylistics! The plan lay dormant for another fifteen or so years, until I decided to try again using a new approach.

Beginning in 2014, my YouTube show *The Saad Truth* had become hugely popular. What if I were to invite Mr. Thompkins for a chat on my show? I decided to explore this possibility and tried to contact his managers. To my disappointment, I did not hear back from anyone. Perhaps a year or so later, I was recounting the story to my young daughter (who must have been around eight years old at the time), and she insisted that I write to them again. And so, I tepidly acquiesced to her nudge but again did not hear from anyone. My daughter, who is a model of persistence, proceeded to then hound me about calling them rather than sending an email. I was finally able to speak to one of Thompkins's managers, who assured me that he was happy to oblige my invitation but perhaps in a few months, after completing a tour. You can guess what happened next: my daughter kept pushing me to follow up, which I did by leaving a voice mail reminding his people of my earlier request to host him on my show. On an otherwise uneventful Saturday morning, as I sat watching a soccer match from the British Premier League, our landline phone rang (it almost never does). My daughter, perhaps sensing that this might be a momentous call, ran to get me the phone. As I looked at the caller ID, I could not believe my eyes. It took Herculean restraint to answer nonchalantly, "Hello." On the line, I heard, "Hi. This is Russell Thompkins Jr. May I please speak to Professor Saad?" Any semblance of calm and collected restraint went out the window when I said excitedly: "Oh my lord!" We ended up scheduling a chat on my show wherein to my delight he sang a few notes of my favorite Stylistics song, "You Are Everything."[46]

Several months later, I was invited to participate in a panel at the Marketing Science conference held that year in Philadelphia. Knowing that Russell lived in the city, I reached out to him and asked if he wanted to hang out. He kindly agreed to do so. While I am hardly one to be starstruck, I could not believe that the man whose voice was omnipresent at countless moments in my life was about to have dinner with me. Russell and I had an extraordinary evening together sharing personal stories as two long-lost friends might do.[47] His grace, humility, and kindness were truly awe-inspiring. After dinner, he offered to take me for a walking tour, which I gladly accepted. As we strolled the sidewalks where famous musicians of Philadelphia were honored with plaques (including one for The Stylistics), he shared stories of his interactions with some of these legendary singers. And all along, people would come up to him to say hello and recount how much his music meant to them. I recall thinking to myself: This needs to be documented. I should have videotaped the evening! Well, I hope that my telling this story serves as a historical record of sorts.

There are two important life lessons to glean from this magical friendship. The first is that to succeed at anything, you have to try. Or to quote the great basketball player Michael Jordan, "I've missed more than 9,000 shots in my career. I've lost almost 300 games. Twenty-six times I've been trusted to take the game-winning shot and missed. I've failed over and over and over again in my life. And that is why I succeed."[48] Well, I decided to take a shot and reach out to Russell. I succeeded in forging a friendship with my childhood musical hero. The second important life lesson is to listen to your children. They are wiser than we give them credit for. Without my daughter's persistence, this story might have never taken place.

On Joe Rogan's podcast I once discussed two entertainment celebrities that I would love to host on my show: actor and director Clint Eastwood and composer Burt Bacharach. I grew up watching Eastwood's spaghetti Western movies (and later appreciating his non-woke positions) and listening to Bacharach's hauntingly beautiful melodies. Imagine my surprise when I received a private message from Bacharach's Instagram account. It was written by Bacharach's son. The son had seen me on the Rogan podcast and said he would try to set up a chat between his dad and yours truly. All it takes to make connections with people is to have a friendly, open spirit. Life can truly be beautiful. Get out there and seize the day.

Baptism by Fire as a Form of Anti-Fragility

Most worthy endeavors in life, be it completing medical school, running a marathon, or starting a new business, require persistence and focus. The late basketball great Kobe Bryant coined the term "Mamba Mentality," which he explained as follows: "Hard work outweighs talent every time. Mamba mentality is about 4 a.m. workouts, doing more than the next guy and then trusting in the work you've put in when it's time to perform. Without studying, preparation and practice, you're leaving the outcome to fate. I don't do fate."[49] Psychologist Angela Lee Duckworth has pioneered the study of the grit trait, which captures this form of stick-to-it-iveness.[50] While grit is correlated with various achievement outcomes (such as academic performance), it has a more general positive effect on happiness and well-being, and this holds true across widely disparate cultures.[51] Part of possessing grit is the capacity to be resilient in overcoming obstacles as you seek to achieve your goals. While resilience is in part shaped by an individual's personality, some forms of childhood adversity foster resilience, which may result in beneficial outcomes.[52] In the same way that one's immune system needs to be challenged during childhood for optimal functioning, overcoming psychological stressors is a key feature of peak functioning. You cannot lead a maximally enriching life if you are never challenged. Developing a proper response to life's stressors is a central feature of resilience.[53] I have experienced some of the worst imaginable childhood adversity growing up during the Lebanese civil war, but those negative experiences have allowed me to develop great resilience in tackling the more mundane challenges of my life in Canada and the United States.

Rigorous training—in specific skills and in how to respond to challenging situations under stress—is a part of many jobs, especially in the military. Pilots go through demanding flight training. Those who want to be Army Rangers or Navy SEALs are compelled to push their minds and bodies to the limit. But there are other occupations and professions that, metaphorically, have grown flabby and weak. That would include, I'm afraid, higher education and my academic colleagues: all those tepid hyper-specialists who are too afraid to utter one word that might offend academic superiors, militant feminists, the Pronoun Taliban, or the Woke Mafia. Knowledge be damned! In the last few years, I have noticed that this weak mindset permeates all layers of academia, but especially when interviewing prospective hires for assistant professorships. When I was a doctoral student at Cornell University, young academics had their first big baptism-by-fire moment when they were invited, as part of a departmental speaker series, to give a lecture from their developing doctoral dissertation. This was a very intimidating platform from which to share one's research because the audience did not suffer fools gladly, and professors prepared senior doctoral students for the eventual grilling they would face when seeking assistant professorships at elite universities.

I faced additional anti-fragility obstacles as I made my way through to my Ph.D. Doctoral students at the Johnson Graduate School of Management (Cornell) had to pass the A-exam, which was made up of two parts:

(1) Professors serving on a student's Ph.D. dissertation committee could ask questions about his specific areas of expertise. While many doctoral students had a supervisor and two additional committee members, my doctoral committee was composed of four outstanding

scholars (Drs. J. Edward Russo, Douglas Stayman, Ali Hadi, and Alberto Segre).

(2) Once the doctoral student presented his dissertation proposal, the committee members would ask pointed questions about the prospective research. No question was out of bounds, as the student had to demonstrate complete mastery of his subject and his proposed dissertation research.

As I presented my dissertation proposal on that fateful day, I noticed that my committee members were not exuding an aura of friendliness. The tone was set by my doctoral supervisor, who began the barrage of tough questions. As I fielded his first question, he took an indignant deep breath and retorted, "I'm going to ask the question a second time hoping that maybe this time you'll understand it." And we were off! When it came time for Professor Hadi (a world-renowned statistician) to ask his questions, he started off by saying, "I know that I told you that I would not ask you detailed technical statistical questions. Well, I lied." He then proceeded to ask me a very detailed technical question, which, because I was well-prepared, I managed to answer. Once the professors had gone through several rounds of very probing and difficult questions, I was asked to step outside the room as they deliberated my fate. I asked my supervisor, "Should I stand by the door outside the room?" He stared at me coldly and responded: "Stand far enough that you cannot hear us."

As I stood outside the room, I felt somewhat frazzled. I thought I had answered all the questions properly, and I certainly knew my material. But based on the harsh tone of some of the questions, I felt quite nervous. After what seemed like an interminable wait, the door swung wide open, and my doctoral supervisor walked toward me with a full smile. I was puzzled and a little unhappy, and asked him what was going on. "Oh, this was some good old-fashioned Ivy League butt-kicking," he said. "It will make a man out of you. We are trying to make sure that you can handle yourself when you go out on the campus visits." As I made my way back into the examination room, the other committee members were all smiling and congratulatory. The tense environment had dissipated into the usual warmth of their supportive mentorship.

Once doctoral students defend their dissertation proposals, they send application packets to universities hoping to land a job. The first round of interviews is usually held at the annual academic conference of their discipline. In my case, as previously mentioned, I had around twenty-five scheduled interviews. The interviewers require that one present one's dissertation work in a cogent and succinct manner. In preparation for that eventuality, my doctoral supervisor had me prepare a one-page summary of my dissertation, which I excitedly agreed to do. He had me rewrite it several times and, in one instance, he feigned falling asleep before telling me, "Now go back and rewrite this so I don't fall asleep reading the first sentence."

Throughout this process I became deeply indebted to my great mentors for testing my resilience and mental toughness. They did not coddle me. They were not concerned with sparing my feelings. They did not give me a participation trophy for showing up. They expected great things of me, and, accordingly, they made sure to test my anti-fragility. For that, I am eternally grateful to them. Incidentally, I recently found out that my doctoral supervisor is retiring from Cornell. Several of his former doctoral students, including yours truly, joined him for a commemorative get-together. Expressing gratitude is not only polite, but also another component of a good and happy life.

Life Lessons Stemming from a Lost Wedding Ring

My wife and I have truly unique wedding rings. Our respective fingerprints are engraved on one another's rings (along with personal inscriptions). Beyond this, I revere my wedding ring because it is a permanent reminder of the beautiful love that I share with my wife. The thought of losing the ring is unthinkable to me, and yet this is precisely what happened in the summer of 2014.[54] My family had spent the day having fun at my in-laws' chalet, located on the edge of a river with a fast-moving current, and at my brother-in-law's chalet, located on a beautiful lake with fresh, albeit dark, water (that is presumably quite deep). The drive back to Montréal took approximately ninety minutes. Before heading home, we picked up some coffees at the Starbucks where I had spent innumerable days writing my first book.[55]

When I realized my ring was missing, the chances of finding it seemed infinitesimal, given that it could have fallen into the lake, or into the river, or somewhere in the woods. The easiest thing would have been to give up and accept that the ring was lost forever. My wife and I decided otherwise. We combed through our photos of the day to see if we could narrow the timeline of when the ring was lost. The first piece of good news was that we found a photo taken after I had last swum in the lake, and my ring was still on my hand. This was a gigantic victory. We then looked at pictures of when we were at the river. The river's current is such that it serves as a type of treadmill; you can swim at one spot for a while. This is precisely what I did in several video clips, one of which captured the exact front-crawl stroke at which I lost my ring! We had identified the precise moment and location where I had lost my ring, but this was hardly a time to rejoice. The riverbed is littered with endless rocks and boulders, and the current is very strong. While we had greatly improved our odds of finding the lost ring, it remained a nearly impossible task.

My wife and I agreed to drive back to her parents' chalet the next morning. Prior to doing so, I realized that we needed to answer a crucial hydraulic question—namely, how would a ring of that weight and size behave in that current? Would it quickly sink to the bottom, or would it be carried downstream by the current, and if so, how far downstream? I asked my wife to find a test ring that we might use in an experiment when we arrived at the river, and we proceeded on our way. Once we arrived at the precise river location, we tied the experimental ring to a string and began the experiment. To our relief, the ring rapidly sank at the spot that it was released. In other words, it was quite conceivable that my wedding ring was somewhere within a five-by-five-foot-square area where I had been swimming against the current. Notwithstanding this good news, it was hardly reason to fully rejoice, as the likelihood of finding the ring in such a rocky riverbed was minimal (the maximal depth was around five to six feet). I wore a set of goggles and a pair of "sticky" water shoes that would allow me to anchor myself on the underwater rocks and began the arduous process of intermittently diving to cover every possible nook and cranny of the stony riverbed. It must have been twenty minutes into the process when I saw a shiny light coming from a crevice between two rocks (the sunlight was reflecting on the ring). I dove to the bottom, and to my utter disbelief, I emerged out of the water with my wedding ring in my hand.

There are many valuable life lessons that can be gleaned from the tale of the lost wedding ring. First, it is always a good idea to be hopeful and optimistic when tackling difficult challenges. Hope is truly an elixir of life that can help you through countless trials and tribulations. The likelihood of finding the ring was next to nothing, and yet my wife and I persisted doggedly in our belief that the problem was tractable. Second, a good marriage requires cooperative teamwork. My wife had the clever idea of going through our photos, and I suggested the "hydraulic" experiment. Our collective brainpower was an asset. Third, the scientific method is an epistemological tool that can be used when navigating through life. Reason, logic, and evidence-based thinking are available for all sorts of everyday decisions. Had we not conducted the "hydraulic" experiment, we would not have been able to prune the search space to such a restricted area. You can think like a scientist in your daily life, even if you are not a professional scientist.

Several years later, the ring yielded a second miracle. If I were Catholic, I might seek to get that ring blessed by a priest, for it seems to be protected by Saint Anthony, the patron saint of lost objects! My wife had loaded the kids in the car and driven to pick me up from our local café. As I was about to enter the passenger side of the car, I heard a weird "ping" and wondered whether I had lost some change from my pocket. My daughter got out of the car and noticed my ring by the car on the pavement. She too had heard the ping and decided to check. Had we not heard the ping, we would have driven home and perhaps have never been able to identify the location where it had fallen off my finger. I have since purchased a plastic contraption that I place on the ring to ensure that it does not fall off my finger. However, as I have lost a tremendous amount of weight over the past eighteen months (and hence my fingers are thinner), I might need to find a new solution for the slippery ring. This leads me to the last of the life lessons as relating to this story: namely, some personal objects carry quasi-sacred status because they are associated with such deep emotional and symbolic valence. My wedding ring's lost-and-found journey is a metaphor of the limitless love that I feel for my wife and children. They make me immeasurably happy.

Many of the worthy pursuits in life involve risks, obstacles, rejections, and the ever-looming potential of failure. By adopting a mindset rooted in well-calibrated persistence, grit, and anti-fragility, we increase the chances of overcoming the barriers that stand in the way of finding purpose, meaning, and happiness in our lives. In many instances, people end up forgoing prospective opportunities because of the fear of failure. But evolution has endowed us with an emotion that might compel us forward and bust through that fear, a topic to which I turn in the next chapter.

CHAPTER EIGHT

It's (Almost) Never Too Late—
Eradicate Regret

Non, je ne regrette rien. [No, I regret nothing.][1]

—Edith Piaf

As children learn good manners.
As young men learn to control the passions.
In middle age be just
In old age give good advice.
Then die without regret.[2]

—Inscription of Delphic maxims at Al Khanoum

At your end be without sorrow.[3]

—Delphic maxim 147

Looking back at your life, are there things that you regret? Do you regret actions that you took, or actions that you didn't take? Regret can eat away at our sense of inner peace. The ancient Greek concept of *ataraxia* refers to a state free from inner turmoil, to tranquility and calmness of the mind. It was a goal of Epicurean and Stoic philosophy. A mind tormented by regret cannot achieve tranquility. Unhappy, intrusive thoughts, manifested in conditions like obsessive-compulsive disorder (OCD), can lead to substantial cognitive and emotional turmoil.[4] Sometimes the thoughts are endless ruminations based on paranoid fears. For example, such a ruminative thought might be "Because of what I said at last night's office party, I'm certain that everyone now views me as an imbecile." In an attempt to alleviate this worry, an OCD sufferer might repeatedly seek confirmation from party attendees that he didn't in fact make a fool of himself. In this, he is like the stereotypical OCD individual who washes his hands incessantly because of a disproportionate fear of germs. Through such repetitive rituals—of handwashing or seeking reassurance—OCD individuals hope that germs or intrusive, negative thoughts can be washed away literally or figuratively. Obviously, not all ruminations on one's actions or inactions lead to dysfunctional outcomes. But for an OCD sufferer, these unpleasantly intrusive thoughts come with an overwhelming intensity and frequency. Regret, however, is one form of existential rumination that many individuals have, revisiting past actions or inactions with a sense of sorrow.

While many of the early studies of regret were conducted in the fields of economics, psychology, and marketing, more recent works have examined the neuronal and physiological signatures of regret. For example, older individuals who experience greater regret intensity have increased morning cortisol (stress response hormone) secretion and worse physical symptoms.[5] Furthermore, as people age and possess fewer opportunities to address sources of regret, they exhibit various negative downstream effects, including an increased likelihood of experiencing depression as reported in this neuroscientific exploration of regret: "The lack of an age-adapted management of regret experiences may thus represent a risk factor for highly prevalent late-life depression. Disengagement from regret experiences at a point of life where the opportunities to undo regrettable behavior are limited may be a protective strategy to maintain emotional well-being and thus can be seen as a resilience factor."[6] The bottom line is that regret not only affects our ability to achieve *ataraxia*, but it can also have a deleterious effect on our physiological and physical health, as well as our psychological adjustment (such as depression scores) and life satisfaction.[7]

There are endless occasions in which we experience regret, from mundane daily contexts (I regret having had a dessert after this heavy meal) to grand existential forms of regret (I regret that I was an absent parent, or I regret that I never pursued my dream of being a pediatrician). If you can look back on your life and think of few, if any, existential regrets, then you will likely be happy and have lived a good life. At this stage of my life, I do have a few regrets, but I'm unsure I could have changed what actually happened anyway. By far my greatest regret is that I was unable to pursue a professional soccer career. I suffered a terrible injury in the U18 (under age 18) Eastern Canadian championship. My club had been crowned champions of Quebec, and we were competing against the champions of Ontario and the Maritime provinces. It was a round-robin tournament that began with my team playing against the Ontario champions. We lost that game 2–0, but I had played extraordinarily well, and the Maritime champions were sure to focus on me next time we played them. Just before that match, my coach advised me to be careful and to get rid of the ball quickly. I was the team playmaker, and nearly always played the right passes, so I asked him why he was so concerned. He said that our opponents would be coming hard after me, and I needed to be aware. The opposing player man-marking me looked to be thirty-five years old, and he kept brutalizing me throughout the game. Finally, just as I had entered the opposing team's eighteen-yard box with the chance of either taking a shot or crossing the ball, the butcher in question tackled me from behind using the extraordinarily dangerous scissors tackle. This is when a player slides behind you and swings his two legs in a scissors motion. If he catches your leg, he can break it. Well, he caught my leg, and the rest is history. The referee did not even whistle a foul, perhaps thinking that

I was faking an injury to have a penalty kick called in my favor. The play went on as I lay on the ground with a shattered leg. It was the opposing goalie who came up to me, saw my pain, and quickly urged the referee to stop the game. I was carried away in an ambulance to a local hospital, where the attending physicians underdiagnosed the severity of my injury.

Upon returning to Montréal, my leg looked wrong. The swelling was not subsiding, and I was unable to put any weight on my leg. An orthopedic surgeon saw me, and the news was not good. When I asked him how long it would take for me to play again, he said, "Forget about playing again. Let's hope that you don't walk with a limp for the rest of your life." I ended up having a closed reduction on my ankle (resetting of the bones without needing to have an open surgery), but the damage was severe. While I did return to some playing (I was one of three rookies to make the nationally ranked McGill University team in 1984, before I quit to focus on my studies), my competitive career was effectively over. I had hoped to make the Canadian national team (I had played for the Quebec team and had become vice champion of Canada), and there were opportunities to pursue a professional soccer career in Europe. But my severe injury, the fact that my family did not support my soccer ambitions, and the additional fact that I lived in Canada (hardly a hotbed for European scouts back in the early 1980s) made it "easy" to accept the career-ending diagnosis and retire. Notwithstanding all these obstacles, I regret that I did not simply pack my bags and move to Europe to at least give it a full attempt. My biggest talent in life was playing soccer, and as Robert De Niro's character in *A Bronx Tale* reminded his son: "Remember, the saddest thing in life is wasted talent. You could have all the talent in the world, but if you don't do the right thing, then nothing happens. But when you do right, guess what, good things happen."[8] Every four years the World Cup of soccer rolls around, and I'm consumed with overwhelming feelings of regret. Did I waste my soccer talent? This is an existential regret that will always haunt me.

Luckily, I was very talented in another domain, academics. I had always planned on becoming a professional soccer player and then eventually a professor, so the career-ending soccer injury accelerated the timeline for my second objective. For the most part, I have nothing to regret professionally. My research productivity and prominence within the public sphere are sizeable. Yet I do have one looming regret. I have always had a deep desire to permanently relocate to Southern California. I have been going to SoCal regularly since 1985, including having lived there from 2001 to 2003 as a visiting professor at UC Irvine. I know with every fiber in my body that I would be maximally happy and fulfilled in the SoCal climate, which agrees with my Lebanese blood. And yet, I have made certain professional decisions that have greatly minimized, if not fully eradicated, the prospects of being offered a professorship there. I never played the expected game in academia, namely, to become an obscure specialist and publish only in the leading "acceptable" journals. As I mentioned earlier, I am an intellectual variety-seeker, publishing scientific papers in many disciplines and in a wide range of academic journals, and such behavior is frowned upon by other academics and thus by college administrators. Furthermore, I never liked to network at academic conferences. I am a very sociable and extroverted person, but I despise interacting with people for real or imagined ulterior motives. I am authentic to a fault. Finally, my maladaptive perfectionism—and my belief that few people could adhere to my brutally exacting ethical and professional standards—has caused me to avoid building large networks of collaborators, which is another part of the academic game. Many scientific endeavors require collaborative teams, but I have largely forgone these opportunities. By being an intellectual variety-seeker, an anti-networker, and a maladaptive perfectionist, I have pleased myself as a researcher and academic, but also made it difficult for other academics to support my candidacy for a professorship at their school. They might admire my professional CV, but I do not fit the expected mold of the "stay in your lane" academic. And it is also true that my popular celebrity and my well-founded but politically incorrect opinions are not approved by the progressives who like to dictate who is hired at universities. I regret that I was unable to better navigate the tensions between my personhood, my desire to live in SoCal, and the careerist expectations required of a modern-day academic. Then again, my "non-modulation" is precisely what garnered me great success, well beyond what the typical academic career might engender, so perhaps my regret is misguided. But if any Southern California university is looking for a top-notch business school professor, I am here!

Two Sources of Regret: Actions vs. Inactions

The psychological study of regret makes a distinction between regret based on actions and regrets that stem from inactions. Dr. Tom Gilovich, my former professor at Cornell, was a pioneer in studying these contrasting regrets. Most people, he discovered, consider their greatest regret to be one of inaction (such as, "I regret that I never went to art school").[9] This insight was also arrived at by the American author Henry Wilson Allen (Will Henry was one of his pseudonyms) when he famously stated: "Fools live to regret their words [actions], wise men to regret their silence [inactions]."[10] Here is part of the Anglican Morning Prayer (general confession), which speaks perfectly to the work of Gilovich on regret: "We have left undone those things which we ought to have done; And we have done those things which we ought not to have done; And there is no health in us."[11]

There is another distinction to make, and this is between short-term and long-term regret. In the short term, one is more likely to regret certain actions, but in the long term, such as reflecting on one's lifetime, it is regret over inactions that dominate. Research showing the dominance of long-term regret over inaction has been replicated across several distinct cultures (including in China, Japan, and Russia).[12] Even though cultures vary in the manner by which they construe time, regret due to inaction over the long term appears to be a universal phenomenon.

Are there elements of regret that do vary cross-culturally? *Intrapersonal* regret dominates in the United States (regret of an outcome that affects oneself), whereas in Taiwan *interpersonal* regret looms larger (regret of an outcome that affects another).[13] This is perhaps not surprising when one recognizes that the United States is an individualistic society, whereas Taiwan is a collectivistic one.

At least one domain of regret is rooted in a clear evolutionary calculus. If you were to ask men and women whether they regret having missed a sexual opportunity (inaction) versus having had a sexual encounter (action), a clear sex difference emerges.[14] Since the benefits and costs of mating are different for the two sexes, women's greater choosiness is such that sexual actions loom larger in their regret calculus, whereas sexual inactions loom larger for men. Hence, when militant feminists in the 1960s and 1970s argued that liberated women should engage in meaningless one-night stands (to be "equal" with men), they were pushing against evolutionary reality. Feminists argued, falsely, that women were no different from men, and from that false premise they went on to say that women should not be subject to the so-called double standard that tolerated promiscuity in men but insisted on chastity in women. That "double standard," so far as it existed, was, however, a mere acceptance of evolutionary reality. The idea pathogen known as militant feminism, in doing away with that double standard and encouraging female promiscuity, pushed many women into a life of unhappiness and sexual regret.

Near-Death and Deathbed Regrets

One's looming mortality has a way of crystallizing the important things in life. There are many testimonies from people near death saying that they experienced a slow-motion replay of important life events. The old phrase "I saw my life flashing before my eyes" is based on human experience.[15] Albert von St. Gallen Heim, a Swiss geologist and mountaineer, was an early researcher into the science of near-death experiences in the late nineteenth century, studying accounts of mountaineers suffering near-fatal falls (including his own).[16] Near-death experiences have been documented across a broad range of cultural traditions and eras, one phenomenon of which is indeed the life review experience ("life flashing before one's eyes").[17] Not surprisingly, one would expect that the images that flash before our eyes are not of our favorite material possessions (the Ferrari, or the spacious five-thousand-square-foot house, or the collection of high heels) but of the most important people and events in our lives. Three Israeli scientists recently conducted both a qualitative and quantitative analysis of life experience reviews and found that regret was a common theme.[18] In other words, as individuals face the imminent end of their lives, regret is a common lens from which to evaluate one's life.

Whereas near-death experiences typically occur as the result of a cataclysmic event (like a heart attack or a fall), palliative patients have a somewhat longer window from which to evaluate their lives. Bronnie Ware worked as a palliative nurse caring for people in the last stages of life. She recorded the top five regrets that people shared with her on their deathbeds. They are:

1. "I wish I'd had the courage to live a life true to myself, not the life others expected of me."
2. "I wish I hadn't worked so hard."

3. "I wish I'd had the courage to express my feelings."
4. "I wish I had stayed in touch with my friends."
5. "I wish I had let myself be happier."[19]

While all five regrets are deeply instructive, I shall focus on regrets one and five for now. The fifth regret is all-encompassing in that it recognizes that our happiness is inherently within our control (at least partially so). When we allow ourselves to be mired in endless negative bile, especially on issues that are out of our control, we need to return to the Stoic Epictetus and heed his timeless advice: "There is only one way to happiness and that is to cease worrying about things which are beyond the power of our will." Take charge of your life and do not worry about what you can't control. Don't regret having not been happy. Make sure to change this reality today. The first regret listed above is arguably the most profound one in that it speaks to existential authenticity. Imagine the number of people who wake up one day to recognize that they have lived a false life. As a teenager, I remember watching the 1982 film *Making Love* starring Kate Jackson, Michael Ontkean, and Harry Hamlin. The plot follows a supposedly happy and successful couple who eventually divorce as the husband comes to terms with his homosexuality. I recall feeling a deep melancholy when watching the movie, realizing that the unnecessary pain felt by the otherwise loving couple could have been avoided had the husband lived his authentic self. What was true in that dramatic circumstance can be true in an endless variety of ways.

Authenticity as Protection against Existential Regret

Because truth and freedom are the two driving ideals of my life, there are few personal traits that I despise more than inauthenticity.

Inauthentic people embody falsehoods and tell many lies, and this violates my love for truth. An authentic person has only one script to remember—the one that corresponds to his true self, and thus he can live freely and honestly. When I watch Hillary Clinton or Kamala Harris in their public lives, I am struck by the extent to which they exude an aura of falsity. There is nothing natural about them. Everything is strained, fake, and phony. This is sinister on multiple levels. It signals to the world that the fraudster is unsure about her real self, and as such she must constantly construct a new personhood for the situation at hand. Who could forget the false accents that Hillary Clinton would affect as a function of the audience that she was addressing? Or the cackling of Kamala Harris whenever she is asked an uncomfortable question? Or her infamously bizarre interaction with children, some of whom were child actors, about the wonders of space research? She advised them that one could see the craters of the moon with their own eyes.[20] Wow, so I can see the moon, the stars, and the sun simply by looking up at the sky and staring at these cosmic realities with my own eyes? Wondrous! I would much rather interact with an authentic person whose character traits I might find disagreeable (like Donald Trump) than an inauthentic person who reeks of duplicity but is otherwise "nice" (like Kamala Harris).

Authentic people are honest with themselves and with those around them. They navigate the world with a honey badger's "I don't give a f**k" attitude. Authentic people never equivocate on their positions to please or placate the crowd. Instead, they tell it like it is whilst being unconcerned about how others might view them. Authentic people are confident, in part because they are honest. They are comfortable in their own skin because they do not desire to dissimulate. They do not pretend to be someone other than themselves. Under pressure, they do not assume the fetal position or prevaricate. They do not sit on the fence when a decision has to be made. They do what they think is right, work to achieve a good result, and accept that they have agency to shape their own lives. Hence, they are much more likely to be happy individuals. A central feature of personal authenticity is "realness" or "genuineness." One is real if there is congruency between one's internal feelings and overt behaviors, even if such genuineness yields negative personal or social outcomes.[21] While being real can at times carry negative consequences, this form of personal authenticity is associated with greater psychological health and well-being across a broad range of measures; being authentic is negatively correlated with neuroticism and depression but positively correlated with agreeableness and conscientiousness.[22] If you are true to your personhood, you minimize the chances of future regret, for you have removed any incongruity between your internal thoughts and feelings and your external actions. It is perhaps not surprising then that authenticity is correlated with life satisfaction and well-being.[23]

Many philosophers have written about the concept of personal authenticity, including Søren Kierkegaard, Martin Heidegger, and Jean-Paul Sartre.[24] But perhaps the best advice comes from the ancient Greek adage: "Know thyself."[25] Students often seek my advice about their career paths. Often, they think in terms of market opportunities: "Professor Saad, should I study big data analytics? I hear the market is hot for this expertise." As a business school professor, I fully appreciate the importance of identifying and exploiting untapped market niches. But this cannot be the sole means by which one makes crucial educational and career decisions. If you wish to live an existentially authentic life, you must look within and ask which career path is best aligned with your true self. Failure to engage in this calculus is what leads to regret later in life. Market conditions might suggest that it is a good idea to become a chartered accountant. But if your main interest in life is art and architecture, then you might regret spending forty years as a tax accountant (notwithstanding the fact that some tax accountants are true "artists" in their ability to skirt the tax code legally). When we study regret we often see that it lies in the discrepancy between one's actual self (tax accountant) and ideal self (architect) or between one's actual self and "ought" self (a feeling that one should be better, more honest, more kindly); it turns out that the most frequent regrets correspond to discrepancies between a person's actual and ideal self.[26] The smaller the discrepancy between your actual and ideal self, the more existentially happy you will be.

Being genuine can lead to professional success. I have hosted hundreds of guests on my show The Saad Truth, the great majority of whom are highly accomplished individuals. They come from a broad range of backgrounds, jobs, and professions, and they are radically different from one another in countless ways. And yet, the common thread is that they all have interesting things to say, and I am lucky enough to be the host who can orchestrate a fascinating dialogue. I have been successful in this role because I am an authentic person. Being authentic serves as a disarming quality because it immediately puts the other person at ease. The guests can relax and know that they need not be on psychological guard, for their interlocutor is genuine. Of all my guests, few have been as beguilingly charming as the journalist and attorney Megyn Kelly. During our chat, we were discussing things that we might have regretted in our lives.[27] To her credit, she stated that there were few, if any, things that she regretted because any experience she had, even if it ended badly, allowed her to grow as an individual. Fair enough. I then proceeded to share my regret that my career has been hampered by my inability to compromise my professional principles, actions, or speech for careerist reasons. She replied that my open and frank manner is precisely what made me attractive to so many people. In other words, rather than regretting any elements of my authentic self, I should embrace them, for they have brought me great rewards. Since we are both no-nonsense honey badgers, it is perhaps not surprising that she would appreciate those uncompromising qualities in me.

In January 2022, I received an email informing me that His Excellency Ajay Bisaria, the high commissioner of India to Canada, wanted to deliver a personal letter to me from the Honorable Narendra Modi, the prime minister of India. During our phone conversation to discuss my visit to the High Commission of India in Ottawa, Mr. Bisaria told me that long ago he had been accepted to pursue a Ph.D. in marketing at Northwestern University (one of the top departments in the world), but he had chosen instead to pursue a career in the Indian foreign service. I asked him whether he ever regretted his decision. His answer was beautiful. He explained that based on his religious beliefs he does not regret his decision. He believes that which happens was meant to be. Many religions offer such metaphysical solace from the potential angst of regret. The idea that things happen for a reason (or that an outcome is God's will, or that providence guides our fates) is one way to achieve tranquility of the mind.

By the way, in case you are wondering about the contents of the letter from Prime Minister Modi to yours truly, I was deeply honored to discover that he wanted to acknowledge my contributions to the world's intellectual life. In the letter, he states: "Writers and thinkers serve society by pushing the boundaries of thought. In a way, such people are explorers who embark on an adventure of the mind and take others along with them, through their power of articulation. There are no limits to what people who *know themselves* can achieve. Your books and thoughts have helped a number of people understand themselves and their own minds better" [emphasis added].[28] Prime Minister Modi was reiterating the importance of the ancient Greek maxim "Know thyself"!

I mentioned earlier that I spent two years as a visiting associate professor at the University of California at Irvine (2001–2003) and was very keen on relocating permanently to Southern California. With that objective in mind, I arranged several interviews with local universities.[29] During my visit to one, I was told that I could not be granted tenure due to religious considerations, as the school was affiliated with a specific religious denomination. My bewildered revulsion was the epitome of authenticity. I was polite but did not hide my views on religious tests as part of the hiring process. I thought that I had long ago escaped the religious tribalism of Lebanon. Apparently not. My near-infinite desire to be in Southern California has its limits. I was not about to convert from Judaism to the religious denomination in question. The other university story is even more comical. I had held a very productive meeting with the chair of the department, and toward the end of our conversation, he advised me that part of the hiring process would require that I face the "God squad" in order to establish the extent to which I had been active within the religious denomination that supported this university. He explained that I would be "coached" regarding what to say, to which I retorted that I found it ironic that a religious institution would promote lying as a central feature of the hiring process. Apparently, in this case, consequentialist ethics win the day! The chair grinned and "corrected" me that it was not lying but coaching, to which I retorted with this nuclear bomb of authenticity: I reminded him that I was an atheist evolutionist Lebanese Jew, and as such it would be a while before I accepted Jesus into my heart as my lord and savior! His smile of resignation said it all. I had hit a dead end in my application. My point in sharing these stories is not to shame either school—the hosts were lovely and hospitable—but to highlight the importance of individual dignity. I would rather return to the socialist frozen tundra known as Quebec rather than modulate any part of my personal identity. I present myself to the world as is. Take it or leave it. Existential authenticity is a pathway to achieving *ataraxia*.

On Becoming a Doctor at the Age of Ninety-One

Sometimes regret comes when we think an opportunity has passed us by. But in many cases, opportunity is still available, if we pursue it. Just as students frequently ask me about potential career paths, they often ask me about whether they should pursue some new academic journey. Their doubts usually revolve around the question of whether they are too old to embark on a new academic path. It might be that they already have a bachelor's degree in business but are now keen to acquire a degree in evolutionary psychology. Or it might be a desire to obtain an M.B.A., but they fear leaving, or being distracted from, their current job. At times, they are keen to explore acquiring a Ph.D., but they feel they will be too old by the time that they graduate. In most such instances, the students seeking my advice are in their twenties or thirties. This is what I usually reply: "Please sit down and let me tell you a story." I then proceed to recount the incredible anecdote of Dr. Dagobert Broh, who obtained his Ph.D. in history at Concordia University (my university) back in 1996. Broh was born in 1904 in Germany. Because of the rise of the Nazis, Broh, who was Jewish, fled to Canada with his family. Life circumstances did not permit him to pursue his university education, but in his sixties, he decided to enroll in some university classes in what was then called Sir George Williams University (SGWU), a Montréal institution that prided itself on being accommodating to mature, nontraditional students. In 1974, SGWU merged with Loyola College (a Jesuit school also known for supporting mature students) to form what eventually became Concordia University. After completing his bachelor's degree at a time when most individuals are thinking about retirement, he completed his M.A. degree in 1985, when he was in his eighties. But Broh was hardly finished; he went on to complete a Ph.D. in 1996 at the age of ninety-one. He passed away in 1999, after having reached an academic pinnacle.[30] At this point, I usually wait for my students' mouths to close (as they are awed by the story) and then playfully ask them, "Do you still believe that you are too old to pursue your dreams?" Broh epitomizes the crucial distinction between intrinsic and extrinsic rewards, and how this shapes our life trajectories. When you pursue something for its intrinsic value, you are engaging in an act of purity. For example, if you obtain a degree in discipline X for no other reason than the desire to grow intellectually, you are doing so for intrinsic reasons. If you obtain the degree because it might improve your position in the job market, that is a classic instance of an extrinsic reward. This is a frequent challenge that I face with M.B.A. students, as many enroll in business school largely for extrinsic reasons. Broh knew that he was at the end of his life. He knew that he was not doing a Ph.D. to start a long academic career. He was not pursuing the Ph.D. to impress his parents, his spouse, or his friends. He obtained the Ph.D. for the most noble of reasons: the pure love of knowledge.

Manfred Steiner has an equally compelling academic trajectory. He obtained his M.D. in 1955 in Vienna. In 1967, he was awarded a Ph.D. in biochemistry from MIT. After he retired from his medical career in 2000, he began taking physics courses at the undergraduate level, as he had always wanted to be a physicist.[31] This past November, at the age of eighty-nine, he defended his Ph.D. dissertation in physics at Brown University, and he is planning on publishing an academic paper based on his doctoral work. Here is Steiner's advice, directed at young people, but really for all of us: "I think young people should follow their dreams whatever they are. They will always regret it if they do not follow their dreams."[32]

Recently, two acquaintances of mine—well into their fifties or sixties—obtained academic degrees. One lady, whom I originally met at our local Italian café, is a working artist who decided to return to Concordia University and pursue a B.F.A. in Film Animation. This was her second undergraduate degree, and she is now contemplating the possibility of enrolling in an M.F.A. program. The second lady is the partner of a man connected to my family by marriage. She pursued a professional CEGEP (Collège d'enseignement général et professionnel [College of General and Professional Studies]) degree in web and graphic design. In Quebec, where I reside, we have a unique educational system. High school students graduate in grade eleven, and they then head off for a two-year CEGEP degree, which is a transitory degree toward being admitted to an undergraduate program in a university. It is similar to a community college in the American context. CEGEP students are typically in their late teens, whereas the typical B.F.A. students are perhaps in their early twenties. In other words, these two lifelong learners were old enough to be the grandmothers of their class cohorts, and yet this did not dissuade them from achieving their educational goals. The same can-do attitude applies to individuals who enroll in medical school after the age of forty. While they constitute a small minority (less than 1 percent within a twenty-year period),[33] they are sufficiently large in number to support the notion that it is truly never too late to pursue some dreams and avoid future regret. Of note, a meta-analysis of the most common life regrets revealed that education was the most frequent one, yielding 32.2 percent of stated regrets (covering the gamut from *I regret that I obtained a degree in this field* to *I regret that I was not more studious* to *I regret that I never obtained my degree*).[34] As should be evident by now, it is seldom too late to assuage education-related regrets.

While it may never be too late to pursue a medical career, Amy Wax did the opposite. She walked away from being a neurologist to pursue a career in law. Well-timed career switches can be just as crucial to avoiding future regret. Amy obtained a B.S. in molecular biophysics and biochemistry from Yale University; she was then a Marshall Scholar in philosophy, physiology, and psychology at Oxford University. This was followed by an M.D. degree at Harvard University. She then completed a residency in neurology and became a consulting neurologist. This is an arduous educational path, and yet Dr. Wax decided to walk away from medicine. At the same time as she became a practicing neurologist, she had graduated with a J.D. degree from Columbia University. She held several legal positions (law clerk to a U.S. court of appeals judge, assistant to the U.S. solicitor general) and then landed a professorship of law at the University of Pennsylvania. Amy and I held a chat on my show where we briefly discussed her incredible career switch.[35] Despite the extraordinary sunk costs associated with becoming a neurologist, she had the courage to switch careers to maximize her occupational happiness. This is the hallmark of a true honey badger, which is further solidified in Amy's case in that she has been fearless and implacable in speaking her mind throughout her academic career. Despite several attempts to get her cancelled, she has been a dogged anti-woke professor unwilling to cave to the perpetually offended campus mobs.[36]

One of my favorite television shows from my childhood back in the 1970s was *Three's Company*. Via the magic of syndication, my young children were recently introduced to *Three's Company*, and it has been a delight for me to experience the show so many years later through their eyes. Even sitcoms can teach life lessons. In one episode that I rewatched recently, one of the lead characters, Janet (played by Joyce DeWitt), is temporarily excited after a dance instructor encourages her to think she could pursue a career as a dancer. He has, of course, ulterior, lecherous motives. But the point of the story comes when Janet realizes that she is in fact too old and insufficiently talented to be a professional dancer. The life lesson here is that while it may never be too late to pursue certain dreams, one also needs to be grounded in reality. The "you can be anything if you set your mind to it" mantra is inspiring, but at times illusory.

The Value of Anticipatory Regret

Regret is considered a negative emotion, but it is also an emotion one learns from, and that can lead to better future behaviors.[37] In contrast to eight other negative emotions (anger, fear, sadness, disappointment, guilt, anxiety, jealousy, and boredom), regret was viewed most positively;[38] and of the nine examined negative emotions, regret was construed as possessing the most functional value.[39] Many entrepreneurs, in particular, recognize the functional value of "anticipatory regret," to which I turn next.

As of September 2020, Amazon's market capitalization was $1.761 trillion. Its founder, Jeff Bezos, was the world's wealthiest individual with a net worth of $201.3 billion.[40] Amazon might have never been founded were it not for the fact that Bezos did not wish to experience future regret at not having taken a shot at starting the company. In a 2001 interview, he stated: "I wanted to project myself forward at age eighty and say, okay, now I'm looking back on my life, I want to have minimized the number of regrets I have. And you know, I knew that when I was eighty, I was not going to regret having tried this. I was not going to regret . . . trying to participate in this thing called the Internet that I thought was going to be a really big deal. I knew that if I failed, I wouldn't regret that. But I knew the one thing I might regret is not ever having tried. And I knew that that would haunt me every day."[41] This is what Bezos referred to as his "regret minimization framework." It is a very powerful mindset to compel people to go for it! Bezos's mental model is also known as anticipatory regret. In other words, it is forward looking; it involves acting now to avoid what you might anticipate as a later regret.

Anthony Robbins is one of the most successful self-help gurus and life coaches. He has sold millions of books and lectured to innumerable people and companies in a career that has spanned well over three decades. Irrespective of whether one agrees with the entirety of his methods and teachings, he has been an undeniable dispenser of well-received advice. When asked about the fear of failure in a 2016 interview, he stated: "The easiest way to deal with the fear of failure is to be more fearful of not taking action."[42] In the interview, Robbins refers to his rocking chair test: not wanting to be eighty-five years old, sitting on a rocking chair, and regretting the things that he did not tackle out of fear, trepidation, or other potential obstacles. A good life might be measured by how easily you sit in your rocking chair, at age eighty-five, reading good books rather than wallowing over lost opportunities.

Some forms of regret are functional and some might be inevitable because of circumstances and choices, but others serve no purpose and are utterly unnecessary. One of the rare occasions that my father visited my wife and me at our home highlights an example of poorly calibrated regret. My dad and I were sitting in the living room, and after a pensive pause, he said, "You know, Gad, I deeply regret that we did not send you to Jewish school." It was uttered in a judgmental tone. I paused, in turn, and said, "You know, Dad, that which you regret most about me is what I have most to thank you for. Having been educated in non-Jewish schools allowed me to interact with a broad range of folks that I would otherwise have been insulated from." He was not pleased with my response. If you are going to regret something, at least make sure it is worth it. His regret was no regret of mine, and he should have let it go; we each have to live our own lives.

Do Not Regret Your Lost Youth—Age Gracefully

Paulina Porizkova was one of the best-known supermodels of the 1980s. She married Ric Ocasek, the lead singer of The Cars, a successful band, popular in the 1980s. He was nearly twenty years her senior when they married. But it is not unusual for older, successful men to wed beautiful, younger women. Porizkova was interviewed recently by *The Times* (of London). She lamented that men no longer show her much attention (her husband passed away in 2019). She stated: "I am now completely invisible. . . . I walk into a party, I try to flirt with guys and they just walk away from me to pursue someone 20 years younger. I'm very single, I'm dressed up, I've made an effort—nothing."[43] I decided to reply to her since many women share her sentiments, shocked at how they no longer hold the same sexual sway over men as they did in their younger years. Here was my response, which I thought was measured and respectful. I told her that she was "hardly invisible but the fact that you do not have the same pull for some men is to be expected. I'm sure that innumerable men have been invisible to you as they approached you in your life. It's called reality. Dynamics change through life stages."[44] Rather than take stock of the important life lesson that I was sharing with her, she decided to retort in the following snarky and rude manner: "Sounds like you speak from experience. I guess the hot babes weren't interested in you, huh?"[45] This led me to reply: "This is an unbecoming response of a serious adult. You are stuck in your irreverent sassy narcissistic teenage years but your birth certificate says otherwise. Stay classy. Oh by the way, my wife is very beautiful on the inside and outside. Be well."[46] I then proceeded to release a *Saad Truth* clip wherein I analyzed the psychological fallacies implicit in her bitterness.[47] When another individual tried to explain to her the "grandmother hypothesis,"[48] which provides an evolutionary explanation for why women live long after the end of their fertility (because they then become childcare help, as grandmothers), Porizkova responded angrily: "Seems like evolution is serving only one section of the population."[49] Her implication was that evolution was inherently sexist. I replied: "Zero understanding of evolution. For most species including humans female mate choice shapes the evolutionary trajectory of male morphology and male behavior. It's called sexual selection."[50] It's also called science and a fact of life.

Porizkova's bitterness, which stems from the idea pathogen known as militant feminism, is an impediment to her leading a happy life, as evidenced in her Twitter bio that contained the following line: "America, you made me a feminist."[51] Based on the furious responses I received from women after my exchanges with Porizkova, this is a deep source of age-related bitterness. Many women lament that their sexual power has an "expiration date" and blame the evil patriarchy for "teaching men to prefer younger women." Well, we all have an expiration date. The speed and grace that I had when I was a seventeen-year-old soccer player and could dribble past four or five opponents with explosive acceleration was missing when I tried to play against my son's soccer team and realized that ten-year-olds could now run faster than me. I did not postulate that the "evil matriarchy" was keeping me down but recognized that I had aged. Male prizefighters are typically not octogenarians, nor are football players (with the exception of Tom Brady of course). Men's sexual vigor is not the same when they are sixty as compared to when they were twenty-one. But older men can compensate for that because of what women look for in a husband. Women around the world desire men with high social status, and not surprisingly men's social status typically increases with age. Men around the world desire young, nubile, and beautiful women, and physical attributes, alas, fade with age. These sex-specific mating preferences are not due to the machinations of the evil patriarchy but are firmly rooted in evolutionary processes. Women's sexual pull on the mating market reaches its zenith when they are younger; that of men when they are older. This is called biology and has nothing to do with sexism. In the words of Christopher Walken in the 2005 film *Wedding Crashers*, "Nature always wins."[52] When you live your life wedded to reality rather than to bitter self-deception rooted in corrosive idea pathogens (in this case militant feminism), it permits you to have *ataraxia*. Failure to do so causes you to direct unnecessary angst and resentment at a unicorn enemy known as the patriarchy.

The Regret of Lost Experiences

When I was a visiting professor at the University of California at Irvine, one of my favorite activities was to scour the numerous extraordinary second-hand bookstores in Southern California accompanied by my wife. I felt like a book archaeologist digging through mounds of "dirt" to uncover the rare jewel. As I type these words, I long for that feeling of elation and happiness that I experienced browsing through the endless aisles of knowledge. Regrettably, most of these bookstores, most notably Acres of Books in Long Beach, California (literally a warehouse of books covering an entire street block), eventually folded in large part due to the powers of Amazon. Was my book hunting a pursuit of material goods or of experiences? After all, I was purchasing tangible goods that would be added to my personal library. But of course, this was greatly overshadowed by the magical experiences both of finding these books and then reading them. This brings me to a very important distinction between two competing drivers of happiness: Are we happier when we collect material possessions or when we amass enriching life experiences? It might at first sound obvious that the latter should be the correct response, and yet as a consumer psychologist I can assure you that the materialism trap is all too real for millions of people. Consumers will go into great debt to purchase a car that they cannot afford, a house for which they can barely cover the mortgage, or a boat that they are likely to use only three times during the summer season. And yet, most research shows that to spend money on life experiences (like a trip around the world) increases an individual's happiness more than spending money on material possessions (like a luxury car).[53] This is consistent with a study that examined the links between various forms of consumption (leisure, personal care, food, health care, vehicles, and housing) on happiness. Only leisure consumption ("consuming" life experiences) was correlated with happiness.[54]

The fact that the consumption of experiences brings us much greater happiness than the purchase of material goods carries over to our regret calculus. Few people when looking back on their lives will rue the lost opportunity of not having purchased a Rolex, a Mercedes, or a Hugo Boss suit. But innumerable people will regret not having visited Paris, not having taken the safari to Namibia, or not having learned how to sail across the Caribbean Sea. This was perfectly captured in a recent Expedia commercial that aired during Super Bowl LVI. The narrator, actor Ewan McGregor, says: "We love stuff, and there's some really great stuff out there. But I doubt that any of us will look back in our lives and think, I wish I had bought an even thinner TV, found a lighter light beer, or had an even smarter smartphone. Do you think any of us will look back in our lives and regret the things we didn't buy—or the places we didn't go?"[55] Spot on. Live your life according to that Expedia motto. The winner at life is the one who collects the greatest number of enriching life experiences, not the one who owns more stuff.

Notwithstanding that when it comes to our happiness, experiences offer us more bang for the buck than material possessions, there remains an important issue to resolve. Experiences are greatly varied. For example, the prescription to "stop and smell the roses" is centered in the here and now, such that we ought to maximally enjoy the simple pleasures of life. On the other hand, contemporary colloquialisms such as YOLO (You Only Live Once) and FOMO (Fear of Missing Out) capture the drive to pursue grand experiences. Enjoying a great cup of coffee whilst reading a great book (as I hope you are doing right now) might be an example of metaphorically stopping and smelling the roses, whereas signing up for that bungee jump in Queenstown, New Zealand, is best captured by the YOLO and/or FOMO ethos. Are our lives better lived if they are composed of ordinary or extraordinary experiences? Of course, as we've seen, variety matters. We should seek an optimal combination of both types of experiences. It turns out, though, that the extent to which we prefer one type of experience over the other is a function of our age. In our youth, we prefer extraordinary experiences over ordinary ones; as we age, both experiences are equally valued.[56]

Regret is an aversive emotion that can gnaw away at our happiness, especially on matters that we cannot retroactively fix (such as marital infidelity leading to divorce). It can, however, also be a useful warning sign to compel us to engage in corrective behavior. In 1999, Barry Cadish set up the website RegretsOnly.com, where individuals could submit their stories of regret. The project proved so successful that he decided to quit his job as an advertising man and focus on writing a book on regret. This book, published in 2001, was titled *Damn! Reflections on Life's Biggest Regrets*. His conclusion, perfectly in line with the scientific findings on regret, was: "Most people regret the things they don't do more than the things they do. If you don't try, you're always going to be left with that nagging question: What if? I didn't want to look back and say, 'I should have done this.'"[57] In his 2022 book *The Power of Regret*, Daniel Pink posits that many regrets stem from failures of boldness (I should have been bold and quit my secure job and started my dream business).[58] Again, this demonstrates that many of our deepest regrets come from inactions that leave us pursuing inauthentic lives. Don't do that. Instead, remember the words of the poet William Ernest Henley: "I am the master of my fate, I am the captain of my soul."[59]

CHAPTER NINE

Don't Worry: Be Happy

*"Do not all men desire happiness? And yet, perhaps, this is
one of those ridiculous questions which I am afraid to ask,
and which ought not to be asked by a sensible man: for
what human being is there who does not desire happiness."*

"There is no one," said Cleinias, "who does not."

*"Well then," I said, "since we all of us desire happiness,
how can we be happy?—that is the next question."*[1]

—Socrates (from *Euthydemus* by Plato)

N ear the beginning of this book, I quoted Seneca: "There is not
any thing in this world, perhaps, that is more talked of, and less
understood, than the business of a *happy life* [emphasis in original]. It
is every man's wish and design; and yet not one of a thousand that
knows wherein that happiness consists."[2] And I quoted Kant: "But it
is a misfortune that the concept of happiness is such an indeterminate
concept that, although every human being wishes to attain this, he can
still never say determinately and consistently with himself what he
really wishes and wills."[3]

I hope that now, as we near the end of this book, we have some answers to Seneca's and Kant's speculations. While there is not one foolproof way to live the good life, I hope to have offered a pathway, illuminated by the light of social science, to being happy. Happiness is not captured in a willful pursuit. Rather, it is a destination one reaches by making optimal decisions, which in turn are the product of specific winning mindsets. In December 2021, on my first trip since the COVID pandemic, I travelled to San Antonio, Texas, to deliver a lecture on *The Parasitic Mind*. An investment banking firm had chosen my book as its book of the year and had invited me to address an audience of esteemed guests and clients, many from the banking and finance industries. At the end of the event, I stuck around to mingle with the guests and sign copies of my book. A young man came up to me and asked me two questions of particular relevance to this book's contents. He asked, first, how he could, as a college student, stay true to his beliefs, given that his grades might depend on the goodwill of ideologically bigoted progressive professors. Unlike me, he said, he was not a tenured professor who could easily withstand the negative consequences of speaking his mind. He also asked me how he should go about becoming a public intellectual. He wanted to be like me. In responding to his first question, I reminded him that tenure does not protect me from the innumerable death threats that I have received. It does not protect me from the consequential costs that I have had to bear professionally (such as losing out on lucrative professorships, grants, and other rewards). Regardless of all this, one must be true to what one believes. One must be authentic. In answering his second question, I told him that there is no 1-2-3 recipe to become a public intellectual. It is not a position you seek; it is something that happens to you if you have valuable and interesting things to say. The psychiatrist and neurologist Viktor E. Frankl made a similar point regarding the pursuit of success and happiness:

Don't aim at success—the more you aim at it and make it a target, the more you are going to miss it. For success, like happiness, cannot be pursued; it must ensue, and it only does so as the unintended side-effect of one's dedication to a cause greater than oneself or as the by-product of one's surrender to a person other than oneself. Happiness must happen, and the same holds for success: you have to let it happen by not caring about it. I want you to listen to what your conscience commands you to do and go on to carry it out to the best of your knowledge. Then you will live to see that in the long-run—in the long-run, I say!—success will follow you precisely because you had *forgotten* to think about it.[4] [Emphasis in original.]

Notwithstanding Frankl's admonition against the willful pursuit of happiness and the empirical evidence highlighting that its dogged pursuit can yield deleterious effects,[5] there appears to be empirical evidence in support of the efficacy of happiness training programs that encourage cognitive reframing, mindfulness, and expressions of gratitude. In a research synthesis of 179 findings of the effects of happiness training programs, 96 percent yielded an increase in happiness, notwithstanding the fact that the positive effects were modest.[6] This is a hopeful message in that it reaffirms the fact that our happiness is in part shaped by the actions we take, the decisions that we make, and the mindsets that we adopt, and that we can learn ways to find the right path to happiness, a path that is lined with such old-fashioned virtues as temperance, gratitude, and hope. Let happiness be the destination, the outcome, and not the primary pursuit.

I next present two brief stories of men who had every reason to be unhappy and miserable and yet, via their winning mindsets, have found existential contentment. They clearly did not willfully pursue happiness but rather conquered their tragic lot in life through positive thinking.

The Existential Gratitude of a Wrongly Imprisoned Man

We all experience stressful periods in our lives. It sometimes seems that the cosmos is conspiring against us. But whenever I find myself wallowing about my lot, I contextualize things; I put my current sources of anger, frustration, and stress within some broader framework. Take the COVID pandemic; it has taken a toll on everyone. The attacks on our personal freedoms have been difficult to endure—and yet, I remembered, I am not doing so badly. I hold a job with a guaranteed income. My experiences have been infinitely less difficult than those of small business owners who have had to make countless sacrifices and be endlessly inventive just to survive. There is an old saying that someone is always worse off than you are; whether you are a business professor or a small business owner or a day laborer, putting your own situation in a broader context can make you count your advantages in any circumstance.

Of all the wonderful guests I have hosted on my show, few have been as memorable as David McCallum. David is not a famous man, but he teaches an important lesson about life. David was exonerated from a murder charge after spending twenty-nine years in prison. I had first heard David's story while watching *David & Me*, a 2014 documentary about his case. I was so moved by his unimaginable grace and sense of forgiveness that I felt compelled to reach out to him. During our conversation, I confessed to David that he was a better man than I am, because I would have been full of anger and venom, and a poisonous desire for revenge, had I experienced his reality. David, however, appeared well-adjusted, enlightened, wise, and forgiving. I asked him how he managed that, and he offered two poignant responses. First, he told me, after he was arrested his mother asked him if he was guilty. He said no, and she never asked again. He felt at peace knowing that his mom believed him. Then he told me that one of his sisters suffered from cerebral palsy. She had been bedridden her entire life. Her example inspired him. She persevered through her own tragic reality, and what he faced was nothing in comparison.[7] I was awestruck by David's purity of spirit, his ineradicable optimism, and his abiding sense of gratitude. I suspect his sense of gratitude—for his life and its own positive aspects—saved his soul from being destroyed by his circumstances. Gratitude offers a partial inoculation against the vagaries of life and is, generally speaking, positively correlated with happiness.[8] To be grateful while unjustly imprisoned is a true accomplishment of character.

The Happy Homeless Scholar

During the COVID pandemic, my wife and I seldom enjoyed the opportunity of going to our favorite restaurants. This had the silver lining, as I mentioned, of helping me lose a sizable amount of weight. We did, however, continue to frequent a Peruvian rotisserie chicken dive. On one such outing, we came across a disheveled and perhaps homeless man sitting on the steps of the establishment. As we waited to be served in the outside queue, I struck up a conversation with him. He asked me what I did for a living. After I told him, he said, "This seems like serious work, but you seem strong to be able to handle it." I was flattered by his response, and it was a highlight of my day. Most people might have ignored this elderly man, but my wife and I chose to engage him. Engaging him brought me the pleasure of his compliment, but that aside, my wife and I believe that all people deserve to be treated with respect and dignity, even when their exteriors might look weathered and destitute. Sometimes we are rewarded with a nice little conversation. Talking with this man reminded me of another extraordinary story involving homelessness. The beginning of that story happened to me nearly twenty years ago, when I lived in Southern California.[9] I was seated at a café working on a project, and I had several books sprawled on the table. An elegant gentleman, speaking with a slight British accent, approached me to comment about some of the books on the table. His name was Bijan Gilani, and he explained to me that he was pursuing a Ph.D. at UC Irvine and was writing a dissertation on the issue of homelessness.[10] As part of his fieldwork, he had integrated himself within the homeless community.

We communicated briefly via email after I moved back to Montréal, but I otherwise lost track of him, only to discover later that, incredibly, Gilani, a once reasonably wealthy man, had eventually become homeless himself. I came across a 2011 article in the OC Weekly that described his extraordinary life trajectory. In reading the article, I was struck by his admirable lack of self-pity. He told the reporter, "I realize people have it a lot worse."[11] Like David McCallum, Gilani never lost sight of the fact that however desperate our plight, it is, within a bigger context, not *that* bad, and that realization affords us an instantaneous jolt of gratitude and psychological well-being. This attitude is not one of schadenfreude (reveling in another's misfortune), but rather of the optimism we should all feel because we are alive. In the article, Bijan continues, "Every morning, I remind myself who I am," and then he adds: "I can write. I can think. I'm educated. I'm a moral person. I like being around people. I'm adaptable, humble, and I love to laugh." To exhibit this level of optimism when so downtrodden is a testament to his positive spirit and mindset. Bijan said that besides owning his SUV (which serves as his home) and a no-frills cellphone, he rejoices at having a gym membership and a card to the Newport Beach Public Library.[12] In other words, in a truly stoic and ascetic manner, he reaffirms the importance of a healthy body and an inquisitive mind as central features in supporting a life of happiness. I am convinced that his life story would constitute a wonderful film, for it would serve as a powerful reminder of the truly important things in life.

Parting Words

I recently held a chat on my show with the classicist and military historian Victor Davis Hanson. As we were saying our goodbyes, Victor ended our conversation with the following: "Thank you, and it's so nice to see an academic who smiles. I don't do it enough, but you do."[13] It is incontestable that our capacity to be happy, and hence smile, is in part shaped by the immutable elements of our personhood. However, as I hope to have convinced you in this book, each of us has the capacity to be the architect of his happiness and well-being. Every moment in life is precious. Savor the infinitesimally small probability of your having ever existed. Of course, life has countless difficult moments that we must overcome, but we have at our disposal several tried and tested antidotes to existential darkness. I have offered you a template or blueprint for maximizing your chances at happiness. To summarize, my recipe for the good life includes:

1. finding the right spouse
2. working in the right profession
3. seeking the sweet spot (moderation) across many life domains
4. engaging life via a playful mindset
5. pursuing variety-seeking at times, across many domains
6. ensuring that one is persistent in the pursuit of meaningful goals
7. being anti-fragile when dealing with failure
8. seeking to minimize future regret, in part by living an authentic life

The successful implementation of each of these prescriptions will draw you closer to the final destination, namely reaching the summit of Mount Happiness. I hope that reading this book has infused you with a sense of happiness and existential inspiration. Thank you for coming on this journey with me.

Acknowledgments

I am grateful to the cosmos for having endowed me with a sunny disposition, which has allowed me to tackle life's challenges with a smile and a sense of hope and optimism. On a personal level, much of my daily happiness stems from the love and solace that I receive from my wife and children. My role as a husband and father provides me a soothing sense of well-being. To build a cohesive family unit rooted in love, respect, and commitment has been one of the great joys of my life. More broadly, I am indebted to all of the individuals, from close friends to random strangers, who have enriched my life in innumerable ways. On a professional level, I am thankful that I am able to pursue my intellectual interests as I see fit.

Many thanks to Harry Crocker, my editor at Regnery, for his careful reading of my manuscript and for his valuable feedback. No author could hope for a better editor. A big thank-you to the rest of the Regnery team for their support throughout the entire process, from first hearing of my idea for this book to the final production stages. It comforts me to know that my publisher is such an enthusiastic champion of my work.

Finally, I am thankful for life. Life is short and fleeting. Every moment is precious and has the potential to be magical.

Notes

Chapter One: On Being the Happy Professor

1. "Declaration of Independence: A Transcription," America's Founding Documents, https://www.archives.gov/founding-docs/declaration-transcript.

2. Richard Layard, *Happiness: Lessons from a New Science* (New York: Penguin Books, 2005), 113.

3. Raj Raghunathan, *If You're So Smart, Why Aren't You Happy?* (New York: Portfolio/Penguin, 2016), 19–20.

4. See references on pages 1 and 2 in Dorit Redlich-Amirav et al., "Psychometric Properties of Hope Scales: A Systematic Review," *International Journal of Clinical Practice* 72, no. 7 (2018), e13213. Emma Pleeging, Martijn Burger, and Job van Exel, "The Relations between Hope and Subjective Well-Being: A Literature Overview and Empirical Analysis," *Applied Research in Quality of Life* 16, no. 3 (2021): 1019–41.

5. Ad Bergsma, "Do Self-Help Books Help?" *Journal of Happiness Studies* 9, no. 3 (2008): 341–60.

6. See, for example, Robyn M. Dawes, *House of Cards: Psychology and Psychotherapy Built on Myth* (New York: Free Press, 1994).

7. Gad Saad, *The Evolutionary Bases of Consumption* (Mahwah, New Jersey: Lawrence Erlbaum, 2007); Gad Saad, *The Consuming Instinct: What Juicy Burgers, Ferraris, Pornography, and Gift Giving Reveal about Human Nature* (Amherst, New York: Prometheus Books, 2011).

8. Gad Saad, "Sex Differences in OCD Symptomatology: An Evolutionary Perspective," *Medical Hypotheses* 67, no. 6 (2006), 1455–59. Gad Saad, "Suicide Triggers as Sex-Specific Threats in Domains of Evolutionary Import: Negative Correlation between Global Male-to-Female Suicide Ratios and Average per Capita Gross National Income," *Medical Hypotheses* 68, no. 3 (2007): 692–96. Gad Saad, "Munchausen by Proxy: The Dark Side of Parental Investment Theory?" *Medical Hypotheses* 75, no. 6 (2010): 479–81.

9. Gad Saad, "My Chat with Media Superstar Glenn Beck (THE SAAD TRUTH_1324)," YouTube, October 25, 2021, https://www.youtube.com/watch?v=vAejgBZplUo, 0:32–1:29.

10. Zhmajaja (@zhmajaja), "I envy the way you have mastered the art of enjoying life," Twitter, November 13, 2021, 3:00 p.m., https://twitter.com/zhmajaja/status/145961 2180484182022?s=20.

11. David Lykken and Auke Tellegen, "Happiness Is a Stochastic Phenomenon," *Psychological Science* 7, no. 3 (1996): 186–89.

12. For a discussion of how genes do not preclude the ability to alter one's happiness, see Ragnhild Bang Nes, "Happiness in Behaviour Genetics: Findings and Implications," *Journal of Happiness Studies* 11, no. 3 (2010): 369–81.

13. Drake Baer and Marguerite Ward, "14 Quotes from Ancient Thinkers That Show They Figured Life out 2,000 Years Ago," Business Insider, May 11, 2020, https://www.businessinsider.com/wise-quotes-from-ancient-philosophers-2016-4.

14. Donald Robertson, *The Philosophy of Cognitive-Behavioural Therapy (CBT): Stoic Philosophy as Rational and Cognitive Psychotherapy* (London: Routledge, 2010).

Chapter Two: Ancient and Modern Wisdom Regarding the Good Life

1. Lucius Annaeus Seneca, *Seneca's Morals of a Happy Life, Benefits, Anger, and Clemency,* trans. Sir Roger L'Estrange (Chicago: Belford, Clarke, & Co., 1882), 125, available at https://archive.org/details/cu31924101956971/page/n125/mode/2up.

2. Immanuel Kant, *Groundwork of the Metaphysics of Morals,* trans. and ed. Mary Gregor (Cambridge, UK: Cambridge University Press, 1997), 28.

3. Øyvind Rabbås et al., eds., *The Quest for the Good Life: Ancient Philosophers on Happiness* (Oxford, UK: Oxford University Press, 2015).

4. Tim Lomas et al., "A Global History of Happiness," *International Journal of Wellbeing* 11, no. 4 (2021): 68–87.

5. Tim Lomas and Colin Lomas, "An Art History of Happiness: Western Approaches to the Good Life through the Last 1000 Years, as Illustrated in Art," *Journal of Positive Psychology and Wellbeing* 2, no. 2 (2018): 214–37.

6. Darrin M. McMahon, *Happiness: A History* (New York: Atlantic Monthly Press, 2006). See also Gad Saad, "My Chat with Dr. Darrin McMahon, Historian of Happiness (THE SAAD TRUTH_1359)," YouTube, January 12, 2022, https://youtu.be/_ktNJxfTJfI.

7. Guoqing Zhang and Ruut Veenhoven, "Ancient Chinese Philosophical Advice: Can It Help Us Find Happiness Today?" *Journal of Happiness Studies* 9, no. 3 (2008): 425–43.

8. David G. Myers and Ed Diener, "The Pursuit of Happiness," *Scientific American* 274, no. 5 (1996): 70–72; David G. Myers and Ed Diener, "The Scientific Pursuit of Happiness," *Perspectives on Psychological Science* 13, no.2 (2018): 218–25; Christopher Kullenberg and Gustaf Nelhans, "The Happiness Turn? Mapping the Emergence of 'Happiness Studies' Using Cited References," *Scientometrics* 103, no. 2 (2015): 615–30.

9. Tim Lomas and Tyler J. VanderWeele, "The Complex Creation of Happiness: Multidimensional Conditionality in the Drivers of Happy People and Societies," *Journal of Positive Psychology* 18, no. 1 (2023): 15–33, https://doi.org/10.1080/17439760.2021.1991453; Richard M. Ryan and Edward L. Deci, "On Happiness and Human Potentials: A Review of Research on Hedonic and Eudaimonic Well-Being," *Annual Review of Psychology* 52, no. 1 (2001): 141–66.

10. Menelaos L. Batrinos, "Testosterone and Aggressive Behavior in Man," *International Journal of Endocrinology & Metabolism* 10, no. 3 (Summer 2012): 563–68.

11. Gad Saad and John G. Vongas, "The Effect of Conspicuous Consumption on Men's Testosterone Levels," *Organizational Behavior and Human Decision Processes* 110, no. 2 (2009): 80–92.

12. Andrew Steptoe, "Happiness and Health," *Annual Review of Public Health* 40 (2019): 339–59; Ruut Veenhoven, "Healthy Happiness: Effects of Happiness on Physical Health and the Consequences for Preventive Health Care," *Journal of Happiness* 9, no. 3 (2008): 449–69; Kostadin Kushlev et al., "Does Happiness Improve Health? Evidence from a Randomized Controlled Trial," *Psychological Science* 31, no. 7 (2020): 807–21.

13. Neal Lathia et al., "Happier People Live More Active Lives: Using Smartphones to Link Happiness and Physical Activity," *PLOS One* 12, no. 1 (2017): e0160589, https://doi.org/10.1371/journal.pone.0160589.

14. For relevant references, see Daisy Coyle, "How Being Happy Makes You Healthier," Healthline, August 27, 2017, https://www.healthline.com/nutrition/happiness-and-health#TOC_TITLE_HDR_6; see also Yoram Barak, "The Immune System and Happiness," *Autoimmunity Reviews* 5, no. 8 (2006): 523–27; Carol D. Ryff, Burton H. Singer, and Gayle Dienberg Love, "Positive Health: Connecting Well-Being with Biology," *Philosophical Transactions of the Royal Society of London. Series B: Biological Sciences* 359, no. 1449 (2004): 1383–94.

15. For the relevant references, please see Allison Abbe, Chris Tkach, and Sonja Lyubomirsky, "The Art of Living by Dispositionally Happy People," *Journal of Happiness Studies* 4, no. 4 (2003): 385–404.

16. That being said, readers might be interested in a satirical clip I posted several years ago: Gad Saad, "Finger Diversity and Fluidity—Let's Stop Focusing on the Number 10 (THE SAAD TRUTH_861)," YouTube, March 3, 2019, https://youtu.be/F84QRYwQWQg.

17. Gordon W. Allport and Henry S. Odbert, "Trait-Names: A Psycho-Lexical Study," *Psychological Monographs* 47, no. 1 (1936): i–171.

18. Oliver P. John, Alois Angleitner, and Fritz Ostendorf, "The Lexical Approach to Personality: A Historical Review of Trait Taxonomic Research," *European Journal of Personality* 2, no. 3 (1988): 171–203; Oliver P. John and Sanjay Srivastava, "The Big Five Trait Taxonomy: History, Measurement, and Theoretical Perspectives," in *Handbook of Personality: Theory and Research*, 2nd ed., eds. Lawrence A. Pervin and Oliver P. John (New York: Guilford Press, 1999), 102–38.

19. Gad Saad, "A Multitude of Environments for a Consilient Darwinian Meta-Theory of Personality: The Environment of Evolutionary Adaptedness, Local Niches, the Ontogenetic Environment, and Situational Contexts," *European Journal of Personality* 21, no. 5 (2007): 624–26; David M. Buss, "How Can Evolutionary Psychology Successfully Explain Personality and Individual Differences?" *Perspectives on Psychological Science* 4, no. 4 (2009): 359–66; Aaron W. Lukaszewski et al., "An Adaptationist Framework for Personality Science," *European Journal of Personality* 34, no. 6 (2020): 1151–74.

20. Gad Saad, "*Homo Consumericus*: Consumption Phenomena as Universals, as Cross-Cultural Adaptations, or as Emic Cultural Instantiations," (working paper, Concordia University, John Molson School of Business, 2007).

21. Jeromy Anglim et al., "Predicting Psychological and Subjective Well-Being from Personality: A Meta-Analysis," *Psychological Bulletin* 146, no. 4 (2020): 279–323.

22. Kristina M. DeNeve and Harris Cooper, "The Happy Personality: A Meta-Analysis of 137 Personality Traits and Subjective Well-Being," *Psychological Bulletin* 124, no. 2 (1998): 197–229.

23. Mariano Rojas, "Life Satisfaction and Satisfaction in Domains of Life: Is It a Simple Relationship?" *Journal of Happiness Studies* 7, no. 4 (2006): 467–97.

24. Barry Schwartz et al., "Maximizing versus Satisficing: Happiness Is a Matter of Choice," *Journal of Personality and Social Psychology* 83, no. 5 (2002): 1178–97.

25. Richard A. Easterlin, "Does Economic Growth Improve the Human Lot? Some Empirical Evidence," in *Nations and Households in Economic Growth: Essays in Honor of Moses Abramovitz*, eds. Paul A. David and Melvin W. Reder (New York: Academic Press, 1974), 89–125.

26. Ed Diener and Shigehiro Oishi, "Money and Happiness: Income and Subjective Well-Being across Nations," in *Culture and Subjective Well-Being*, eds. Ed Diener and Eunkook M. Suh (Cambridge, Massachusetts: MIT Press, 2000), 185–218; Ed Diener and Robert Biswas-Diener, "Will Money Increase Subjective Well-Being?" *Social Indicators Research* 57 (2002): 119–69; Cf. the references on p. 148 of Shigehiro Oishi, *The Psychological Wealth of Nations: Do Happy People Make a Happy Society?* (West Sussex, United Kingdom: Wiley-Blackwell, 2012).

27. Matthew A. Killingsworth, "Experienced Well-Being Rises with Income, Even above $75,000 per Year," *Proceedings of the National Academy of Sciences of the United States of America* 118, no. 4 (2021): e2016976118, https://doi.org/10.1073/pnas.2016976118.

28. Philip Brickman, Dan Coates, and Ronnie Janoff-Bulman, "Lottery Winners and Accident Victims: Is Happiness Relative?" *Journal of Personality and Social Psychology* 36, no. 8 (1978): 917–27; Erik Lindqvist, Robert Östling, and David Cesarini, "Long-Run Effects of Lottery Wealth on Psychological Well-Being," *Review of Economic Studies* 87, no. 6 (2020): 2703–26.

29. Joseph Henrich, Steven J. Heine, and Ara Norenzayan, "The Weirdest People in the World?" *Behavioral and Brain Sciences* 33, no. 2–3 (2010): 61–83.

30. Ruut Veenhoven "How Universal Is Happiness?" in *International Differences in Well-Being*, eds. Ed Diener, Daniel Kahneman, and John Helliwell (New York: Oxford University Press, 2010), 328–50; Tim Lomas, "Positive Cross-Cultural Psychology: Exploring Similarity and Difference in Constructions and Experiences of Wellbeing," *International Journal of Wellbeing* 5, no. 4 (2015): 60–77; Gwendolyn Gardiner et al., "Happiness around the World: A Combined Etic-Emic Approach across 63 Countries," *PLOS One* 15, no. 12 (2020): e0242718.

31. Ed Diener, "Subjective Well-Being: The Science of Happiness and a Proposal for a National Index," *American Psychologist* 55, no. 1 (2000): 34–43, 34.

32. Ed Diener, Shigehiro Oishi, and Katherine L. Ryan, "Universals and Cultural Differences in the Causes and Structure of Happiness: A Multilevel Review," in *Mental Well-Being: International Contributions to the Study of Positive Mental Health*, ed. Corey L. M. Keyes (Dordrecht, Netherlands: Springer, 2013), 153–176.

33. Mohsen Joshanloo, Evert Van de Vliert, and Paul E. Jose, "Four Fundamental Distinctions in Conceptions of Wellbeing across Cultures," in *The Palgrave Handbook of Positive Education*, eds. Margaret L. Kern and Michael L. Wehmeyer (Cham, Switzerland: Palgrave Macmillan, 2021), 675–702, https://doi.org/10.1007/978-3-030-64537-3_26.

34. John F. Helliwell et al., eds., *World Happiness Report* (New York: Sustainable Development Solutions Network, 2021), https://worldhappiness.report/ed/2021/.

35. See figure 2.3. John F. Helliwell, Richard Layard, and Jeffrey Sachs, eds., *World Happiness Report* (New York: Sustainable Development Solutions Network, 2012), 30, https://s3.amazonaws.com/happiness-report/2012/World_Happiness_Report_2012.pdf.

36. See figure 2.1. Helliwell et al., *World Happiness Report* (2021), 20, https://happiness-report.s3.amazonaws.com/2021/WHR+21.pdf.

37. Frank Martela et al., "The Nordic Exceptionalism: What Explains Why the Nordic Countries Are Constantly among the Happiest in the World," in *The World Happiness Report 2020*, eds. John Helliwell, Richard Layard, Jeffrey Sachs, and Jan Emmanuel De Neve (New York: Sustainable Development Solutions Network, 2020), https://worldhappiness.report/ed/2020/the-nordic-exceptionalism-what-explains-why-the-nordic-countries-are-constantly-among-the-happiest-in-the-world/.

38. Fred R. Shapiro, ed., *The New Yale Book of Quotations* (New Haven, Connecticut: Yale University Press, 2021), 307.

39. Abraham P. Buunk and Frederick X. Gibbons, "Social Comparison: The End of a Theory and the Emergence of a Field," *Organizational Behavior and Human Decision Processes* 102, no. 1 (2007): 3–21.

40. Robert H. Frank and Philip J. Cook, *The Winner-Take-All Society: Why the Few at the Top Get So Much More Than the Rest of Us* (New York: The Free Press, 1995); Robert H. Frank, *The Darwin Economy: Liberty, Competition, and the Common Good* (Princeton, New Jersey: Princeton University Press, 2011); see also Gad Saad, "My Chat with Economist Robert Frank, Author of *Success and Luck* (THE SAAD TRUTH_171)," YouTube, May 14, 2016, https://youtu.be/VkGZRQ-ICwI.

41. Gad Saad and Tripat Gill, "Gender Differences When Choosing between Salary Allocation Options," *Applied Economics Letters* 8, no. 8 (2001): 531–33.

42. David G. Blanchflower and Andrew J. Oswald, "Money, Sex, and Happiness: An Empirical Study," *Scandinavian Journal of Economics* 106, no. 3 (2004): 393–415.

43. Tim Wadsworth, "Sex and the Pursuit of Happiness: How Other People's Sex Lives Are Related to Our Sense of Well-Being," *Social Indicators Research* 116, no. 1 (2014): 115–35.

44. James H. Fowler and Nicholas A. Christakis, "Dynamic Spread of Happiness in a Large Social Network: Longitudinal Analysis over 20 Years in the Framingham Heart Study," *British Medical Journal* 337 (2008): a2338, https://doi.org/10.1136/bmj.a2338.

45. Victoria Husted Medvec, Scott F. Madey, and Thomas Gilovich, "When Less Is More: Counterfactual Thinking and Satisfaction among Olympic Medalists," *Journal of Personality and Social Psychology* 69, no. 4 (1995): 603–10.

46. Daniel Kahneman, "Objective Happiness," in *Well-Being: The Foundations of Hedonic Psychology*, eds. Daniel Kahneman, Ed Diener, and Norbert Schwarz (New York: Russell Sage Foundation, 1999), 3–25; Simon Kemp, Christopher D. B. Burt, and Laura Furneaux, "A Test of the Peak–End Rule with Extended Autobiographical Events," *Memory & Cognition* 36, no. 1 (2008): 132–38.

47. Shankar Vedantam et al, "Daniel Kahneman on Misery, Memory, and Our Understanding of the Mind," KRWG Public Media, March 12, 2018, https://www.krwg.org/post/daniel-kahneman-misery-memory-and-our-understanding-mind.

48. S. Boyd Eaton, Melvin Konner, and Marjorie Shostak, "Stone Agers in the Fast Lane: Chronic Degenerative Diseases in Evolutionary Perspective," *American Journal of Medicine* 84, no. 4 (1988): 739–49; Norman P. Li, Mark van Vugt, and Stephen M. Colarelli, "The Evolutionary Mismatch Hypothesis: Implications for Psychological Science," *Current Directions in Psychological Science* 27, no. 1 (2018): 38–44; Yuqian Chang and Kristina M. Durante, "Why Consumers Have Everything but Happiness: An Evolutionary Mismatch Perspective," *Current Opinion in Psychology* 46 (2022): 101347. I learned of this paper after I had written up the section in question but thought it was appropriate to cite it even if identified after the fact.

49. David M. Buss, "The Evolution of Happiness," *American Psychologist* 55, no. 1 (2000): 15–23; Bjørn Grinde, "Darwinian Happiness: Can the Evolutionary Perspective on Well-Being Help Us Improve Society?" *World Futures* 61, no. 4 (2005): 317–29; Bjørn Grinde, "Happiness in the Perspective of Evolutionary Psychology," *Journal of Happiness Studies* 3, no. 4 (2002): 331–54.

50. Robin I. M. Dunbar, "The Social Brain: Mind, Language, and Society in Evolutionary Perspective," *Annual Review of Anthropology* 32 (2003): 163–81.

51. Melikşah Demir, Metin Özdemir, and Lesley A. Weitekamp, "Looking to Happy Tomorrows with Friends: Best and Close Friendships as They Predict Happiness," *Journal of Happiness Studies* 8, no. 2 (2007): 243–71; Austen R. Anderson and Blaine J. Fowers, "An Exploratory Study of Friendship Characteristics and Their Relations with Hedonic and Eudaimonic Well-Being," *Journal of Social and Personal Relationships* 37, no. 1 (2020): 260–80.

52. Joe Keohane, *The Power of Strangers: The Benefits of Connecting in a Suspicious World* (New York: Random House, 2021); Gillian M. Sandstrom and Elizabeth W. Dunn, "Is Efficiency Overrated? Minimal Social Interactions Lead to Belonging and Positive Affect," *Social Psychological and Personality Science* 5, no. 4 (2014): 437–42; Gillian M. Sandstrom and Erica J. Boothby, "Why Do People Avoid Talking to Strangers? A Mini Meta-Analysis of Predicted Fears and Actual Experiences Talking to a Stranger," *Self and Identity* 20, no. 1 (2021): 47–71; Nicholas Epley and Juliana Schroeder, "Mistakenly Seeking Solitude," *Journal of Experimental Psychology: General* 143, no. 5 (2014): 1980–99.

53. Josh Getlin, "Natural Wonder: At Heart, Edward Wilson's an Ant Man. But It's His Theories on Human Behavior That Stir Up Trouble," *Los Angeles Times*, October 21, 1994, https://www.latimes.com/archives/la-xpm-1994-10-21-ls-53158-story.html.

54. See, for instance, Thomas J. DiLorenzo, *The Problem with Socialism* (Washington, D.C.: Regnery Publishing, 2016) and Robert Lawson and Benjamin Powell, *Socialism*

Sucks: Two Economists Drink Their Way through the Unfree World (Washington, D.C.: Regnery Publishing, 2019).

55. Betsey Stevenson and Justin Wolfers, "The Paradox of Declining Female Happiness," *American Economic Journal: Economic Policy* 1, no. 2 (2009): 190–225.

56. Shawn Grover and John F. Helliwell, "How's Life at Home? New Evidence on Marriage and the Set Point for Happiness," *Journal of Happiness Studies* 20, no. 2 (2019): 373–90.

57. See chapter 7 of my book *The Parasitic Mind* (Washington, D.C.: Regnery Publishing, 2020), wherein I provide several lines of evidence in support of this universal fact.

58. Erika D. Smith, "Larry Elder Is the Black Face of White Supremacy. You've Been Warned," *Los Angeles Times*, August 20, 2021, https://www.latimes.com/california/story/2021-08-20/recall-candidate-larry-elder-is-a-threat-to-black-californians.

59. Kay S. Hymowitz, "The Black Family: 40 Years of Lies," *City Journal*, Summer 2005, https://www.city-journal.org/html/black-family-40-years-lies-12872.html.

60. Tim Lomas, "Positive Politics: Left-Wing versus Right-Wing Policies, and Their Impact on the Determinants of Wellbeing," in *The Routledge International Handbook of Critical Positive Psychology*, eds. Nicholas J. L. Brown, Tim Lomas, and Francisco Jose Eiroa-Orosa (New York: Routledge, 2018), 351–67; David B. Newman et al., "Conservatives Report Greater Meaning in Life Than Liberals," *Social Psychological and Personality Science* 10, no. 4 (2019): 494–503; Jaime L. Napier and John T. Jost, "Why Are Conservatives Happier Than Liberals?" *Psychological Science* 19, no. 6 (2008): 565–72; Adam Okulicz-Kozaryn, Oscar Holmes IV, and Derek R. Avery, "The Subjective Well-Being Political Paradox: Happy Welfare States and Unhappy Liberals," *Journal of Applied Psychology* 99, no. 6 (2014): 1300–1308; Benjamin Radcliff, "Politics, Markets, and Life Satisfaction: The Political Economy of Human Happiness," *American Political Science Review* 95, no. 4 (2001): 939–52; Olga Khazan, "Why Conservatives Find Life More Meaningful Than Liberals," *The Atlantic*, July 26, 2018, https://www.theatlantic.com/science/archive/2018/07/why-conservatives-find-life-more-meaningful-than-liberals/566105/.

61. Michael Savage (@ASavageNation), "Occasional-Cortex Caught Lying about Capital Riot Fears-CNN covers for her!" Twitter, February 5, 2021, 11:35 a.m., https://twitter.com/asavagenation/status/1357729488033882112?lang=en.

62. Gad Saad, in *A Better Life: 100 Atheists Speak Out on Joy and Meaning in a World without God*, ed. Christopher Johnson (New York: Cosmic Teapot, Inc., 2013), 88–89.

63. See Gad Saad, *The Evolutionary Bases of Consumption* (Mahwah, New Jersey: Lawrence Erlbaum, 2007), 211–14, and the references therein.

64. Gad Saad, *The Consuming Instinct: What Juicy Burgers, Ferraris, Pornography, and Gift Giving Reveal about Human Nature* (Amherst, New York: Prometheus Books, 2011), chapter 8.

65. Daniela Villani et al., "The Role of Spirituality and Religiosity in Subjective Well-Being of Individuals with Different Religious Status," *Frontiers in Psychology* 10 (2019): 1525, https://doi.org/10.3389/fpsyg.2019.01525; Christopher Alan Lewis and Sharon Mary Cruise, "Religion and Happiness: Consensus, Contradictions,

Comments and Concerns," *Mental Health, Religion & Culture* 9, no. 3 (2006): 213–25; Christopher Alan Lewis, John Maltby, and Sue Burkinshaw, "Religion and Happiness: Still No Association," *Journal of Beliefs & Values* 21, no. 2 (2000): 233–36; Liesbeth Snoep, "Religiousness and Happiness in Three Nations: A Research Note," *Journal of Happiness Studies* 9, no. 2 (2008): 207–11.

66. Michael Minkov, Christian Welzel, and Michael Schachner, "Cultural Evolution Shifts the Source of Happiness from Religion to Subjective Freedom," *Journal of Happiness Studies* 21, no. 8 (2020): 2873–88.

67. Mark D. Holder, Ben Coleman, and Judi M. Wallace, "Spirituality, Religiousness, and Happiness in Children Aged 8–12 Years," *Journal of Happiness Studies* 11, no. 2 (2010): 131–50.

Chapter Three: Key Life Decisions: The Right Life Partner and the Ideal Job

1. Bertrand Russell, *The Conquest of Happiness* (London, UK: George Allen & Unwin Ltd., 1932), 185.

2. Kenneth Tynan, "Fifteen Years of the Salto Mortale," *New Yorker*, February 20, 1978, https://www.newyorker.com/magazine/1978/02/20/fifteen-years-salto-mortale.

3. In my 2011 book *The Consuming Instinct*, I suggested the adage *I consume therefore I am.*

4. Christine M. Proulx, Heather M. Helms, and Cheryl Buehler, "Marital Quality and Personal Well-Being: A Meta-Analysis," *Journal of Marriage and Family* 69, no. 3 (2007): 576–93; Tom W. Smith, "Job Satisfaction in the United States," (working paper, NORC/University of Chicago, 2007), http://www-news.uchicago.edu/releases/07/pdf/070417.jobs.pdf; Jan-Emmanuel De Neve and the Workplace Well-Being Committee, "Work and Well-Being: A Global Perspective," chapter 5 in *Global Happiness Policy Report*, ed. Global Council for Happiness and Wellbeing (New York: Sustainable Development Solutions Network, 2018), 74–127.

5. Aliya Alimujiang et al., "Association between Life Purpose and Mortality among US Adults Older Than 50 Years," *JAMA Network Open* 2, no. 5 (2019), e194270, doi:10.1001/jamanetworkopen.2019.4270.

6. Barry Schwartz and Kenneth E. Sharpe, "Practical Wisdom: Aristotle Meets Positive Psychology," *Journal of Happiness Studies* 7, no. 3, (2006): 377–95.

7. Liz Mineo, "Good Genes Are Nice, but Joy Is Better," *Harvard Gazette*, April 11, 2017, https://news.harvard.edu/gazette/story/2017/04/over-nearly-80-years-harvard-study-has-been-showing-how-to-live-a-healthy-and-happy-life/.

8. As quoted in Alice Ghent, "The Happiness Effect," *Bulletin of the World Health Organization* 89, no. 4 (2011): 246–47.

9. TED, "Robert Waldinger: What Makes a Good Life? Lessons from the Longest Study on Happiness—TED," YouTube, January 25, 2016, https://www.youtube.com/watch?v=8KkKuTCFvzI&t=7s, 8:11–8:31.

10. Julianne Holt-Lunstad, Timothy B. Smith, and J. Bradley Layton, "Social Relationships and Mortality Risk: A Meta-Analytic Review," *PLOS Medicine* 7, no. 7 (2010), e1000316.

11. "Marriage and Couples," Gottman Institute, https://www.gottman.com/about/research/couples/.

12. Michael M. Roy and Nicholas J. S. Christenfeld, "Do Dogs Resemble Their Owners?" *Psychological Science* 15, no. 5 (2004): 361–63; Christina Payne and Klaus Jaffe, "Self Seeks Like: Many Humans Choose Their Dog Pets Following Rules Used for Assortative Mating," *Journal of Ethology* 23, no. 1 (2005): 15–18; Sadahiko Nakajima, Mariko Yamamoto, and Natsumi Yoshimoto, "Dogs Look Like Their Owners: Replications with Racially Homogenous Owner Portraits," *Anthrozoös* 22, no. 2 (2009): 173–81.

13. Borbála Turcsán et al., "Birds of a Feather Flock Together? Perceived Personality Matching in Owner-Dog Dyads," *Applied Animal Behaviour Science* 140, no. 3–4 (2012): 154–60.

14. M. Joseph Sirgy, "Self-Congruity Theory in Consumer Behavior: A Little History," *Journal of Global Scholars of Marketing Science* 28, no. 2 (2018): 197–207.

15. Georg W. Alpers and Antje B. M. Gerdes, "Another Look at 'Look-Alikes': Can Judges Match Belongings with Their Owners?" *Journal of Individual Differences* 27, no. 1 (2006): 38–41; Stefan Stieger and Martin Voracek, "Not Only Dogs Resemble Their Owners, Cars Do, Too," *Swish Journal of Psychology* 73, no. 2 (2014): 111–17.

16. Beth Vallen et al., "Shape- and Trait-Congruency: Using Appearance-Based Cues as a Basis for Product Recommendations," *Journal of Consumer Psychology* 29, no. 2 (2019): 271–84.

17. Shanhong Luo and Eva C. Klohnen, "Assortative Mating and Marital Quality in Newlyweds: A Couple-Centered Approach," *Journal of Personality and Social Psychology* 88, no. 2 (2005): 304–26; Shanghong Luo, "Assortative Mating and Couple Similarity: Patterns, Mechanisms, and Consequences," *Social and Personality Psychology Compass* 11, no. 8 (2017), https://doi.org/10.1111/spc3.12337; Ruth Gaunt, "Couple Similarity and Marital Satisfaction: Are Similar Spouses Happier?" *Journal of Personality* 74, no. 5 (2006): 1401–20.

18. The scientific findings have been equivocal, but there is some evidence that humans, via their sense of smell, can distinguish and have a preference for mates whose immunological profile augments their own for the protection of their offspring. Jan Havlíček and S. Craig Roberts, "MHC-Correlated Mate Choice in Humans: A Review," *Psychoneuroendocrinology* 34, no. 4 (2009): 497–512; Jan Havlíček, Jamie Winternitz, and S. Craig Roberts, "Major Histocompatibility Complex-Associated Odour Preferences and Human Mate Choice: Near and Far Horizons," *Philosophical Transactions of the Royal Society of London. Series B, Biological Sciences* 375, no. 1800 (2020), 20190260.

19. John E. Edlund and Brad J. Sagarin, "The Mate Value Scale," *Personality and Individual Differences* 64 (2014): 72–77; Daniel Conroy-Beam et al., "Assortative Mating and the Evolution of Desirability Covariation," *Evolution and Human Behavior* 40, no. 5 (2019): 479–91.

20. Helen E. Fisher, "Lust, Attraction, and Attachment in Mammalian Reproduction," *Human Nature* 9, no. 1 (1998): 23–52.

21. Mandy Erickson, "Setting Your Biological Clock, Reducing Stress While Sheltering in Place," *Scope* (blog), Stanford Medicine, June 3, 2020, https://scopeblog.stanford.edu/2020/06/03/setting-your-biological-clock-reducing-tress-while-sheltering-in-place/.

22. Jessica Wapner, "Vision and Breathing May Be the Secrets to Surviving 2020," *Scientific American*, November 16, 2020, https://www.scientificamerican.com/article/vision-and-breathing-may-be-the-secrets-to-surviving-2020/.

23. Gad Saad, "My Chat with Political Scientist Dr. Charles Murray (THE SAAD TRUTH_1322)," YouTube, October 20, 2021, https://youtu.be/YiQo1fQtv1U, 83:24–83:29.

24. Corinthians 13:4–8, New International Version, Bible Gateway, https://www.biblegateway.com/passage/?search=1%20Corinthians%2013%3A4-8&version=NIV.

25. Yohsuke Ohtsubo and Esuka Watanabe, "Do Sincere Apologies Need to Be Costly? Test of a Costly Signaling Model of Apology," *Evolution and Human Behavior* 30, no. 2 (2009): 114–23.

26. Gad Saad, "Suicide Triggers as Sex-Specific Threats in Domains of Evolutionary Import: Negative Correlation between Global Male-to-Female Suicide Ratios and Average per Capita Gross National Income," *Medical Hypotheses* 68, no. 3 (2007): 692–96.

27. "Global Study on Homicide," United Nations Office on Drugs and Crime, 2019, https://www.unodc.org/unodc/en/data-and-analysis/global-study-on-homicide.html; E. Ann Carson, "Prisoners in 2020—Statistical Tables," Bureau of Justice Statistics, December 2021, https://bjs.ojp.gov/content/pub/pdf/p20st.pdf, Table 1; *Data Matters* 1, United Nations Office on Drugs and Crime, 2021, https://www.unodc.org/documents/data-and-analysis/statistics/DataMatters1_prison.pdf; "Demographic Data Project," National Alliance to End Homelessness, https://endhomelessness.org/demographic-data-project-gender-and-individual-homelessness/.

28. Thor Norström and Hans Grönqvist, "The Great Recession, Unemployment and Suicide," *Journal of Epidemiology & Community Health* 69, no. 2 (2014): 110–16.

29. David G. Blanchflower et al., "The Happiness Trade-Off between Unemployment and Inflation," *Journal of Money, Credit and Banking* 46, no. S2 (2014): 117–41.

30. Jamie Chamberlin, "Retiring Minds Want to Know," *Monitor on Psychology* 45, no. 1 (January 2014), https://www.apa.org/monitor/2014/01/retiring-minds.

31. Yitzhak Fried and Gerald R. Ferris, "The Validity of the Job Characteristics Model: A Review and Meta-Analysis," *Personnel Psychology* 40, no. 2 (1987): 287–322; Stephen E. Humphrey, Jennifer D. Nahrgang, and Frederick P. Morgeson, "Integrating Motivational, Social, and Contextual Work Design Features: A Meta-Analytic Summary and Theoretical Extension of the Work Design Literature," *Journal of Applied Psychology* 92, no. 5 (2007): 1332–56.

32. Robert Karasek et al., "Job Decision Latitude, Job Demands, and Cardiovascular Disease: A Prospective Study of Swedish Men," *American Journal of Public Health* 71, no. 7 (1981): 694–705.

33. Yamna Taouk et al., "Psychosocial Work Stressors and Risk of All-Cause and Coronary Heart Disease Mortality: A Systematic Review and Meta-Analysis," *Scandinavian Journal of Work, Environment & Health* 46, no. 1 (2020): 19–31.

34. Michael Marmot, *The Status Syndrome: How Social Standing Affects Our Health and Longevity* (New York: Henry Holt, 2004).

35. Andrew Steptoe, Jane Wardle, and Michael Marmot, "Positive Affect and Health-Related Neuroendocrine, Cardiovascular, and Inflammatory Processes," *Proceedings of the National Academy of Sciences of the United States of America* 102, no. 18 (2005): 6508–12; Wolff Schlotz et al., "Perceived Work Overload and Chronic Worrying Predict Weekend-Weekday Differences in the Cortisol Awakening Response," *Psychosomatic Medicine* 66, no. 2 (2004): 207–14.

36. Peter L. Schnall and Paul A. Landsbergis, "Job Strain and Cardiovascular Disease," *Annual Review of Public Health* 15 (1994): 381–411; Md Omar Faruque et al., "Psychosocial Work Factors and Blood Pressure among 63,800 Employees from the Netherlands in the Lifelines Cohort Study," *Journal of Epidemiology & Community Health* 76, no. 1 (2022): 60–66, doi:10.1136/jech-2021-216678; Sohrab Amiri and Sepideh Behnezhad, "Job Strain and Mortality Ratio: A Systematic Review and Meta-Analysis of Cohort Studies," *Public Health* 181 (2020): 24–33.

37. Paul B. Lester et al., "Happy Soldiers Are Highest Performers," *Journal of Happiness Studies* 23, no. 3 (2022): 1099–1120.

38. Mika Kivimäki et al., "Justice at Work and Reduced Risk of Coronary Heart Disease among Employees: The Whitehall II Study," *Archives of Internal Medicine* 165, no. 19 (2005): 2245–51.

39. Gad Saad, "Two Paths to Immortality, Neither of Which Requires Religion: Ways to Be Immortal without the Help of God," *Psychology Today*, May 31, 2010, https://www.psychologytoday.com/ca/blog/homo-consumericus/201005/two-paths-immortality-neither-which-requires-religion.

40. It should be mentioned that even those who hate their jobs can become workaholics. Often work is an escape from other unhappy circumstances in their lives.

Chapter Four: The Sweet Spot: All Good Things in Moderation

1. Daniel M. Fatovich, "The Inverted U Curve and Emergency Medicine: Overdiagnosis and the Law of Unintended Consequences," abstract, *Emergency Medicine Australasia* 28, no. 4 (2016): 480–82.

2. Evangelos Markopoulos and Hannu Vanharanta, *The Company Democracy Model: Creating Innovative Democratic Work Cultures for Effective Organizational Knowledge-Based Management and Leadership* (New York: Routledge, 2022), Table 2.1.

3. Maimonides, "De'ot—Chapter One," trans. Eliyahu Touger, Chabad, https://www.chabad.org/library/article_cdo/aid/910340/jewish/Deot-Chapter-One.htm.

4. Benoit B. Mandelbrot, *The Fractal Geometry of Nature* (San Francisco: W. H. Freeman, 1982); Nikk Ogasa, "How Romanesco Cauliflower Forms Its Spiraling

Fractals," *Science News*, July 8, 2021, https://www.sciencenews.org/article/romanesco-cauliflower-fractal-spiral-genetics-biology; "Fractal Geometry," IBM, https://www.ibm.com/ibm/history/ibm100/us/en/icons/fractal/.

5. Edward O. Wilson, *Consilience: The Unity of Knowledge* (London: Abacus, 1998).

6. Tommie W. Singleton, "Understanding and Applying Benford's Law," *ISACA Journal* (May 1, 2011), https://www.isaca.org/resources/isaca-journal/past-issues/2011/understanding-and-applying-benfords-law; Steven J. Miller, ed., *Benford's Law: Theory & Applications* (Princeton, New Jersey: Princeton University Press, 2015).

7. I learned of this example from the *Connected* Netflix series hosted by Latif Nasser.

8. Ana Bajželj, "Middle Way (Buddhism)," *Buddhism and Jainism*, in *Encyclopedia of Indian Religions*, eds. K. T. S. Sarao and Jeffrey Long (Dordrecht, Netherlands: Springer, 2017), https://doi.org/10.1007/978-94-024-0852-2_280.

9. James Legge, *The Life and Teachings of Confucius with Explanatory Notes*, 6th ed. (London: Trübner & Co., 1887), 285.

10. Aurelian Craiutu, *A Virtue for Courageous Minds: Moderation in French Political Thought, 1748–1830* (Princeton, New Jersey: Princeton University Press, 2012).

11. Amy Muise, Ulrich Schimmack, and Emily A. Impett, "Sexual Frequency Predicts Greater Well-Being, but More Is Not Always Better," *Social Psychological and Personality Science* 7, no. 4 (2016): 295–302.

12. Ronald A. Cohen, "Yerkes–Dodson Law," in *Encyclopedia of Clinical Neuropsychology*, eds. Jeffrey S. Kreutzer, John DeLuca, and Bruce Caplan (New York: Springer, 2011), https://doi.org/10.1007/978-0-387-79948-3_1340.

13. Yun Jun Yang, "An Overview of Current Physical Activity Recommendations in Primary Care," *Korean Journal of Family Medicine* 40, no. 3 (2019): 135–42.

14. Peter Warr, "Happiness and Mental Health: A Framework of Vitamins in the Environment and Mental Processes in the Person," in *The Handbook of Stress and Health: A Guide to Research and Practice*, eds. Cary L. Cooper and James Campbell Quick (Malden, Massachusetts: John Wiley & Sons Ltd., 2017), 57–74.

15. Edward J. Calabrese and Linda A. Baldwin, "U-Shaped Dose-Responses in Biology, Toxicology, and Public Health," *Annual Review of Public Health* 22 (2001): 15–33; Edward J. Calabrese and Linda A. Baldwin, "The Frequency of U-Shaped Dose Responses in the Toxicological Literature," *Toxicological Sciences* 62, no. 2 (2001): 330–38.

16. Stanford, "1. Introduction to Human Behavioral Biology," YouTube, February 1, 2011, https://www.youtube.com/watch?v=NNnIGh9g6fA&list=PLD7E21BF91F3F9683&index=1. [The first of his 25-part lecture series.]

17. Robert M. Sapolsky, "Stress and the Brain: Individual Variability and the Inverted-U," *Nature Neuroscience* 18, no. 10 (2015): 1344–46.

18. Biyu J. He and John M. Zempel, "Average Is Optimal: An Inverted-U Relationship between Trial-to-Trial Brain Activity and Behavioral Performance," *PLOS Computational Biology* 9, no. 11 (2013), e1003348, doi:10.1371/journal.pcbi.1003348; Elisabetta Baldi and Corrado Bucherelli, "The Inverted 'U-Shaped' Dose-Effect Relationships in Learning and Memory: Modulation of Arousal and Consolidation," *Nonlinearity in Biology, Toxicology, and Medicine* 3, no. 1 (2005):

9–21; Roshan Cools and Mark D'Esposito, "Inverted-U Shaped Dopamine Actions on Human Working Memory and Cognitive Control," *Biological Psychiatry* 69, no. 12 (2011): e113–e125; Georg Northoff and Shankar Tumati, "'Average Is Good, Extremes Are Bad'—Non-Linear Inverted U-Shaped Relationship between Neural Mechanisms and Functionality of Mental Features," *Neuroscience & Biobehavioral Reviews* 104 (2019): 11–25.

19. Anna Abraham, "Is There an Inverted-U Relationship between Creativity and Psychopathology?" *Frontiers in Psychology* 5, no. 750 (2014), https://doi.org/10.3389/fpsyg.2014.00750.

20. Remy M. J. P. Rikers, Henk G. Schmidt, and Henny P. A. Boshuizen, "Knowledge Encapsulation and the Intermediate Effect," *Contemporary Educational Psychology* 25, no. 2 (2000): 150–66.

21. Matthew E. Falagas, Vrettos Ierodiakonou, and Vangelis G. Alexiou, "At What Age Do Biomedical Scientists Do Their Best Work?" *The FASEB Journal* 22, no. 12 (2008): 4067–70.

22. Bobby J. Calder and Brian Sternthal, "Television Commercial Wearout: An Information Processing View," *Journal of Marketing Research* 17, no. 2 (1980): 173–86; Susanne Schmidt and Martin Eisend, "Advertising Repetition: A Meta-Analysis on Effective Frequency in Advertising," *Journal of Advertising* 44, no. 4 (2015): 415–28.

23. Xi Lu, Xiaofei Xie, and Lu Liu, "Inverted U-Shaped Model: How Frequent Repetition Affects Perceived Risk," *Judgment and Decision Making* 10, no. 3 (2015): 219–24.

24. James Price Dillard et al., "Fear Responses to Threat Appeals: Functional Form, Methodological Considerations, and Correspondence between Static and Dynamic Data," *Communication Research* 44, no. 7 (2017): 997–1018; James Price Dillard, Ruobing Li, and Yan Huang, "Threat Appeals: The Fear-Persuasion Relationship Is Linear and Curvilinear," *Health Communication* 32, no. 11 (2017): 1358–67. For a counter view regarding the inverted-U curve and fear appeals see Shu Scott Li and James Price Dillard, "Everything in Moderation? Not for Threat Appeals," Society for Personality and Social Psychology, June 18, 2021, https://www.spsp.org/news-center/blog/li-dillard-threat-appeals.

25. Adam M. Grant and Barry Schwartz, "Too Much of a Good Thing: The Challenge and Opportunity of the Inverted U," *Perspectives on Psychological Science* 6, no. 1 (2011): 61–76.

26. Willoughby B. Britton, "Can Mindfulness Be Too Much of a Good Thing? The Value of a Middle Way," *Current Opinion in Psychology* 28 (2019): 159–65.

27. Stephanie Tom Tong et al., "Too Much of a Good Thing? The Relationship between Number of Friends and Interpersonal Impressions on Facebook," *Journal of Computer-Mediated Communication* 13, no. 3 (2008): 531–49.

28. Anthony Chmiel and Emery Schubert, "Back to the Inverted-U for Music Preference: A Review of the Literature," *Psychology of Music* 45, no. 6 (2017): 886–909.

29. Gad Saad, "My Chat with Professor Amy Chua, Tiger Mom Extraordinaire (THE SAAD TRUTH_1320)," YouTube, October 18, 2021, https://youtu.be/1I2YLia09Hg.

30. Lawrence A. Kurdek, Mark A. Fine, and Ronald J. Sinclair, "School Adjustment in Sixth Graders: Parenting Transitions, Family Climate, and Peer Norm Effects," *Child Development* 66, no. 2 (1995): 430–45, 439, Figure 1.

31. Simon Kuznets, "Economic Growth and Income Inequality," *The American Economic Review* 45, no. 1 (1955): 1–28; John Thornton, "The Kuznets Inverted-U Hypothesis: Panel Data Evidence from 96 Countries," *Applied Economics Letters* 8, no. 1 (2001): 15–16.

32. Zonghuo Yu and Fei Wang, "Income Inequality and Happiness: An Inverted U-Shaped Curve," *Frontiers in Psychology* 8, no. 2052 (2017), doi: 10.3389/fpsyg.2017.02052.

33. Soumyananda Dinda, "Environmental Kuznets Curve Hypothesis: A Survey," *Ecological Economics* 49, no. 4 (2004): 431–55.

34. Philippe Aghion et al., "Competition and Innovation: An Inverted-U Relationship," *Quarterly Journal of Economics* 120, no. 2 (2005): 701–28.

35. Yuichi Furukawa, "Intellectual Property Protection and Innovation: An Inverted-U Relationship," *Economics Letters* 109, no. 2 (2010): 99–101; Nikolaos Papageorgiadis and Abhijit Sharma, "Intellectual Property Rights and Innovation: A Panel Analysis," *Economics Letters* 141 (April 2016): 70–72.

36. Aleksandra Cichocka et al., "What Inverted U Can Do for Your Country: A Curvilinear Relationship between Confidence in the Social System and Political Engagement," *Journal of Personality and Social Psychology* 115, no. 5 (2018): 883–902.

37. Janet L. Gamble and Jeremy J. Hess, "Temperature and Violent Crime in Dallas, Texas: Relationships and Implications of Climate Change," *Western Journal of Emergency Medicine* 13, no. 3 (2012): 239–46.

38. Margaret A. Allen and Gloria J. Fischer, "Ambient Temperature Effects on Paired Associated Learning," *Ergonomics* 21, no. 2 (1978): 95–101.

39. The ensuing four stages of corporate responsibility were originally discussed in this article: Gad Saad, "The Evolving Role of Corporate Responsibility over the Past Century," *Arabian Business*, March 29, 2021, https://www.arabianbusiness.com/spotlight/461046-the-evolving-role-of-corporate-responsibility-over-the-past-century.

40. Sanja Pekovic, Gilles Grolleau, and Naoufel Mzoughi, "Environmental Investments: Too Much of a Good Thing?" *International Journal of Production Economics* 197 (2018): 297–302; Hidemichi Fujii et al., "Corporate Environmental and Economic Performance of Japanese Manufacturing Firms: Empirical Study for Sustainable Development," *Business Strategy and the Environment* 22, no. 3 (2013): 187–201.

41. James Anthony, "Get Woke, Go Broke: Disney Revenue Plummets after Woke Corporate Culture Revealed," The Post Millennial, May 14, 2021, https://thepostmillennial.com/get-woke-go-broke-disney-revenues-plummet-after-woke-corporate-culture-revealed; Jessica Guynn, "Why Elon Musk Believes 'Woke Mind Virus' and 'Wokeness' Are Threats to Modern Civilization," *USA Today*, April 20, 2022, https://www.usatoday.com/story/money/2022/04/20/elon-musk-woke-mind-virus-netflix/7388590001/.

42. Vincent Harinam, "Is Woke Capitalism Profitable?" Quillette, July 21, 2020, https://quillette.com/2020/07/21/is-woke-capitalism-profitable/.

43. Jason R. Pierce and Herman Aguinis, "The Too-Much-of-a-Good-Thing Effect in Management," *Journal of Management* 39, no. 2 (2013): 313–38. Please also see the relevant references cited in the article in question in support of the various inverted-U effects.

44. See also Huy Le et al., "Too Much of a Good Thing: Curvilinear Relationships between Personality Traits and Job Performance," *Journal of Applied Psychology* 96, no. 1 (2011): 113–33.

45. Sebastian E. Baumeister et al., "Alcohol Consumption and Cardiorespiratory Fitness in Five Population-Based Studies," *European Society of Cardiology* 25, no. 2 (2018): 164–72; Johannes T. Neumann et al., "Alcohol Consumption and Risks of Cardiovascular Disease and All-Cause Mortality in Healthy Older Adults," *European Journal of Preventive Cardiology* 29, no. 6 (2022): e230–e232, doi:10.1093/eurjpc/zwab177; J. Bruce German and Rosemary L. Walzem, "The Health Benefits of Wine," *Annual Review of Nutrition* 20 (2000): 561–93.

46. Renate Helena Maria de Groot, Carolijn W. I. Ouwehand, and Jelle Jolles, "Eating the Right Amount of Fish: Inverted U-Shape Association between Fish Consumption and Cognitive Performance and Academic Achievement in Dutch Adolescents," *Prostaglandins, Leukotrienes and Essential Fatty Acids* 86, no. 3 (2012): 113–17.

47. Kaili Yang et al., "Association of the Frequency of Spicy Food Intake and the Risk of Abdominal Obesity in Rural Chinese Adults: A Cross-Sectional Study," *BMJ Open* 9, no. 11 (2019), e028736, doi:10.1136/bmjopen-2018-028736.

48. Avni M. Shah and George Wolford, "Buying Behavior as a Function of Parametric Variation of Number of Choices," *Psychological Science* 18, no. 5 (2007): 369–70; Erika A. Patall, Harris Cooper, and Jorgianne Civey Robinson, "The Effects of Choice on Intrinsic Motivation and Related Outcomes: A Meta-Analysis of Research Findings," *Psychological Bulletin* 134, no. 2 (2008): 270–300. The following two meta-analyses examined choice overload, the first of which did not document a significant effect whereas the second explored moderators of choice overload. Benjamin Scheibehenne, Rainer Greifeneder, and Peter M. Todd, "Can There Ever Be Too Many Options? A Meta-Analytic Review of Choice Overload," *Journal of Consumer Research* 37, no. 3 (2010): 409–25; Alexander Chernev, Ulf Böckenholt, and Joseph Goodman, "Choice Overload: A Conceptual Review and Meta-Analysis," *Journal of Consumer Psychology* 25, no. 2 (2015): 333–58; Yoel Inbar, Simona Botti, and Karlene Hanko, "Decision Speed and Choice Regret: When Haste Feels Like Waste," *Journal of Experimental Social Psychology* 47, no. 3 (2011): 533–40.

49. Sheena S. Iyengar and Mark R. Lepper, "When Choice Is Demotivating: Can One Desire Too Much of a Good Thing?" *Journal of Personality and Social Psychology* 79, no. 6 (2000): 995–1006.

50. Rémi Desmeules, "The Impact of Variety on Consumer Happiness: Marketing and the Tyranny of Freedom," *Academy of Marketing Science Review* 12, no. 1 (2002): 1–18, 10, Figure 2.

51. Hilke Brockmann and Jan Delhey, eds., *Human Happiness and the Pursuit of Maximization: Is More Always Better?* (Heidelberg, Germany: Springer, 2013).

52. Shigehiro Oishi, Ed Diener, and Richard E. Lucas, "The Optimum Level of Well-Being: Can People Be Too Happy?" *Perspectives on Psychological Science* 2, no. 4 (2007): 346–60.

53. June Gruber, Iris B. Mauss, and Maya Tamir, "A Dark Side of Happiness? How, When, and Why Happiness Is Not Always Good," *Perspectives on Psychological Science* 6, no. 3 (2011): 222–33.

54. F. H. Peters, trans., *The Nichomachean Ethics of Aristotle*, 10th ed. (London: Kegan Paul, Trench, Trübner & Co., 1906), 46.

55. Aimee Drolet et al., "The Preference for Moderation Scale," *Journal of Consumer Research* 47, no. 6 (2021): 831–54.

Chapter Five: Life as a Playground

1. Stuart Brown with Christopher Vaughn, *Play: How It Shapes the Brain, Opens the Imagination, and Invigorates the Soul* (New York: Penguin, 2009), 5.

2. "Oreo: Stay Playful by the Martin Agency," The Drum, February 2019, https://www.thedrum.com/creative-works/project/the-martin-agency-oreo-stay-playful.

3. From his 1908 essay titled "Oxford from Without," in the book *All Things Considered*, 9th ed. (London: Methuen, 1915). See https://www.gutenberg.org/files/11505/11505-h/11505-h.htm#OXFORD_FROM_WITHOUT.

4. "Play Quotes," The Strong National Museum of Play, https://www.museumofplay.org/about/play-quotes/.

5. Carl G. Jung, *Psychological Types* (New York: Routledge Classics, 2016; originally published 1921), 112; David Elkind, "The Power of Play: Learning What Comes Naturally," *American Journal of Play* 1, no. 1 (2008): 1–6, 1.

6. Charalampos Mainemelis and Sarah Ronson, "Ideas Are Born in Fields of Play: Towards a Theory of Play and Creativity in Organizational Settings," *Research in Organizational Behavior* 27 (2006): 81–131; Claire Aislinn Petelczyc et al., "Play at Work: An Integrative Review and Agenda for Future Research," *Journal of Management* 44, no. 1 (2018): 161–90.

7. Henry Ford with Samuel Crowther, *My Life and Work* (New York: Doubleday, Page & Company, 1922), chapter 6, available at https://www.gutenberg.org/cache/epub/7213/pg7213.html.

8. For relevant references regarding the proximate-ultimate distinction, see Gad Saad, "On the Method of Evolutionary Psychology and Its Applicability to Consumer Research," *Journal of Marketing Research* 54, no. 3 (2017), 465.

9. For relevant references regarding the adaptive roots of pregnancy sickness, see ibid., 466.

10. Peter Gray, "Evolutionary Functions of Play: Practice, Resilience, Innovation, and Cooperation," in *The Cambridge Handbook of Play: Developmental and Disciplinary Perspectives*, eds. Peter K. Smith and Jaipaul L. Roopnarine (Cambridge, UK: Cambridge University Press, 2019), 84–102. For other evolutionary-based analyses of play, please see: Peter K. Smith, "Does Play Matter? Functional and Evolutionary Aspects of Animal and Human Play," *Behavioral and Brain Sciences* 5, no. 1 (1982): 139–55; Anthony D. Pellegrini, Danielle Dupuis, and Peter K. Smith, "Play in Evolution and Development," *Developmental Review* 27, no. 2 (2007):

261–76; Rohit Mehta et al., "'Let Children Play!': Connecting Evolutionary Psychology and Creativity with Peter Gray," *TechTrends* 64, no. 5 (2020): 684–89; Peter LaFreniere, "Evolutionary Functions of Social Play: Life Histories, Sex Differences, and Emotion Regulation," *American Journal of Play* 3, no. 4 (2011): 464–88; Paul E. Smaldino et al., "The Evolution of Two Types of Play," *Behavioral Ecology* 30, no. 5 (2019): 1388–97.

11. Daniel Feldman, "Children's Play in the Shadow of War," *American Journal of Play* 11, no. 3 (2019): 288–307.

12. Ellipsis in the original. Ibid., 293.

13. Roger Diwan (@RogerDiwan), "really, shame on you. how low can you go?" Twitter, March 1, 2022, 5:42 p.m., https://twitter.com/RogerDiwan/status/1498790765018 898440?s=20&t=qsfoCPdECekTNwJ_QoN_Lw.

14. Cindy Dell Clark, "A Clown Most Serious: Patch Adams," *International Journal of Play* 2, no. 3 (2013): 163–73.

15. George Eisen, *Children and Play in the Holocaust: Games among the Shadows* (Amherst, Massachusetts: University of Massachusetts Press, 1990).

16. Sue C. Bratton et al., "The Efficacy of Play Therapy with Children: A Meta-Analytic Review of Treatment Outcomes,"*Professional Psychology: Research and Practice* 36, no 4 (2005): 376–90.

17. Michael Yogman et al., "The Power of Play: A Pediatric Role in Enhancing Development in Young Children," *Pediatrics* 142, no. 3 (2018): 1–17.

18. Jamie Ahloy-Dallaire, Julia Espinosa, and Georgia Mason, "Play and Optimal Welfare: Does Play Indicate the Presence of Positive Affective States?" *Behavioural Processes* 156 (November 2018): 3–15; Sanne L. Nijhof et al., "Healthy Play, Better Coping: The Importance of Play for the Development of Children in Health and Disease," *Neuroscience & Biobehavioral Reviews* 95 (December 2018): 421–29; David Elkind, *The Power of Play: Learning What Comes Naturally* (Philadelphia, Pennsylvania: Da Capo Press, 2007).

19. Rene T. Proyer, "The Well-Being of Playful Adults: Adult Playfulness, Subjective Well-Being, Physical Well-Being, and the Pursuit of Enjoyable Activities," *European Journal of Humour Research* 1, no. 1 (2013): 84–98.

20. Nansook Park, Christopher Peterson, and Martin E. P. Seligman, "Strengths of Character and Well-Being," *Journal of Social and Clinical Psychology* 23, no. 5 (2004): 603–19.

21. Gad Saad, "My Thoughts on Dave Chappelle (THE SAAD TRUTH_1319)," YouTube, October 16, 2021, https://youtu.be/eLeKnY6WOUc.

22. Srdja Popovic and Mladen Joksic, "Why Dictators Don't Like Jokes," *Foreign Policy*, April 5, 2013, https://foreignpolicy.com/2013/04/05/why-dictators-dont-like-jokes/.

23. Gad Saad, "My Chat with Megyn Kelly (THE SAAD TRUTH_1301)," YouTube, September 27, 2021, https://youtu.be/Hs33J3XNJDc.

24. Gad Saad, "My Apology Letter Regarding My Friendship with Jordan Peterson (THE SAAD TRUTH_1365)," YouTube, January 19, 2022, https://youtu.be/ wsoqH2oPK3o. See also Gad Saad, "I Self-Flagellate Therefore I Am—I Apologize for Everything (THE SAAD TRUTH_1376)," YouTube, February 4, 2022, https:// youtu.be/hSvb5mLGl7E.

25. Gad Saad, "Tell My Wife That I Love Her (THE SAAD TRUTH_343)," YouTube, January 20, 2017, https://youtu.be/LquFudV-nLA.

26. Joseph O. Polimeni and Jeffrey P. Reiss, "The First Joke: Exploring the Evolutionary Origins of Humor," *Evolutionary Psychology* 4, no. 1 (2006): 347–66; Matthew Gervais and David Sloan Wilson, "The Evolution and Functions of Laughter and Humor: A Synthetic Approach," *Quarterly Review of Biology* 80, no. 4 (2005): 395–430.

27. Brandon M. Savage et al., "Humor, Laughter, Learning, and Health! A Brief Review," *Advances in Physiology Education* 41, no. 3 (2017): 341–47; JongEun Yim, "Therapeutic Benefits of Laughter in Mental Health: A Theoretical Review," *Tohoku Journal of Experimental Medicine* 239, no. 3 (2016): 243–49.

28. Solfrid Romundstad et al., "A 15-Year Follow-Up Study of Sense of Humor and Causes of Mortality: The Nord-Trøndelag Health Study," *Psychosomatic Medicine* 78, no. 3 (2016): 345–53.

29. Neza Stiglic and Russell M. Viner, "Effects of Screentime on the Health and Well-Being of Children and Adolescents: A Systematic Review of Reviews," *BMJ Open* 9, no. 1 (2019): e023191, doi:10.1136/bmjopen-2018-023191.

30. Richard Louv, *Last Child in the Woods: Saving Our Children from Nature-Deficit Disorder* (Chapel Hill, North Carolina: Algonquin Books, 2005).

31. See, for example, Elizabeth K. Nisbet, John M. Zelenski, and Steven A. Murphy, "Happiness Is in Our Nature: Exploring Nature Relatedness as a Contributor to Subjective Well-Being," *Journal of Happiness Studies* 12, no. 2 (2011): 303–22, and relevant references therein.

32. Edward O. Wilson, *Biophilia* (Cambridge, Massachusetts: Harvard University Press, 1986); Bjørn Grinde and Grete Grindal Patil, "Biophilia: Does Visual Contact with Nature Impact on Health and Well-Being?" *International Journal of Environmental Research and Public Health* 6, no. 9 (2009): 2332–43.

33. Roger S. Ulrich, "View through a Window May Influence Recovery from Surgery," *Science* 224, no. 4647 (1984): 420–21. For a review of the effects of optimal design choices in healthcare settings, see Roger S. Ulrich et al., "A Review of the Research Literature on Evidenced-Based Healthcare Design," *HERD: Health Environments Research & Design Journal* 1, no. 3 (2008): 61–125.

34. Won Sop Shin, "The Influence of Forest View through a Window on Job Satisfaction and Job Stress," *Scandinavian Journal of Forest Research* 22, no. 3 (2007): 248–53.

35. Friedrich Nietzsche, *Twilight of the Idols: Or, How to Philosophize with the Hammer*, trans. Richard Polt (Indianapolis: Hackett Publishing, 1997), 10.

36. Marily Oppezzo and Daniel L. Schwartz, "Give Your Ideas Some Legs: The Positive Effect of Walking on Creative Thinking," *Journal of Experimental Psychology: Learning, Memory, and Cognition* 40, no. 4 (2014): 1142–52.

37. Jim Holt, "Time Bandits: What Were Einstein and Gödel Talking About?" *New Yorker*, February 20, 2005, https://www.newyorker.com/magazine/2005/02/28/time-bandits-2.

38. Baba Brinkman, "I'm A African—Baba Brinkman—Rap Guide to Evolution Music Videos," YouTube, February 8, 2012, https://www.youtube.com/watch?v=G6r6POHC8zg.

39. Linda Rosa et al., "A Close Look at Therapeutic Touch," *JAMA* 279, no. 13 (1998): 1005–10.

40. Gad Saad, "My Chat with Darren Dahl, Co-Editor of the Journal of Consumer Research (THE SAAD TRUTH_149)," YouTube, March 26, 2016, https://youtu.be/ti_BRx8f2Fw.

41. Elina Halonen, "Darren Dahl Presidential Address—SCP Annual Conference 2014," YouTube, March 27, 2014, https://www.youtube.com/watch?v=fYN7N-GdmEk.

42. Pierre Laszlo, "Macroscope: Science as Play," *American Scientist* 92, no. 5 (2004): 398.

43. Ibid., 400.

44. P. S. Blackawton et al., "Blackawton Bees," *Biology Letters* 7, no. 2 (2011), 168.

45. Chester Raymo, "Science as Play," *Science Education* 57, no. 3 (1973), 280.

46. Ibid., 288.

47. Nick Butler and Sverre Spoelstra, "Academics at Play: Why the 'Publication Game' Is More than a Metaphor," *Management Learning* 51, no. 4 (2020): 414–30.

48. Johan Huizinga, *Homo Ludens: A Study of the Play-Element in Culture* (London, UK: Routledge & Kegan Paul, 1980), originally printed in Dutch in 1938.

49. Murray S. Davis, "That's Interesting! Towards a Phenomenology of Sociology and a Sociology of Phenomenology," *Philosophy of Social Science* 1, no. 2 (1971): 309–44.

50. Cara Ocobock et al., "Organized Adult Play and Stress Reduction: Testing the Absorption Hypothesis in a Comedy Improv Theater," *Adaptive Human Behavior and Physiology* 6, no. 4 (2020): 436–46.

51. Garry Chick et al., "Do Birds of a Playful Feather Flock Together? Playfulness and Assortative Mating," *American Journal of Play* 12, no. 2 (2021): 178–215; Kay Brauer, René T. Proyer, and Garry Chick, "Adult Playfulness: An Update on an Understudied Individual Differences Variable and Its Role in Romantic Life," *Social and Personality Psychology Compass* 15, no. 4 (2021): e12589.

52. Gad Saad (@GadSaad), "Me to my wife: 'Come see this gorgeous body . . . ,'" Twitter, April 12, 2021, 11:23 a.m., https://twitter.com/GadSaad/status/1381629149631111169?s=20.

53. Glenn E. Weisfeld et al., "Do Women Seek Humorousness in Men Because It Signals Intelligence? A Cross-Cultural Test," *Humor* 24, no. 4 (2011): 435–62.

54. Jeffrey A. Hall, "Humor in Romantic Relationships: A Meta-Analysis," *Personal Relationships* 24, no. 2 (2017): 306–22.

55. Geoffrey F. Miller, *The Mating Mind: How Sexual Choice Shaped the Evolution of Human Nature* (New York: Doubleday, 2000); Jeffrey A. Hall, "Sexual Selection and Humor in Courtship: A Case for Warmth and Extroversion," *Evolutionary Psychology* 13, no. 3 (2015), https://doi.org/10.1177/1474704915598918; Eric R. Bressler, Rod A. Martin, and Sigal Balshine, "Production and Appreciation of Humor as Sexually Selected Traits," *Evolution and Human Behavior* 27, no. 2 (2006): 121–30.

56. For an example, see Gad Saad, "My wife and daughter went to an all-girl 5km mud race . . . ," Twitter, September 19, 2021, 11:00 a.m., https://twitter.com/GadSaad/status/1439605247018782731?s=20.

57. Gad Saad, "Rapid-Fire Poetry in the Saad Household (THE SAAD TRUTH_1034)," YouTube, April 14, 2020, https://youtu.be/-tM73qjxdKs.

58. While it is likely that the agents were from the Mossad, they could have also been from Shin Bet (internal security service). That said, given that I'm an Arabic-speaking Jew, it is not difficult to imagine that this was likely a testing ground to see whether I would eventually be a worthy Mossad agent (given my background).

59. Federica Pirrone and Mariangela Albertini, "Olfactory Detection of Cancer by Trained Sniffer Dogs: A Systematic Review of the Literature," *Journal of Veterinary Behavior* 19 (May–June 2017): 105–17.

60. See references in Kaitlyn Arford, "10 Science-Based Benefits of Having a Dog," American Kennel Club, October 20, 2020, https://www.akc.org/expert-advice/lifestyle/10-science-based-benefits-dog; see also Katherine Jacobs Bao and George Schreer, "Pets and Happiness: Examining the Association between Pet Ownership and Well-Being," *Anthrozoös* 29, no. 2 (2016): 283–96; Lauren Powell et al., "Companion Dog Acquisition and Mental Well-Being: A Community-Based Three-Arm Controlled Study," *BMC Public Health* 19, no. 1 (2019): 1428, https://doi.org/10.1186/s12889-019-7770-5.

61. Rebecca Sommerville, Emily A. O'Connor, and Lucy Asher, "Why Do Dogs Play? Function and Welfare Implications of Play in the Domestic Dog," *Applied Animal Behaviour Science* 197 (December 2017): 1–8.

62. Michael W. White et al., "Give a Dog a Bone: Spending Money on Pets Promotes Happiness," *Journal of Positive Psychology* 17, no. 4 (2022): 589–95, https://doi.org/10.1080/17439760.2021.1897871.

Chapter Six: Variety as the Spice of Life (Sometimes)

1. Darius Lyman, *The Moral Sayings of Publius Syrus, a Roman Slave: From the Latin* (Boston: L. E. Barnard & Company, 1856), 40, Maxim 406.

2. James Wood, *Dictionary of Quotations: From Ancient and Modern, English and Foreign Sources* (London: Frederick Warne and Co., 1899), 380.

3. Eddie Deezen, "The Sexual Prowess of Wilt Chamberlain: 20,000 Women?" *The Atlantic*, August 22, 2012, https://www.theatlantic.com/health/archive/2012/08/the-sexual-prowess-of-wilt-chamberlain-20-000-women/261429/.

4. Bertrand Russell, *The Conquest of Happiness* (London: George Allen & Unwin Ltd., 1932), 157.

5. Barbara E. Kahn and Hoori Rafieian, "More Than Just the Spice of Life: Using Variety as a Signal for Change and Diversification," *Consumer Psychology Review* 5, no. 1 (2022): 87–106. For a recent summary of the variety-seeking literature in consumer behavior, see Yuan Zhang, "Variety-Seeking Behavior in Consumption: A Literature Review and Future Research Directions," *Frontiers in Psychology* 13 (2022), doi:10.3389/fpsyg.2022.874444.

6. Kennon M. Sheldon, Julia Boehm, and Sonja Luybomirsky, "Variety Is the Spice of Happiness. The Hedonic Adaptation Prevention Model," in *The Oxford Handbook*

of Happiness, eds. Ilona Boniwell, Susan A. David, and Amanda Conley Ayers (Oxford, UK: Oxford University Press, 2013), 901–14.

7. Acacia C. Parks et al., "Pursuing Happiness in Everyday Life: The Characteristics and Behaviors of Online Happiness Seekers," *Emotion* 12, no. 6 (2012): 1222–34.

8. Karynna Okabe-Miyamoto, Seth Margolis, and Sonja Lyubomirsky, "Is Variety the Spice of Happiness? More Variety Is Associated with Lower Efficacy of Positive Activity Interventions in a Sample of Over 200,000 Happiness Seekers," *Journal of Positive Psychology* (2021): 1–12, https://doi.org/10.1080/17439760.2021.2006760.

9. Jan-Benedict E. M. Steenkamp and Hans Baumgartner, "The Role of Optimum Stimulation Level in Exploratory Consumer Behavior," *Journal of Consumer Research* 19, no. 3 (1992): 434–48; Hyewook Genevieve Jeong, Kate Christensen, and Aimee Drolet, "The Short-Lived Benefits of Variety Seeking among the Chronically Indecisive," *Journal of Experimental Psychology: Applied* 22, no. 4 (2016): 423–35.

10. Kelley Gullo et al., "Does Time of Day Affect Variety-Seeking?" *Journal of Consumer Research* 46, no. 1 (2019): 20–35.

11. Richard E. Nisbett and David E. Kanouse, "Obesity, Food Deprivation, and Supermarket Shopping Behavior," *Journal of Personality and Social Psychology* 12, no. 4 (1969): 289–94; Alison Jing Xu, Norbert Schwarz, and Robert S. Wyer Jr., "Hunger Promotes Acquisition of Nonfood Objects," *Proceedings of the National Academy of Sciences of the United States of America* 112, no. 9 (2015): 2688–92.

12. Caroline Goukens et al., "Wanting a Bit(e) of Everything: Extending the Valuation Effect to Variety Seeking," *Journal of Consumer Research* 34, no. 3 (2007): 386–94.

13. Zhongqiang Huang et al., "The Sleepy Consumer and Variety Seeking," *Journal of Marketing Research* 56, no. 2 (2019): 179–96.

14. Jing Tian, Yicheng Zhang, and Cheng Zhang, "Predicting Consumer Variety-Seeking through Weather Data Analytics," *Electronic Commerce Research and Applications* 28 (2018): 194–207.

15. Jungkeun Kim et al., "COVID-19 Restrictions and Variety Seeking in Travel Choices and Actions: The Moderating Effects of Previous Experience and Crowding," *Journal of Travel Research* 61, no. 7 (2022): 1648–65, https://doi.org/10.1177/00472875211037744.

16. Bruce Barry and Greg L. Stewart, "Composition, Process, and Performance in Self-Managed Groups: The Role of Personality," *Journal of Applied Psychology* 82, no. 1 (1997): 62–78. For a meta-analysis of how team members' distribution of scores (including their variability) on the Big-Five personality traits affect team performance, see Miranda A. G. Peeters et al., "Personality and Team Performance: A Meta-Analysis," *European Journal of Personality* 20, no. 5 (2006): 377–96.

17. Daniel Fernandes and Naomi Mandel, "Political Conservatism and Variety-Seeking," *Journal of Consumer Psychology* 24, no. 1 (2014): 79–86.

18. Shigehiro Oishi and Erin C. Westgate, "A Psychologically Rich Life: Beyond Happiness and Meaning," *Psychological Review* 129, no. 4 (2022): 790–811, http://dx.doi.org/10.1037/rev0000317.

19. Ibid., abstract.

20. Gad Saad et al., "Are Identical Twins More Similar in Their Decision Making Styles Than Their Fraternal Counterparts?" *Journal of Business Research* 120 (November 2020): 638–43; Gad Saad and John G. Vongas, "The Effect of Conspicuous Consumption on Men's Testosterone Levels," *Organizational Behavior and Human Decision Processes* 110, no. 2 (2009): 80–92; Gad Saad and Eric Stenstrom, "Calories, Beauty, and Ovulation: The Effects of the Menstrual Cycle on Food and Appearance-Related Consumption," *Journal of Consumer Psychology* 22, no. 1 (2012): 102–13; Gad Saad, "Advertised Waist-to-Hip Ratios of Online Female Escorts: An Evolutionary Perspective," *International Journal of E-Collaboration*, 4, no. 3 (2008): 40–50; Gad Saad, Aliza Eba, and Richard Sejean, "Sex Differences When Searching for a Mate: A Process-Tracing Approach," *Journal of Behavioral Decision Making* 22, no. 2 (2009): 171–90; Sigal Tifferet et al., "Gift Giving at Israeli Weddings as a Function of Genetic Relatedness and Kinship Certainty," *Journal of Consumer Psychology* 28, no. 1 (2018): 157–65.

21. Jerry A. Jacobs and Scott Frickel, "Interdisciplinarity: A Critical Assessment," *Annual Review of Sociology* 35 (2009): 43–65.

22. Leroy Hood and Lee Rowen, "The Human Genome Project: Big Science Transforms Biology and Medicine," *Genome Medicine* 5, no. 9 (2013): 1–8.

23. Moti Nissani, "Ten Cheers for Interdisciplinarity: The Case for Interdisciplinary Knowledge and Research," abstract, *The Social Science Journal* 34, no. 2 (1997): 201–16, 201.

24. Shiji Chen, Clément Arsenault, and Vincent Larivière, "Are Top-Cited Papers More Interdisciplinary?" *Journal of Informetrics* 9, no. 4 (2015): 1034–46.

25. Vincent Larivière, Stefanie Haustein, and Katy Börner, "Long-Distance Interdisciplinarity Leads to Higher Scientific Impact," *PLOS One* 10, no. 3 (2015), e0122565.

26. Jian Wang, Bart Thijs, and Wolfgang Glänzel, "Interdisciplinarity and Impact: Distinct Effects of Variety, Balance, and Disparity," *PLOS One* 10, no. 5 (2015), e0127298.

27. See chapter 5 in David Epstein, *Range: Why Generalists Triumph in a Specialized World* (New York: Riverhead Books, 2019); Dedre Gentner, "Analogy in Scientific Discovery: The Case of Johannes Kepler," in *Model-Based Reasoning: Science, Technology, Values*, eds. Lorenzo Magnani and Nancy J. Nersessian (New York: Kluwer Academic/ Plenum Publishers, 2002), 21–39.

28. Kevin Dunbar, "How Scientists Really Reason: Scientific Reasoning in Real-World Laboratories," in *The Nature of Insight*, eds. Robert J. Sternberg and Janet E. Davidson (Cambridge, Massachusetts: MIT Press, 1995), 365–95.

29. Eduardo Melero and Neus Palomeras, "*The Renaissance Man* Is Not Dead! The Role of Generalists in Teams of Inventors," *Research Policy* 44, no. 1 (2015): 154–67.

30. Florenta Teodoridis, Michaël Bikard, and Keyvan Vakili, "Creativity at the Knowledge Frontier: The Impact of Specialization in Fast- and Slow-Paced Domains," *Administrative Science Quarterly* 64, no. 4 (2019): 894–927.

31. Wai Fong Boh, Roberto Evaristo, and Andrew Ouderkirk, "Balancing Breadth and Depth of Expertise for Innovation: A 3M Story," *Research Policy* 43, no. 2 (2014): 349–66.

32. "Solve the World's Greatest Challenges," InnoCentive, https://www.innocentive.com/.

33. Don R. Swanson, "Undiscovered Public Knowledge," *The Library Quarterly* 56, no. 2 (1986): 103–18.

34. Don R. Swanson and Neil R. Smalheiser, "Undiscovered Public Knowledge: A Ten-Year Update," in *KDD'96: Proceedings of the Second International Conference on Knowledge Discovery and Data Mining*, eds. Evangelos Simoudis, Jiawei Han, and Usama Fayyad (Palo Alto, California: AAAI Press, 1996), 295–98, https://www.researchgate.net/profile/Neil-Smalheiser/publication/221653369_Undiscovered_Public_Knowledge_A_Ten-Year_Update/links/00b7d53550ec2b5077000000/Undiscovered-Public-Knowledge-A-Ten-Year-Update.pdf.

35. Robert Root-Bernstein et al., "Arts Foster Scientific Success: Avocations of Nobel, National Academy, Royal Society, and Sigma Xi Members," *Journal of Psychology of Science and Technology* 1, no. 2 (2008): 51–63.

36. Dawei Li, Yijuan Wang, and Zhi-Ping Liu, "Academic Background of Nobel Prize Laureates Reveals the Importance of Multidisciplinary Education in Medicine," *Social Sciences & Humanities Open* 3, no. 1 (2021), 100114.

37. Gad Saad, "Which Ten Historical Figures Would You Invite for Dinner?" *Psychology Today*, December 29, 2014, https://www.psychologytoday.com/ca/blog/homo-consumericus/201412/which-ten-historical-figures-would-you-invite-dinner.

38. Michael Araki, "Scientific Polymathy: The End of a Two-Cultures Era," *The Lancet* 395, no. 10218 (2020): 113–14.

39. The curated playlist of all guests on *The Saad Truth*: Gad Saad, "One-on-One Chats," YouTube, https://www.youtube.com/watch?v=2TZzznMefcg&list=PLa-VfOWrqWJozkpqegu5BTq6iJI3mFTgy.

40. Mart R. Gross, "The Evolution of Parental Care," *The Quarterly Review of Biology* 80, no. 1 (2005): 37–45.

41. Joseph Henrich, Robert Boyd, and Peter J. Richerson, "The Puzzle of Monogamous Marriage," *Philosophical Transactions of the Royal Society B: Biological Sciences* 367, no. 1589 (2012): 657–69.

42. Cynthia M. Beall and Melvyn C. Goldstein, "Tibetan Fraternal Polyandry: A Test of Sociobiological Theory," *American Anthropologist* 83, no. 1 (1981): 5–12.

43. Eric Alden Smith, "Is Tibetan Polyandry Adaptive? Methodological and Metatheoretical Analyses," *Human Nature* 9, no. 3 (1998): 225–61.

44. Susan M. Hughes et al., "Experimental Evidence for Sex Differences in Sexual Variety Preferences: Support for the Coolidge Effect in Humans," *Archives of Sexual Behavior* 50, no. 2 (2021): 495–509.

45. David P. Schmitt and 118 Members of the International Sexuality Description Project, "Universal Sex Differences in the Desire for Sexual Variety: Tests from 52 Nations, 6 Continents, and 13 Islands," *Journal of Personality and Social Psychology* 85, no. 1 (2003): 85–104.

46. Robin Baker, *Sperm Wars: Infidelity, Sexual Conflict and Other Bedroom Battles* (London: Fourth Estate, 1996).

47. For an examination of key evolutionary reasons that drive women's pursuit of sexual variety including in the context of short-term mating, see Elizabeth G. Pillsworth and Martie G. Haselton, "Women's Sexual Strategies: The Evolution of Long-Term Bonds and Extrapair Sex," *Annual Review of Sex Research* 17, no. 1 (2006): 59–100. See also Heidi Greiling and David M. Buss, "Women's Sexual Strategies: The Hidden Dimension of Extra-Pair Mating," *Personality and Individual Differences* 285, no. 2 (2000): 929–63 [and relevant references therein on p. 931].

48. Some researchers have questioned the veracity of the sperm heteromorphism hypothesis, but see the following rebuttal: Robin Baker, "Robin Baker and Mark Bellis: Pioneers of Research on Human Sperm Competition," in *Encyclopedia of Evolutionary Psychological Science*, eds. Todd K. Shackelford and Viviana A. Weekes-Shackelford (Cham, Switzerland: Springer, 2021), 6734–43, https://doi.org/10.1007/978-3-319-16999-6_3590-1 [online entry].

49. Alexander H. Harcourt et al., "Testis Weight, Body Weight and Breeding System in Primates," *Nature* 293, no. 5827 (1981): 55–57; Alan F. Dixson, "Copulatory and Postcopulatory Sexual Selection in Primates," *Folia Primatologica* 89, no. 3–4 (2018): 258–86.

50. Shawn Grover and John F. Helliwell, "How's Life at Home? New Evidence on Marriage and the Set Point for Happiness," *Journal of Happiness Studies* 20, no. 2 (2019): 373–90; Nicholas H. Wolfinger, "Does Sexual History Affect Marital Happiness?" Institute for Family Studies, October 22, 2018, https://ifstudies.org/blog/does-sexual-history-affect-marital-happiness.

51. David A. Frederick et al., "What Keeps Passion Alive? Sexual Satisfaction Is Associated with Sexual Communication, Mood Setting, Sexual Variety, Oral Sex, Orgasm, and Sex Frequency in a National US Study," *The Journal of Sex Research* 54, no. 2 (2017): 186–201.

52. Jean M. Twenge, Ryne A. Sherman, and Brooke E. Wells, "Declines in Sexual Frequency among American Adults, 1989–2014," *Archives of Sexual Behavior* 46, no. 8 (2017): 2389–2401.

53. Lars Penke and Jens B. Asendorpf, "Beyond Global Sociosexual Orientations: A More Differentiated Look at Sociosexuality and Its Effects on Courtship and Romantic Relationships," *Journal of Personality and Social Psychology* 95, no. 5 (2008): 1113–35.

54. Sarah E. Hill, Marjorie L. Prokosch, and Danielle J. DelPriore, "The Impact of Perceived Disease Threat on Women's Desire for Novel Dating and Sexual Partners: Is Variety the Best Medicine?" *Journal of Personality and Social Psychology* 109, no. 2 (2015): 244–61.

55. Kristina M. Durante and Ashley Rae Arsena, "Playing the Field: The Effect of Fertility on Women's Desire for Variety," *Journal of Consumer Research* 41, no. 6 (2015): 1372–91; Ali Faraji-Rad, Mehrad Moeini-Jazani, and Luk Warlop, "Women Seek More Variety in Rewards When Closer to Ovulation," *Journal of Consumer Psychology* 23, no. 4 (2013): 503–8.

56. Gad Saad, "On Animal Cruelty, Veganism, and Human Nature (THE SAAD TRUTH_594)," YouTube, February 22, 2018, https://youtu.be/f8MMNOwjiYE [see the slide starting at the 4:55 mark]; Gad Saad, "Animal Welfare—The Sequel (THE SAAD TRUTH_595)," YouTube, February 23, 2018, https://youtu.be/Nzs7pV6-TYo.

57. Gad Saad (@GadSaad), "My wife walked up to the server . . . ," Twitter, October 27, 2021, 10:26 a.m., https://twitter.com/GadSaad/status/1453367468769095685?s=20.

58. Valerie Bertinelli (@Wolfiesmom), "'Hi' 'Pardon me'. . . ," Twitter, October 27, 2021, 3:37 p.m., https://twitter.com/Wolfiesmom/status/1453445814215348227?s=20.

59. Gad Saad (@GadSaad), "She wanted to say to the server's colleague . . . ," Twitter, October 28, 2021, 8:18 a.m., https://twitter.com/GadSaad/status/1453697767331835905?s=20. I discussed this unfortunate episode in two *Saad Truth* clips: Gad Saad, "The Twitter Mob Has Sent Me into Hiding (THE SAAD TRUTH_1326)," YouTube, October 27, 2021, https://youtu.be/5gODUnVoqn4; Gad Saad, "My Message to Valerie Bertinelli and the Fierce Pronoun Keyboard Warriors (THE SAAD TRUTH_1329)," YouTube, November 1, 2021, https://youtu.be/kds-w6KO-oE.

60. See Gad Saad, *The Consuming Instinct: What Juicy Burgers, Ferraris, Pornography, and Gift Giving Reveal about Human Nature* (Amherst, New York: Prometheus Books, 2011), 50–54 and references therein.

61. Rochelle Embling et al., "Effect of Food Variety on Intake of a Meal: A Systematic Review and Meta-Analysis," *The American Journal of Clinical Nutrition* 113, no. 3 (2021): 716–41.

62. Kelly L. Haws et al., "Exploring the Relationship between Varieties of Variety and Weight Loss: When More Variety Can Help People Lose Weight," *Journal of Marketing Research* 54, no. 4 (2017): 619–35.

63. Joseph P. Redden and Stephen J. Hoch, "The Presence of Variety Reduces Perceived Quantity," *Journal of Consumer Research* 36, no. 3 (2009): 406–17.

64. Judith A. Juvancic-Heltzel, Ellen L. Glickman, and Jacob E. Barkley, "The Effect of Variety on Physical Activity: A Cross-Sectional Study," *The Journal of Strength & Conditioning Research* 27, no. 1 (2013): 244–51; Jacob E. Barkley et al., "The Variety of Exercise Equipment and Physical Activity Participation in Children," *Journal of Sport Behavior* 34, no. 2 (2011): 137–49.

65. Jordan Etkin and Cassie Mogilner, "Does Variety among Activities Increase Happiness?" *Journal of Consumer Research* 43, no. 2 (2016): 210–29.

66. Ashley V. Whillans et al., "Buying Time Promotes Happiness," *Proceedings of the National Academy of Sciences of the United States of America* 114, no. 32 (2017): 8523–27.

67. Aaron S. Heller et al., "Association between Real-World Experiential Diversity and Positive Affect Relates to Hippocampal–Striatal Functional Connectivity," *Nature Neuroscience* 23, no. 7 (2020): 800–804.

Chapter Seven: On Persistence and the Anti-Fragility of Failure

1. Elizabeth Knowles, ed., *The Oxford Dictionary of Quotations*, 5th ed. (Oxford, UK: Oxford University Press, 2001), 454.

2. Lucius Annaeus Seneca, *Of Providence*, 13, available at https://archive.org/details/seneca-of-providence.

3. Jonathan Gerber and Ladd Wheeler, "On Being Rejected: A Meta-Analysis of Experimental Research on Rejection," *Perspectives on Psychological Science* 4, no. 5 (2009): 468–88.

4. James Fair, "Apex Predators in the Wild: Which Mammals Are the Most Dangerous?" *Discover Wildlife*, November 24, 2021, https://www.discoverwildlife.com/animal-facts/mammals/hunting-success-rates-how-predators-compare/.

5. Neil Hammerschlag, R. Aidan Martin, and Chris Fallows, "Effects of Environmental Conditions on Predator–Prey Interactions between White Sharks (*Carcharodon carcharias*) and Cape Fur Seals (*Arctocephalus pusillus pusillus*) at Seal Island, South Africa," *Environmental Biology of Fishes* 76 (2006): 341–50, https://doi.org/10.1007/s10641-006-9038-z.

6. "Why Does Poor Quality Soil Make Such Great Wine?" Vivino, https://www.vivino.com/wine-news/why-does-poor-quality-soil-make-such-great-wine; Tom Marquardt and Patrick Darr, "Wine, Etc.: Difficult Growing Conditions Can Lead to Extraordinary Wines," *Baltimore Sun*, August 14, 2013, https://www.baltimoresun.com/maryland/carroll/cct-arc-d49eedf1-7386-553e-bab5-acbff6254b4c-20130814-story.html.

7. Jeff Cox, *The Essential Book of Fermentation: Great Taste and Good Health with Probiotic Foods* (New York: Penguin Books, 2013), 137.

8. I thank my good friend and colleague Andrew Ryder for having alerted me to this example.

9. See the relevant references in Phil W. West, *Tree and Forest Measurement*, 2nd ed. (Heidelberg, Germany: Springer-Verlag, 2009), 37; see also references 42 and 52 cited in the last sentence on p. 104 in Norman L. Biddington, "The Effects of Mechanically-Induced Stress in Plants—A Review," *Plant Growth Regulation* 4, no. 2 (1986): 103–23.

10. Martha Henriques, "How Japan's Skyscrapers Are Built to Survive Earthquakes," BBC, January 16, 2019, https://www.bbc.com/future/article/20190114-how-japans-skyscrapers-are-built-to-survive-earthquakes.

11. H. Okada et al., "The 'Hygiene Hypothesis' for Autoimmune and Allergic Diseases: An Update," *Clinical & Experimental Immunology* 160, no. 1 (2010): 1–9.

12. Steve Stankevicius, "Intellectually Sterile Universities Are Causing Idea Allergies," The Daily Banter, March 8, 2016, http://thedailybanter.com/2016/03/intellectually-sterile-universities-are-causing-idea-allergies/.

13. For a thorough discussion of anti-fragility, please refer to Nassim Nicholas Taleb, *Antifragile: Things That Gain from Disorder* (New York: Random House, 2012).

14. I have edited this exchange slightly for clarity. Salem Center for Policy, "The Parasitic Mind: How Infectious Ideas Are Killing Common Sense," YouTube, May 10, 2022, from 1:28:25 to 1:32:40, https://www.youtube.com/watch?v=O5S5ImEZAlw&t=5317s.

15. "Oprah: Clerk Thinks I Can't Afford $38K Handbag?" *USA Today*, August 9, 2013, https://www.usatoday.com/story/money/business/2013/08/09/a-38000-handbag-not-unheard-of-in-luxury-market/2635871/.

16. Cady Lang, "The Core Message of Meghan and Harry's Oprah Interview: Racism Drove Us from the Royal Family," *Time*, March 8, 2021, https://time.com/5944613/meghan-markle-oprah-racism/.

17. Steerpike, "Fact Check: Why Isn't Archie a Prince," *The Spectator*, March 8, 2021, https://www.spectator.co.uk/article/fact-check-why-isn-t-archie-a-prince/.

18. Freddy Gray, "Have Harry and Meghan Been Driven Mad by Fame," *The Spectator*, November 18, 2021, https://spectatorworld.com/topic/harry-meghan-palace-vs-sussexes/.

19. Gad Saad, *The Parasitic Mind: How Infectious Ideas Are Killing Common Sense* (Washington, D.C.: Regnery Publishing, 2020), 94.

20. Russell D. Clark III and Elaine Hatfield, "Gender Differences in Receptivity to Sexual Offers," *Journal of Psychology & Human Sexuality* 2, no. 1 (1989): 39–55.

21. Jia Jiang, "100 Days of Rejection Therapy," Rejection Therapy with Jia Jiang, https://www.rejectiontherapy.com/100-days-of-rejection-therapy. See also Jia Jiang, *Rejection Proof: How I Beat Fear and Became Invincible through 100 Days of Rejection* (New York: Harmony Books, 2015). Many thanks to my sister-in-law, who alerted me to Jiang's rejection project via his TED Talk on the topic.

22. Andrew McKenzie, "Zidane the Flawed Genius," BBC Sport, July 10, 2006, http://news.bbc.co.uk/sport2/hi/football/world_cup_2006/teams/france/5165296.stm.

23. "Barcelona Initially Unconvinced That Leo Messi Would Succeed as a Pro," *Sports Illustrated*, February 6, 2012, https://www.si.com/soccer/2012/02/06/barca-extract.

24. Memories of Air, "September 16, 1997—Michael Jordan Interview—The Tonight Show Jay Leno," YouTube, July 13, 2017, from 3:25 to 5:00, https://www.youtube.com/watch?v=Oxdoqg Kc1rg.

25. Justin Hartwig, "The Top Selling Book Series of All Time," Investopedia, November 19, 2020, https://www.investopedia.com/highest-selling-book-series-5087534.

26. Anjelica Oswald, "J. K. Rowling Shares Photos of Her Rejection Letters for 'Inspiration,'" Business Insider, March 25, 2016, https://www.businessinsider.com/jk-rowling-rejection-letters-2016-3.

27. Noor Zainab Hussain and Esha Vaish, "The Eight-Year-Old Who Gave Publisher Bloomsbury Pottermania," Reuters, October 28, 2016, https://www.reuters.com/article/us-bloomsbury-pubg-harry-potter-idUSKCN12S1ME.

28. Katie Baillie, "Harry Potter and the Philosopher's Stone Turns 21: Fans Reminisce over Where They Were When They Read the First Book," Metro, June 26, 2018, https://metro.co.uk/2018/06/26/harry-potter-philosophers-stone-turns-21-fans-reminisce-read-first-book-7661951/.

29. Emily Temple, "The Most-Rejected Books of All Time: (Of the Ones That Were Eventually Published)," Literary Hub, December 22, 2017, https://lithub.com/the-most-rejected-books-of-all-time/.

30. Ken Dunn, "5 Self-Publishing Book Tips from the 'Chicken Soup for the Soul' Author Who Has Sold over 500 Million Copies," *Entrepreneur*, July 29, 2020, https://www.entrepreneur.com/article/352513.

31. Laurel Wamsley, "'Zen and the Art of Motorcycle Maintenance' Author Robert M. Pirsig Dies at 88," NPR, April 24, 2017, https://www.npr.org/sections/

thetwo-way/2017/04/24/525443040/-zen-and-the-art-of-motorcycle-maintenance-author-robert-m-pirsig-dies-at-88.

32. "William Golding Biography," CliffsNotes, https://www.cliffsnotes.com/literature/l/lord-of-the-flies/william-golding-biography.

33. "How Dr. Seuss Got His Start 'on Mulberry Street,'" NPR, January 24, 2012, https://www.npr.org/2012/01/24/145471724/how-dr-seuss-got-his-start-on-mulberry-street.

34. Jenny Desborough, "The Beatles: When Did the Beatles Get a Record Deal? 'Twice Rejected,'" *Daily Express*, October 12, 2020, https://www.express.co.uk/entertainment/music/1345844/The-Beatles-When-the-Beatles-get-record-deal-TWICE-rejected-paul-endacott-evg; "Love Me Do: Management Lessons from the Fifth Beatle," Knowledge at Wharton, March 18, 2016, https://knowledge.wharton.upenn.edu/article/love-management-lessons-fifth-beatle/.

35. Stephen Galloway, "How USC Film School Got Millions from Steven Spielberg (and He Didn't Even Go There)," *Hollywood Reporter*, March 1, 2019, https://www.hollywoodreporter.com/lifestyle/lifestyle-news/how-usc-film-school-got-millions-steven-spielberg-1190637/.

36. Carsten Wrosch, Michael F. Scheier, and Gregory E. Miller, "Goal Adjustment Capacities, Subjective Well-Being, and Physical Health," *Social and Personality Psychology Compass* 7, no. 12 (2013): 847–60.

37. "Editorial Criteria and Processes," *Nature*, https://www.nature.com/nature/for-authors/editorial-criteria-and-processes; "About NEJM," *New England Journal of Medicine*, https://www.nejm.org/about-nejm/about-nejm.

38. "Summary Report of Journal Operations, 2017," *American Psychologist* 73, no. 5 (2018): 683–84, https://doi.org/10.1037/amp0000347.

39. Sigal Tifferet et al., "Gift Giving at Israeli Weddings as a Function of Genetic Relatedness and Kinship Certainty," *Journal of Consumer Psychology* 28, no. 1 (2018): 157–65.

40. Liza M. Rubenstein et al., "Cognitive Attributions in Depression: Bridging the Gap between Research and Clinical Practice," *Journal of Psychotherapy Integration* 26, no. 2 (2016): 103–15; Lei Wang and Meizhen Lv, "Internal-External Locus of Control Scale," in *Encyclopedia of Personality and Individual Differences*, eds. Virgil Zeigler-Hill and Todd K. Shackelford (Cham, Switzerland: Springer, 2020), 2339–43, https://doi.org/10.1007/978-3-319-24612-3_41.

41. Roderick E. White, Stewart Thornhill, and Elizabeth Hampson, "Entrepreneurs and Evolutionary Biology: The Relationship between Testosterone and New Venture Creation," *Organizational Behavior and Human Decision Processes* 100, no. 1 (2006): 21–34.

42. Neil Patel, "90% of Startups Fail: Here's What You Need to Know about the 10%," *Forbes*, January 16, 2015, https://www.forbes.com/sites/neilpatel/2015/01/16/90-of-startups-will-fail-heres-what-you-need-to-know-about-the-10/?sh=2c34e6e76679.

43. "Fail Faster," d.school, Stanford, https://dschool.stanford.edu/classes/fail-faster.

44. Kevin D. Hall and Scott Kahan, "Maintenance of Lost Weight and Long-Term Management of Obesity," *Medical Clinics of North America* 102, no. 1 (2018):

183–97; Samantha M. McEvedy et al., "Ineffectiveness of Commercial Weight-Loss Programs for Achieving Modest but Meaningful Weight Loss: Systematic Review and Meta-Analysis," *Journal of Health Psychology* 22, no. 12 (2017): 1614–27.

45. I discussed my weight loss secrets on my most recent appearance on Joe Rogan's podcast. Powerful JRE, "Gad Saad on Maintaining His 86 Pound Weight Loss," YouTube, May 11, 2022, https://www.youtube.com/watch?v=oO-Bv4iRZKI.

46. Gad Saad, "My Chat with Legendary Lead Singer of The Stylistics, Russell Thompkins Jr. (THE SAAD TRUTH_584)," YouTube, February 8, 2018, https://youtu.be/aorkR100P_s.

47. Gad Saad, "On Forging a Friendship with a Legendary Singer (THE SAAD TRUTH_674)," YouTube, June 16, 2018, https://youtu.be/PEQ8g4pFwwM.

48. Eric Zorn, "Without Failure, Jordan Would Be False Idol," *Chicago Tribune*, May 19, 1997, https://www.chicagotribune.com/news/ct-xpm-1997-05-19-9705190096-story.html.

49. Kirsten Moran, "The Meaning of Kobe Bryant's 'Mamba Mentality' One Year after His Death," Nevada Sports Net, January 26, 2021, https://nevadasportsnet.com/news/reporters/the-meaning-of-kobe-bryants-mamba-mentality-one-year-after-his-death.

50. Angela Lee Duckworth and Patrick D. Quinn, "Development and Validation of the Short Grit Scale (Grit-S)," *Journal of Personality Assessment* 91, no. 2 (2009): 166–74; Angela Duckworth, *Grit: The Power of Passion and Perseverance* (Toronto, Ontario: HarperCollins Publishers Ltd., 2016). For a critique of the grit construct and associated literature, see Marcus Credé, Michael C. Tynan, and Peter D. Harms, "Much Ado about Grit: A Meta-Analytic Synthesis of the Grit Literature," *Journal of Personality and Social Psychology* 113, no. 3 (2017): 492–511.

51. David J. Disabato, Fallon R. Goodman, and Todd B. Kashdan, "Is Grit Relevant to Well-Being and Strengths? Evidence across the Globe for Separating Perseverance of Effort and Consistency of Interests," *Journal of Personality* 87, no. 2 (2019): 194–211; Hye Won Kwon, "Are Gritty People Happier Than Others?: Evidence from the United States and South Korea," *Journal of Happiness Studies* 22, no. 7 (2021): 2937–59; Jesus Alfonso D. Datu et al., "Is Grittiness Next to Happiness? Examining the Association of Triarchic Model of Grit Dimensions with Well-Being Outcomes," *Journal of Happiness Studies* 22, no. 2 (2021): 981–1009.

52. Bruce J. Ellis et al., "Beyond Risk and Protective Factors: An Adaptation-Based Approach to Resilience," *Perspectives on Psychological Science* 12, no. 4 (2017): 561–87.

53. Ruud J. R. Den Hartigh and Yannick Hill, "Conceptualizing and Measuring Psychological Resilience: What Can We Learn from Physics?" *New Ideas in Psychology* 66 (August 2022): 100934.

54. Gad Saad, "5 Life Lessons from a Lost Ring (THE SAAD TRUTH_646)," YouTube, May 11, 2018, https://youtu.be/KOoChcW5RVA.

55. Gad Saad, *The Evolutionary Bases of Consumption* (Mahwah, New Jersey: Lawrence Erlbaum, 2007). When I was writing the book, a barista once asked me what my job was. I told him I was a professor. He looked disappointed. I asked him why, and he said that he assumed I was a porn producer interviewing young actors

and actresses. Those, I had to inform him, were students of mine discussing their research projects!

Chapter Eight: It's (Almost) Never Too Late—Eradicate Regret

1. Édith Piaf, "Non, Je Ne Regrette Rien," lyrics by Michel Vaucaire, music by Charles Dumont, 1960.
2. Inscription of Delphic maxims at Ai-Khanoum quoted from Michael Wood, *In the Footsteps of Alexander the Great: A Journey from Greece to Asia* (Berkeley and Los Angeles, California: University of California Press, 2001), 160–61.
3. Evangelos Markopoulos and Hannu Vanharanta, *The Company Democracy Model: Creating Innovative Democratic Work Cultures for Effective Organizational Knowledge-Based Management and Leadership* (New York: Routledge, 2022), Table 2.1.
4. Dominic Julien, Kieron P. O'Connor, and Frederick Aardema, "Intrusive Thoughts, Obsessions, and Appraisals in Obsessive-Compulsive Disorder: A Critical Review," *Clinical Psychology Review* 27, no. 3 (2007): 366–83.
5. Carsten Wrosch et al., "Regret Intensity, Diurnal Cortisol Secretion, and Physical Health in Older Individuals: Evidence for Directional Effects and Protective Factors," *Psychology and Aging* 22, no. 2 (2007): 319–30.
6. Stefanie Brassen et al., "Don't Look Back in Anger! Responsiveness to Missed Chances in Successful and Nonsuccessful Aging," *Science* 336, no. 6081 (2012): 614. For another neuroscientific examination of regret, see Giorgio Coricelli et al., "Regret and Its Avoidance: A Neuroimaging Study of Choice Behavior," *Nature Neuroscience* 8, no. 9 (2005): 1255–62.
7. Len Lecci, Morris A. Okun, and Paul Karoly, "Life Regrets and Current Goals as Predictors of Psychological Adjustment," *Journal of Personality and Social Psychology* 66, no. 4 (1994): 731–41.
8. *A Bronx Tale*, directed by Robert De Niro, screenplay by Chazz Palminteri (Savoy Pictures, 1993).
9. Thomas Gilovich and Victoria Husted Medvec, "The Experience of Regret: What, When, and Why," *Psychological Review* 102, no. 2 (1995): 379–95.
10. DeWitt Wallace and Lila Acheson Wallace, eds., *The Reader's Digest*, vol. 104 (Pleasantville, New York: Reader's Digest Association, 1974), 137 [as obtained via an electronic search of the quote in Google Books].
11. *The Book of Common Prayer*, in *Oxford Essential Quotations*, ed. Susan Ratcliffe, 5th ed. (Oxford, UK: Oxford University Press, 2017), https://www.oxfordreference.com/view/10.1093/acref/9780191843730.001.0001/q-oro-ed5-00001833.
12. Thomas Gilovich et al., "Regrets of Action and Inaction across Cultures," *Journal of Cross-Cultural Psychology* 34, no. 1 (2003): 61–71.
13. Seger M. Breugelmans et al., "Generality and Cultural Variation in the Experience of Regret," *Emotion* 14, no. 6 (2014): 1037–48.
14. Andrew Galperin et al., "Sexual Regret: Evidence for Evolved Sex Differences," *Archives of Sexual Behavior* 42, no. 7 (2013): 1145–61; Neal J. Roese et al., "Sex Differences in Regret: All for Love Or Some for Lust?" *Personality & Social Psychology Bulletin* 32, no. 6 (2006): 770–80; Leif Edward Ottesen Kennair, Trond

Viggo Grøntvedt, and Mons Bendixen, "The Function of Casual Sex Action and Inaction Regret: A Longitudinal Investigation," *Evolutionary Psychology* 19, no. 1 (2021): 1474704921998333.

15. Steve Taylor, "'My Life Flashed before My Eyes': A Psychologist's Take on What Might Be Happening," The Conversation, June 10, 2021, https://theconversation. com/my-life-flashed-before-my-eyes-a-psychologists-take-on-what-might-be-happening-162320; Christof Koch, "What Near-Death Experiences Reveal about the Brain," *Scientific American*, June 1, 2020, https://www.scientificamerican.com/ article/what-near-death-experiences-reveal-about-the-brain/.

16. Russell Noyes Jr. and Roy Kletti, "The Experience of Dying from Falls," *OMEGA—Journal of Death and Dying* 3, no. 1 (1972): 45–52.

17. Ana León, "Near-Death Experiences throughout the History of Art and Science: Challenges for the XXI Century," in *Death, Dying, Culture: An Interdisciplinary Interrogation*, eds. Lloyd Steffen and Nate Hinerman (Oxfordshire, UK: Inter-Disciplinary Press, 2013), 205–15; Bruce Greyson, "Western Scientific Approaches to Near-Death Experiences," *Humanities* 4, no. 4 (2015): 775–96.

18. Judith Katz, Noam Saadon-Grosman, and Shahar Arzy, "The Life Review Experience: Qualitative and Quantitative Characteristics," *Consciousness and Cognition* 48 (February 2017): 76–86.

19. Bronnie Ware, *The Top Five Regrets of the Dying: A Life Transformed by the Dearly Departing* (Carlsbad, California: Hay House, 2012).

20. Samuel Chamberlain, "Child Actors Used for Kamala Harris' Bizarre Space Video," *New York Post*, October 12, 2021, https://nypost.com/2021/10/12/ kamala-harris-bizarre-space-video-uses-child-actors/.

21. Christopher J. Hopwood et al., "Realness Is a Core Feature of Authenticity," *Journal of Research in Personality* 92 (June 2021), article 104086.

22. Ibid.

23. Güler Boyraz, J. Brandon Waits, and Victoria A. Felix, "Authenticity, Life Satisfaction, and Distress: A Longitudinal Analysis," *Journal of Counseling Psychology* 61, no. 3 (2014): 498–505; Anna Sutton, "Living the Good Life: A Meta-Analysis of Authenticity, Well-Being and Engagement," *Personality and Individual Differences* 153 (January 2020), article 109645.

24. Jacob Golomb, *In Search of Authenticity: From Kierkegaard to Camus* (New York: Routledge, 1995).

25. For the historical origins of this edict, see Michael A. Peters, "Truth and Self-Knowledge," *Educational Philosophy and Theory* 53, no. 2 (2021): 105–11.

26. Shai Davidai and Thomas Gilovich, "The Ideal Road Not Taken: The Self-Discrepancies Involved in People's Most Enduring Regrets," *Emotion* 18, no. 3 (2018): 439–52.

27. Gad Saad, "My Chat with Megyn Kelly (THE SAAD TRUTH_1301)," YouTube, September 27, 2021, https://youtu.be/Hs33J3XNJDc.

28. "Author Gad Saad Says He Was Astonished to Receive a Letter from PM Modi on Republic Day, Says First Politician He Followed on Twitter Is Modi," OpIndia, January 27, 2022, https://www.opindia.com/2022/01/canadian-writer-gad-saad-delighted-after-receiving-a-letter-from-pm-modi/.

29. I first reported these two anecdotes in a 2010 *Psychology Today* article: Gad Saad, "Religious Discrimination in Universities: A Personal Story," *Psychology Today*, April 3, 2010, https://www.psychologytoday.com/ca/blog/homo-consumericus/201004/religious-discrimination-in-universities-personal-story.

30. Gad Saad, "Age Ain't Nothing but a Number (Sometimes)," *Psychology Today*, September 8, 2013, https://www.psychologytoday.com/ca/blog/homo-consumericus/201309/age-ain-t-nothing-number-sometimes; "Life Begins at 91 for Oldest PhD," *Times Higher Education*, June 21, 1996, https://www.timeshighereducation.com/news/life-begins-at-91-for-oldest-phd/94178.article; "Dagobert Broh Left Legacy to History Graduate Students," *Concordia's Thursday Report*, May 1, 2003, http://ctr.concordia.ca/2002-03/May_1/22-dagobert/index.shtml.

31. Pete Bilderback, "Brown Physics Student Manfred Steiner Earns Ph.D. at Age 89," Brown University, 2021, https://www.brown.edu/academics/physics/news/2021/11/brown-physics-student-manfred-steiner-earns-phd-age-89.

32. Ibid. See our recent conversation, Gad Saad, "My Chat with Physician & Physicist Dr. Manfred Steiner—Obtained 2nd PhD at 89 (THE SAAD TRUTH_1448)," YouTube, August 26, 2022, https://youtu.be/jIoHJMtxgzk.

33. Patrick Boyle, "Med School after 40," AAMC, February 28, 2020, https://www.aamc.org/news-insights/med-school-after-40.

34. Neal J. Roese and Amy Summerville, "What We Regret Most…and Why," *Personality and Social Psychology Bulletin* 31, no. 9 (2005): 1273–85.

35. Gad Saad, "My Chat with Law Professor and Neurologist Dr. Amy Wax (THE SAAD TRUTH_1368)," YouTube, January 24, 2022, https://youtu.be/AhyeUd7vOe4.

36. Aidan Iacobucci, "Princeton-Based Academic Freedom Group Backs Amy Wax as Upenn Starts Review Process over Anti-Asian Remarks," *Daily Princetonian*, January 27, 2022, https://www.dailyprincetonian.com/article/2022/01/professor-amy-wax-faculty-review-racist-remarks.

37. Marcel Zeelenberg and Rik Pieters, "A Theory of Regret Regulation 1.0," *Journal of Consumer Psychology* 17, no. 1 (2007): 3–18.

38. Colleen Saffrey, Amy Summerville, and Neal J. Roese, "Praise for Regret: People Value Regret above Other Negative Emotions," *Motivation and Emotion* 32, no. 1 (2008): 46–54.

39. Ibid.

40. "Jeff Bezos," *Forbes*, https://www.forbes.com/profile/jeff-bezos/?sh=34d0b9d11b23.

41. Full quote starts at the 3:48 mark and continues until 4:34. Academy of Achievement, "Jeff Bezos, Academy Class of 2001, Full Interview," YouTube, July 12, 2016, https://www.youtube.com/watch?v=s7ZvBy1SROE.

42. Joe Avella and Richard Feloni, "Tony Robbins: How to Get over Your Fear of Failure," Business Insider, July 15, 2016, https://www.businessinsider.com/tony-robbins-fear-failure-not-your-guru-2016-7?utm_source=yahoo&utm_medium=referral.

43. The Times and The Sunday Times (@thetimes), "'I am now completely invisible…,'" Twitter, January 8, 2022, 9:05 a.m., https://twitter.com/thetimes/status/1479816424378052608?s=20&t=K6IridQwiwv8zqwqNa9vSw.

44. Gad Saad (@GadSaad), "Dear @paulinaporizkov, you are hardly invisible . . . ," Twitter, January 8, 2022, 5:51 p.m., https://twitter.com/GadSaad/status/14799489 41181468672?s=20.

45. Paulina Porizkova (@paulinaporizkov), "Sounds like you speak from experience. I guess the hot babes weren't interested in you, huh?" Twitter, January 8, 2022, 10:41 p.m., https://twitter.com/paulinaporizkov/status/1480021766718300163?s=20.

46. Gad Saad (@GadSaad), "This is an unbecoming response of a serious adult . . . ," Twitter, January 9, 2022, 7:40 a.m., https://twitter.com/GadSaad/status/14801575 78936078340?s=20.

47. Gad Saad, "On Aging Gracefully—Former Supermodel Paulina Porizkova Is Angry with Men (THE SAAD TRUTH_1357)," YouTube, January 9, 2022, https://youtu. be/LdvyvaaQQ_k.

48. Kristen Hawkes and James E. Coxworth, "Grandmothers and the Evolution of Human Longevity: A Review of Findings and Future Directions," *Evolutionary Anthropology: Issues, News, and Reviews* 22, no. 6 (2013): 294–302.

49. Paulina Porizkova (@paulinaporizkov), "Because the same guys who run the world today would have been long dead . . . ," Twitter, January 8, 2022, 11:48 p.m., https:// twitter.com/paulinaporizkov/status/1480038684212744192.

50. Gad Saad (@GadSaad), "Zero understanding of evolution . . . ," Twitter, January 9, 2022, 7:37 a.m., https://twitter.com/GadSaad/status/1480156807868055555?s=20.

51. Paulina Porizkova (@paulinaporizkov), "Accidental former supermodel. Occasional actress. Current writer. America, you made me a feminist.," Twitter bio, https:// twitter.com/paulinaporizkov.

52. *Wedding Crashers*, written by Steve Faber and Bob Fisher, directed by David Dobkin (New Line Cinema, 2005).

53. Thomas Gilovich and Iñigo Gallo, "Consumers' Pursuit of Material and Experiential Purchases: A Review," *Consumer Psychology Review* 3, no. 1 (2020): 20–33; Thomas Gilovich, Amit Kumar, and Lily Jampol, "A Wonderful Life: Experiential Consumption and the Pursuit of Happiness," *Journal of Consumer Psychology* 25, no. 1 (2015): 152–65; Leaf Van Boven and Thomas Gilovich, "To Do or to Have? That Is the Question," *Journal of Personality and Social Psychology* 85, no. 6 (2003): 1193–1202; Amit Kumar, Matthew A. Killingsworth, and Thomas Gilovich, "Spending on Doing Promotes More Moment-to-Moment Happiness than Spending on Having," *Journal of Experimental Social Psychology* 88 (May 2020), article 103971.

54. Thomas DeLeire and Ariel Kalil, "Does Consumption Buy Happiness? Evidence from the United States," *International Review of Economics* 57, no. 2 (2010): 163–76. For a recent review of the relationship between happiness and consumption, see Ruut Veenhoven et al., "Happiness and Consumption: A Research Synthesis Using an Online Finding Archive," *SAGE Open* 11, no. 1 (2021): 1–21.

55. Rachel West, "Ewan McGregor Wants You to See the World Instead of Buying 'Stuff' in New Expedia Super Bowl Ad," ET Canada, February 10, 2022, https://etcanada. com/news/866222/ewan-mcgregor-wants-you-to-see-the-world-instead-of-buying-stuff-in-new-expedia-super-bowl-ad/.

56. Amit Bhattacharjee and Cassie Mogilner, "Happiness from Ordinary and Extraordinary Experiences," *Journal of Consumer Research* 41, no. 1 (2014): 1–17.

57. Kristi Turnquist, "Regrets, You've Had a Few?" *Seattle Times*, June 18, 2001, https://archive.seattletimes.com/archive/?date=20010618&slug=regret18.

58. Daniel H. Pink, *The Power of Regret: How Looking Backward Moves Us Forward* (New York: Riverhead Books, 2022).

59. William Ernest Henley, "Invictus," Poetry Foundation, https://www.poetryfoundation.org/poems/51642/invictus.

Chapter Nine: Don't Worry: Be Happy

1. Plato, *Euthydemus*, trans. Benjamin Jowett (Project Gutenberg, 2013), available at https://www.gutenberg.org/files/1598/1598-h/1598-h.htm.

2. Lucius Annaeus Seneca, *Seneca's Morals of a Happy Life, Benefits, Anger, and Clemency*, trans. Sir Roger L'Estrange (Chicago: Belford, Clarke, & Co., 1882), 125, available at https://archive.org/details/cu31924101956971/page/n125/mode/2up.

3. Immanuel Kant, *Groundwork of the Metaphysics of Morals*, trans. and ed. Mary Gregor (Cambridge, UK: Cambridge University Press, 1997), 28.

4. Viktor E. Frankl, *Man's Search for Meaning: An Introduction to Logotherapy*, 4th ed. (Boston: Beacon Press, 1992), 12–13.

5. Felicia K. Zerwas and Brett Q. Ford, "The Paradox of Pursuing Happiness," *Current Opinion in Behavioral Sciences* 39 (June 2021): 106–12; Iris B. Mauss et al., "Can Seeking Happiness Make People Unhappy? Paradoxical Effects of Valuing Happiness," *Emotion* 11, no. 4 (2011): 807–15.

6. Ad Bergsma, Ivonne Buijt, and Ruut Veenhoven, "Will Happiness-Trainings Make Us Happier? A Research Synthesis Using an Online Findings-Archive," *Frontiers in Psychology* 11 (2020), article 1953, https://doi.org/10.3389/fpsyg.2020.01953.

7. Gad Saad, "My Chat with Ken Klonsky, Director of Innocence International (THE SAAD TRUTH_580)," YouTube, January 30, 2018, https://youtu.be/iE5GEZ3iDF8; Gad Saad, "My Chat with David McCallum, 29 Years in Prison as an Innocent Man (THE SAAD TRUTH_581)," YouTube, January 31, 2018, https://youtu.be/w6Bx1pvng3Q.

8. Philip C. Watkins et al., "Gratitude and Happiness: Development of a Measure of Gratitude, and Relationships with Subjective Well-Being," *Social Behavior and Personality* 31, no. 5 (2003): 431–52.

9. Gad Saad, "The Incredible Tale of a Homeless Man—The Case of Dr. Bijan Gilani (THE SAAD TRUTH_1295)," YouTube, September 18, 2021, https://www.youtube.com/watch?v=3zKLjSL2pvo&t=3s.

10. Dr. Gilani's doctoral dissertation, which he defended in 2003: Bijan Gilani, "The Emergence of Resistant Poverty and the Perception of Low Self-Efficacy," (Ph.D. dissertation, University of California, Irvine, 2003), https://bit.ly/2XGewoa.

11. R. Scott Moxley, "Give Bijan Gilani a Job," *OC Weekly*, December 15, 2011, https://www.ocweekly.com/give-bijan-gilani-a-job-6420199.

12. Ibid.

13. Gad Saad, "My Chat with Classicist and Military Historian Dr. Victor Davis Hanson (THE SAAD TRUTH_1383)," YouTube, February 21, 2022, https://youtu.be/G8x_BLFMamk.

Index

Y
Yerkes-Dodson law, 70

Z
Zidane, Zinedine, 142